# The Boomerang AGE

| DATE DUE | |
|---|---|
| | |
| | |
| | |
| | |
| | |
| | |
| | |
| | |
| | |
| | |
| | |
| | |
| | |
| | |
| | |
| | |
| | PRINTED IN U.S.A. |

# The
# Boomerang
# AGE

**Transitions to Adulthood in Families**

# Barbara A. Mitchell

**ALDINETRANSACTION**
**A Division of Transaction Publishers**
**New Brunswick (U.S.A.) and London (U.K.)**

First paperback printing 2007

Copyright © 2006 by Transaction Publishers, New Brunswick, New Jersey.

This book is printed on acid-free paper that meets the American National Standard for Permanence of Paper for Printed Library Materials.

Library of Congress Catalog Number: 2005053552
ISBN: 978-0-202-30838-8 (cloth); 978-0-202-30978-1 (paper)
Printed in the United States of America

Library of Congress Cataloging-in-Publication Data

Mitchell, Barbara Ann, 1961-
    The boomerang age : transitions to adulthood in families / Barbara A.
        Mitchell.
        p. cm.
    Includes bibliographical references and index.
    ISBN: 0-202-30838-3 (cloth : alk. paper)
        1. Adult children living with parents. 2. Parent and adult child. 3. Family.
    4. Adulthood. I. Title.

HQ755.86.M57 2005
306.874--dc22

                                                          2005053552

# Acknowledgements

This book is dedicated to the memory of Ellen M. Gee, my mentor, colleague, and friend. Professor Gee was a prominent family sociologist and life course theorist who played a significant role in the development of my ideas and in the establishment of my career. I would also like to thank the several individuals who provided assistance to me throughout the writing of this book. I acknowledge the valuable direction and insight offered by Professor Victor Marshall, Director of the Institute on Aging at the University of North Carolina, Chapel Hill, provided during the development of this manuscript. I also am appreciative of the research assistance that I received from Mary Rogers and the statistical work of Doug Talling. Last, but not least, I gratefully acknowledge the ongoing support and patience provided by my husband, Andrew V. Wister, and my daughter, Kayzia.

# Contents

# List of Tables and Figures

# 1

# Introduction and Overview

Dramatic changes are taking place in the lives of young adults in Western industrialized societies, whom we conceptualize as members of the "boomerang age." This term reflects the fact that, relative to their earlier predecessors, today's young people often experience less permanency and more movement in and out of a variety of family-related roles, statuses and living arrangements. This has occurred largely in part because of significant alterations to both public realms (e.g., economic, educational, work, and technological) and private spheres (e.g., emergence of new family forms and structures, gender roles). Changing cultural contexts and multiculturalism in rapidly globalizing environments also profoundly affect the timing and nature of family-related youth transitional trends.

As a result, family-related youth transitional behaviors have become increasingly dynamic, complex, and fluid (Corijn and Klijzing, 2001; Hogan and Astone, 1986; Irwin, 1985; Rossi, 1997; Sherrod, 1996). They are also more likely to become "reversed." For example, young adults commonly experiment with "alternative" lifestyles, such as non-marital cohabitation. This living arrangement has been shown to be considerably more fragile than traditional, legal marital unions in most Western societies (Wu and Balakrishnan, 1995). Marriage, however, particularly during young adulthood, is also subject to relatively high rates of dissolution (Wolf, 1996). Moreover, we have also witnessed an increased phenomenon of "boomerang kids" in North America, or young adults returning to the parental home after an initial "launch." Goldscheider and Goldscheider (1999), for example, calculate that more than 40 percent of American youth leaving home at age eighteen or younger return to the parental nest at least once after an initial departure. This trend is unprecedented from a historical perspective and has obvious consequences for family dynamics and the "complete" transition to adulthood. Indeed, due

1

to the impermanence of many transitional behaviors, coupled with the extensive diversity that characterizes the family-related behaviours of young adults, we cannot assume a fixed or "normal" life cycle pattern of youth transitions (e.g., see Booth et al., 1999; Corijn and Klijzing, 2001; McDaniel and Tepperman, 2000).

Given the current complexity and possible instability of many family-related youth transitions, it is clear that we require more careful analysis of their evolution against a changing socio-cultural, economic and demographic landscape. The main focus of this work is to document and elaborate contemporary trajectories to adulthood from a life course perspective within the context of historical and structural change. The primary family-related transitions for young adults (typically aged nineteen to thirty-five) that will be examined throughout this book include: homeleaving and returning to parental households, non-marital cohabitation, marriage, parenthood, and divorce/union break-up.

This book fills important gaps in the literature by focusing on an often-neglected period of the family life course in the fields of families and aging—the transition to adulthood, which typically occurs during midlife family development. Although this "middle territory" is the longest period of family development, it has not received the attention that younger and older families have, particularly in family sociology, family studies, and developmental psychology. Instead, research has concentrated on younger families with infants or children, the middle generations' caregiving to elderly parents, or older parents as grandparents (e.g., McDaniel, 1996; Ryff and Seltzer, 1996). However, as young adults continue to live with their parents for longer periods of time in North America and Europe (e.g., see Aquilino, 1999; Cherlin et al., 1997; Côté and Allahar, 1994; Boyd and Norris, 1999; Mitchell, Wister; and Gee, 2004 in press; Goldscheider and Goldscheider, 1999), and life spans become extended, it becomes apparent that families (of origin) play an increasingly pivotal role in the life course of young adults.

This work is also important because it complements the expansive body of research that examines the movement from secondary school to university and from school to work during young adulthood (e.g., see Anisef and Axelrod, 1993; Côté and Allahar, 1994; Crysdale and MacKay, 1994; Galaway and Hudson, 1996). This literature implicitly treats many family and household patterns (i.e., homeleaving) as a function of other status changes, especially educational and occupational attainment. Therefore, this volume also adds to existing literature by explicating young adults' family-related transitional behaviors in relation to themes of intergenerational relationships, aging, family continuity, and change.

Moreover, this work is comprehensive in that it provides a comparative, international perspective by integrating major research findings and by highlighting selected socio-demographic trends, with a strong orientation to Western industrialized societies, particularly North American countries (United States and Canada). This will entail documentation of important trends and patterns from nationally representative data sets (e.g., U.S. National Survey of Families and Households, U.S. Census Bureau, Statistics Canada, Population and General Social Surveys, Family and Fertility Surveys). Additional international comparisons will also be made to selected European countries, including: Great Britain, Germany, France, Sweden, The Netherlands, and Italy using comparable empirical studies. This will allow for comparative analyses across a number of diverse industrialized nations.

Key family-related transitions will be examined separately in this volume, once the theoretical groundwork has been laid in chapter 2. Specifically, in chapter 3, we begin with a focus on young adult's family-related transitions within a socio-historical perspective (1950s-2000s). This enables an appreciation of how and why transitional behaviors have changed over time and establishes the decline of a standardized, institutionalized life course. Historical insights also help us to clarify whether modern patterns are distinctive or whether there are important continuities in the life course of young adults and their families. Contemporary research on patterns of homeleaving and home returning, which generally precede other family-related transitions, such as parenthood, are presented in chapter 4. The family formation patterns of young adults will be the emphasis of chapter 5, since the majority of young adults do not marry or cohabit until they have left the parental home. This will include analysis of non-marital cohabitation (heterosexual and homosexual), marriage patterns, childbearing, and divorce among young adults (in this sequence).

Particular attention will be paid to themes of continuity, disruption, diversity, and social change. In this way, the reader will be able to appreciate and recognize uniformities and regularities, but also the variability that occur within sub-groups of the population and over time. Individual factors related to socio-demographic and economic variables (i.e., young adult's gender, age, educational and work activities), family background (i.e., family structure, socio-economic status) and cultural environment (e.g., race/ethnicity, religiosity), as well as geographical and regional factors will be used as a comparative schema upon which family-related transitions will be analyzed.

The material presented in chapters 3 through 5 are situated within a life course perspective, which is initially outlined in chapter 2 to provide a foundation for the book. A life course approach (e.g., Giele and Elder, 1998; Elder, 1985; Hareven, 1996, Riley, 1998) offers a dynamic and flexible model of social behavior that encompasses socio-historical variability, structural constraints and human agency. The family is perceived as a micro social group within a macro social context—a "collection of individuals with shared history who interact within ever-changing social contexts" (Bengston and Allen, 1993: 470). Transitions are conceptualized as discrete life changes or events, such as leaving home or getting married. As such, the life course emphasizes the ways in which transitions, in addition to their pathways and trajectories, are socially organized. And, in keeping with our "boomerang age" metaphor, the strength of this approach lies in the acknowledgement of possible "reversibility" in transitions rather than assuming static or fixed life cycle stages.

One of the major tenets of the life course perspective, and a central theme of this book, is that a young adult's developmental path is embedded in and transformed by conditions and events that occur during the historical and geographical locations in which they live. For example, geo-political events (e.g., war), economic cycles and factors (e.g., recessions, housing costs), and social and cultural ideologies (e.g., ethnocultural and religious identification) can shape young people's perceptions and choices, such as when to leave home or marry. In other words, behavior and decisions do not occur "in a vacuum," since young adults and their families interact within a specific socio-historical time. Indeed, an understanding of various cohorts or generations in their respective historical and geographical contexts aid scholars and policymakers to identify circumstances that have differentially affected people's respective life course histories.

Another central theme of the life course perspective that we draw upon is the notion of "linked lives." Societal and individual experiences are "linked" through the family and its network of shared relationships (Elder, 1998). These shared networks of relations form the basis of an important resource for young adults—"social capital." Social capital "exists in the relations among persons" (Coleman, 1988:11) and represents the ability of actors to secure benefits by virtue of membership in social networks or other social structures (Portes, 1998). It manifests itself as family connectedness or support and can be influenced by cultural factors. For example, cultural groups often reproduce "traditional" norms and expectations via "social timetables" that influence the timing and circumstances of many family-related transitional events (e.g., when to marry and have children).

Moreover, individuals are influenced by changes that occur within families, and families, in turn, are affected by the behavior and developmental life trajectories of individual family members. This tenet underscores the importance of intergenerational relationship exchanges, including "social capital" and other family resources. For example, the unemployment or divorce of an adult child can trigger a return back to the parental home, if parents are supportive of this decision. Parent-child relations are inadvertently affected when young adults "refill" a previously empty nest. Therefore, the effects of transitional events and processes on mid-life family solidarity and exchanges of support will be elaborated, whenever possible, throughout the book in order to consider the effect of these behaviors on family dynamics and intergenerational relations.

Yet another hallmark of the life course perspective is that earlier life course decisions, opportunities, and conditions shape later outcomes. Thus, the past has the potential to affect the present and future, which can be viewed as a "ripple" or "domino effect." The timing and conditions under which earlier life events and behaviors occur (e.g., teenage pregnancy, becoming a "street kid") can set up a chain reaction of experiences for individuals and their families. This long-term view, with its recognition of cumulative advantage or disadvantage is particularly valuable for understanding social inequality later in life and for creating effective social policy and programs (O'Rand, 1996).

In keeping with this latter theme, social policy issues and social action are also considered in chapter 6. And, in order to appreciate the power of human agency or the active role that young people can play in affecting their own choices, circumstances, and opportunities, the implications of our findings will be discussed in terms of their significance for action-oriented social change. Specifically, readers will garner important skills and knowledge so that they will have the tools to critically analyze current social policy issues and influence future policy initiatives.

Finally, in chapter 7 we conclude with a summary of dominant theoretical, conceptual, and research themes and ideas. This will include discussion of how family-related transitional behaviors intersect with young adults' schooling and work trajectories, technological advances, and cultural/attitudinal and socio-demographic change. Attention is also paid to predicting future family life course trends over the next twenty-five years, based upon past and current patterns. In particular, we will explore two possible future scenarios— the first scenario considers increased individualization and "free choice" while the second explores the likelihood of increased familism or a return to so-called "traditional" family-based behaviors. It is concluded that the first scenario, with a heavy emphasis on flexibility and diversity, will likely characterize future family-related transitions. However, it is also speculated that some sub-groups will continue to exhibit many traditional, family-oriented behaviors.

In closing, the theoretical contributions and empirically based research presented in this book will provide key knowledge on historical and contemporary family-related youth transitions to adulthood from a North American and international perspective. While this book is primarily aimed at upper-level undergraduate and graduate students, this information will be valuable to a broad audience. For example, it can be used by students, educators, researchers, and professionals who wish to develop an expertise in life course research and youth transitions within several disciplines, especially sociology of families, gerontology, aging and human development, family studies, and family social demography/population studies.

# 2

# In Theoretical Perspective: The Life Course Approach

This chapter cultivates the theoretical groundwork for subsequent chapters, which will present a synthesis of empirical work on major family-related transitions to adulthood, as well as their implications for major policy issues. It begins by providing a conceptualization of "the boomerang age," including discussion of how this somewhat elusive temporal period diverges from concepts such as "generation" and "cohort." The remaining sections will outline the core concepts and assumptions underlying the life course perspective, which is the organizing framework of this book. Particular attention will be paid to highlighting terms and ideas that have significant value for studying the family-related transitional behavior of young adults. This includes the recognition that family lives need to be contextualized within their historical, socio-economic, and geographic locations. Also, young adults and their families are seen as having the potential to adapt to their unique and changing sociocultural environments.

Moreover, the theme of diversity will be addressed, based on the premise that we should not "over homogenize" young adulthood. Instead, heterogeneity will be emphasized in order to capture variability in family-related transitions as young people (aged nineteen to thirty-five) navigate their way to adult roles and statuses. In addition, the notion of "linked lives" is addressed, since all family-life decisions involve more than one individual (Burch and Matthews, 1987). In chapters 4 and 5 we provide an emphasis on this postulate in order to appreciate reciprocal processes and effects of transitional behaviors on both a societal and familial level. Notably, young adult's transitional behaviors are viewed as both affecting, and affected by, the quality of their intergenerational relationships. Attention is also directed to how the timing of prior family-related transitions shape later outcomes (e.g., day-to-day family interactions), an idea that alerts us to the cumulative "chain reaction" effects of transitional behaviors on young adults and their parents over the life course.

Finally, although it is recognized that human behavior is often constrained by structural "forces" or external factors, the role of human agency in transitional behaviors is also given due weight. This fundamental notion alerts us to the fact that individuals are not just passive recipients of social structure but can play important roles as "innovators" of life course processes. As a result, young people have the capacity to be important players in the shaping of their own life course patterns, as well as the world around them. This theme will be revisited and given particular prominence when we address social policy issues and recommendations to young adults for social action in chapter 7.

### What is the Boomerang Age?

As previously discussed, the term "boomerang age" is used to characterize the contemporary socio-cultural environment in which young adults in most industrialized countries develop and mature. This metaphor is used to reflect the fact that, relative to earlier decades, today's young people experience less permanency and more movement in and out of a variety of family-related roles, statuses and living arrangements. Yet, in many ways, young adults of today are swinging back to behaviors that were characteristic of family life over a century ago. Our primary historical "benchmark" that is used to compare these patterns are the decades following the second half of the twentieth century, that is, since the 1950s. The 1950s have been chosen as a major reference point for several reasons. First, this is a time period in which comparable, international data became more widely available. The 1950s also constitute one of our most powerful visions of "traditional" family life (Coontz, 1992). Indeed, when I pose the question to my students: "What images (and time period) come to mind when you think of traditional family life?" an overwhelming number refer to this time period, with adjacent stereotypes of early marriage and parenthood, conformity to social timetables, and a strictly gendered division of labor within fairly monolithic family structures. Moreover, many scholars document that this time period was somewhat anomalous with regard to the stability and near universality of many family-related behaviors, such as marriage. Prior to that time, marriages often ended relatively early due to death, although divorce was almost non-existent. Since that time, we have experienced massive social and economic change in many family-related realms such as family structure, gender roles, and living arrangements. In particular, a wider diversity and proliferation of new family forms and structures have emerged and predominant.

Of particular importance to this book are two emergent trends that have surfaced to create a "boomerang age": (1) the greater instability and reversibility of partnership formation, and (2) the increased likelihood that once young adults leave home, they are not necessarily "gone for good." Fuelling these phenomena are macrolevel, socio-demographic, economic, and ethnocultural factors associated with social change. Notably, changing economic opportunities, the increased labor force participation of young women, and the need for higher education have affected the kinds of choices young adults make in marital family formation domains.

However, while it is recognized that these broad changes have contributed to transformations in patterns, social change cannot always be attributed to the same set of factors, and at times, can even occur as the result of opposing forces. Generally, there has been a shift toward growing individualism, secularization, egalitarian gender roles, and urbanization in many Western industrialized countries. These trends have no doubt prompted young people to question much traditional behavior, such as marriage (particularly at an early age) and have contributed to the popularity of alternative life styles such as non-marital heterosexual cohabitation. On the other hand, both Canada and the U.S. have become increasingly multicultural societies, such that some families may display patterns of behavior consistent with their cultural traditions, and they cannot be considered individualistic per se.

For example, some traditional ethnic groups, although living in North America, still consider cohabitation as "immoral" and as "living in sin" (Mitchell, 2001). Also, delayed homeleaving has become increasingly common and it is more likely among traditional ethnic groups due to cultural traditions. Yet, changing economic opportunities and the need for higher education may also make living at home a preferred life style for many young adults associated with more "liberalized" cultural backgrounds. As a result, intergenerational "doubling-up" can be conceptualized as a "profamilistic" living arrangement that appears to run counter toward the trend toward non-family living and the "rise of the primary individual" (Glenn, 1987; Kobrin, 1976).

Therefore, while we can identify general trends and patterns in industrialized countries, it is important not to assume that all societies (and families) are "linear products" of the great forces of modernization. William J. Goode (1963), for instance, in his seminal book *World Revolutions and Family Patterns* argued that there is a global trend toward worldwide convergence around the nuclear family system—what he calls the "western conjugal family system." His central premise is that the movement toward the conjugal family may be attributed in large part to the forces of industrialization. For example, an industrial economy requires geographic mobility, and extended families can be cumbersome to move. However, as McDaniel and Tepperman (2000:36) observe, "there is no evidence of a single evolutionary path in family life—from simple to complex, extended to nuclear family." For example, two major industrialized countries—Japan and Sweden—exhibit very different patterns of family life, including gender norms and family forms. Cognizant of these points, the goal of this book is to recognize the value in showing general processes of family change that have occurred across many Westernized industrialized societies, yet to make note of countries that diverge from modal patterns.

With regard to the first major emergent trend—the changing nature and greater impermanence of partnership patterns (which will be documented in chapter 5)—it is first important to note that the majority of North Americans and most Europeans continue to (legally) marry at least once. It is also vital to recognize that marital patterns have always been diverse, and that we should not assume that families of the past were monolithic structures, characterized by high degrees of stability. For example, many marriages "broke-up" during the 1930s in North America, creating levels of single-parent-hood not that different from today. However, the factors accounting for single-parent families have radically changed—today the chief reason is separation/divorce, whereas in the past it was due to the death of a spouse (Gee, 2000).

Using our comparison period of trends since the 1950s, however, we can see that marriages have become dramatically less stable. In particular, divorce rates have skyrocketed over the past thirty years in North America and many European countries. Indeed, it is estimated that almost half of first marriages in the United States will end in divorce (Bumpass, Raley, and Sweet, 1995). Remarriages are also increasingly frequent (which illustrates how people are not abandoning marriage since they are reverting back again to marital statuses), yet they are even less likely to be as stable as first marriages (Cherlin, 1992).

In addition, since the 1970s, increasing numbers of young adults in North America and many European countries are choosing nonmarital cohabitation rather than legal marriage. Prior to this time, unmarried heterosexual cohabitation was relatively rare and taboo (Wu and Schimmele, 2003). Moreover, cohabitation is generally a considerably fragile type of union, since they are less stable than marriages (Riedmann, Lamanna, and Nelson, 2003). Indeed in Europe, the most fragile partnerships are cohabiting unions that do not covert into marriages, with the exception of countries such as Sweden (Kiernan, 1999). In many countries, couples that live together before marriage also have a higher risk of marital dissolution (Gee, 2000; Wu and Schimmele, 2003).

The second trend that has emerged over time is the tendency for young adults to leave home at later ages in North American and many European countries (Cherlin et al., 1999; Boyd, 2000; Goldscheider and Goldscheider, 1999). Part of the increase in coresidence rates can be attributed to the increasing prevalence of home returning, a phenomenon that is unprecedented from a historical point of view. Commonly dubbed the "boomerang kid" phenomenon, this trend of circular migration has been on the rise since the 1950s, particularly in North America, and appears to have reached its highest levels. For example, Goldscheider and Goldscheider (1999) found an overall increase from 22 percent to 40 percent in returning home between those reaching adulthood before World War II and those who did so in the 1980s. There was a sharp rise in the odds of returning home for the Vietnam cohort, who came of age between 1966 and 1972, but that level has held steady. Furthermore, multiple home returning is not that uncommon in the U.S. and Canada, with a significant number of young people returning home more for more than two four-month periods (Mitchell and Gee, 1996).

Finally, although not the focus of this book (mainly due to existing data limitations), there are a few additional emergent trends in living arrangements that are worth mentioning (and will be revisited in chapter 6). These trends also signify important revolutions that have occurred in family life over time and provide additional support for a "boomerang age" conceptualization. The first is the rise is the growing number of long-distance relationships or stable relationships that are developing without the spouses living together (Jackson, Brown and Patterson-Stewart, 2000; MacDonald, 2001; Rhodes, 2002). Termed "commuter couples" or "living together apart" by European sociologists (McDaniel and Tepperman, 2000), these "true couple relationships" (Nault and Belanger, 1996:1) are formed when each partner maintains their own household. Partners are typically young adults or are middle-aged professionals who typically live in separate cities or countries. They may live with one another for sporadic periods of time and they engage in frequent visits to each other's home.

For example, in 1998 the U.S. Bureau of the Census indicated that 2.4 million Americans reported that they were married (and not separated), but that there spouse did not live in the same home. This represented a 21 percent increase over the previous four years. It is also interesting to note that despite the rise in "nomadic" relationships, preliminary research documents their relatively low odds of long-term survival (Guldner, 2003). With regard to prevalence in other industrialized countries, no known research has been reported on commuter marriages in countries other than the U.S. Yet researchers surmise that this trend is occurring in other industrialized countries as well (Lovin, 2004).

Similarly, another parallel trend in family-related living arrangements is that of dual-family of orientation residences, often dubbed "astronaut families" with "parachute children." Increasing multiculturalism and high rates of immigration mean that many young adults will still have parents living abroad in different countries. In U.S. and Canadian cities, for example, there is the recent emergence of the "astronaut family," in which Taiwanese and Hong Kong family households are literally split across the Pacific Ocean (Waters, 2002). Young adults may live in one parental household for a time period and then switch residences, for example, while attending college or university.

It is also intriguing to note that over time, young adults have generally become more mobile. They are more likely to travel for leisure or business pursuits and to move from country to country. Cultural values of independence and autonomy, improved transportation methods, the relatively cheap cost of airline travel, corporate business travel in an increasingly global work environment have no doubt made this possible. Prior to the 1960s, for example, it was relatively rare for young adults (particularly single women) to spend time travelling, or for them to work in other countries on visas for a short time period. Now, it is relatively common for college students (especially American females) to travel abroad during spring and summer breaks (Field, 1999). Moreover, many major companies report dramatic increases in expenditures on international business in addition to domestic travel for their "globetrotting" workers (e.g. see Travel Industry Assoc. of America, 2005).

## How Does the "Boomerang Age" Differ from Generation and Cohort?

Some readers may wonder how the "boomerang age" differs from demographic concepts such as "generation" and "cohort." Indeed, the commonly used term "generation" represents a "polysemous" concept (Kertzer, 1983) with a multitude of definitions that are often contradictory, imprecise and colloquial. One of the earliest definitions appeared in one of the twentieth-century social science classics entitled *The Polish Peasant in Europe and America.* In this landmark study, Thomas and Znaniecki (1918-1920/1927) documented the lives of Polish immigrants through the core concept of "immigration generation." First generation referred to "foreign-born," while their native-born children are the second generation. They also referred to generation in terms of the kinship relations of parents and offspring. However, although these writers were successful in relating the experiences of one generation to another, they have been criticized for failing to relate these lives to their historical times (Elder and Pellerin, 1998).

More recently, writers have tended to view generation as a synonym for a set of birth cohorts or as a label for a historical or cultural period. From this perspective, a generation is usually made up of a set of individual birth cohorts usually encompassing an age span as wide as thirty years (Hareven, 1996). Cohorts are distinguishable from generations because they typically refer more to persons born at the same time with distinct years of birth that has shared a common historical experience. A generation, then, can consist of several cohorts, each of whom has encountered different historical periods. If a historical event differentially affects people of different cohorts (or different ages), then this is considered a cohort effect (Uhlenberg and Miner, 1996). The Vietnam War era and the counterculture it produced in the 1960s, for instance, had a different effect on youth than it did on middle-aged persons. Conversely, if a historical period has the same effect on persons for all cohorts (ages), a period effect has occurred (Chappell, Gee, McDonald, and Stones, 2003).

Furthermore, generations are characterized as having a unique set of characteristics based on the persons comprising them. This sets them apart from those born prior or subsequent to them and this may be related to the size or composition of the cohorts from which it is comprised. For example, in his 1996 book, *Boom, Bust, and Echo: How to Profit from the Coming Demographic Shift*, David Foot focuses on three main generations. These are: the baby boomers (born between 1947 and 1966); the baby bust generation (born between 1967 and 1979); and the baby-boom-echo generation (born between 1980 and 1995). At the back end of the baby boom generation is "Generation X." This includes about 2.6 million persons born between 1960 and 1966 (who at the time were in their early to mid-thirties). Being born within one of these generations can affect choices and opportunities in profound ways. For example, persons born in Generation X faced much competition for jobs due to economic recessionary periods and they were exposed to a culture of youth consumerism. In this sense, there is some overlap with the term "boomerang age," with a focus on young adults aged nineteen to thirty-five since many were born soon after the years identified with "Generation X" and share similar economic and cultural experiences.

Other popular definitions focus on generation as a position within a continuum of kinship descent or as a distinct life stage (e.g., the college student generation). Three or four generations can co-exist at one time, starting from great-grandparenthood down to great-grand childhood. Members of specific generations can vary as much as forty years, but there can be considerable overlap in age. Age similarity implies a common historical location and corresponding temporal relation to major historical events. Similar to many of these ideas, we conceptualize the "boomerang age" as a temporal period that implies a common historical location and related experiences (Elder and Pellerin, 1998). It includes young adults who were aged nineteen to thirty-five during the 1990s, as well as those in this age range at the current time.

However, as Mannheim (1952:297) wisely cautioned, "the fact that people are born at the same time...does not in itself involve similarity of location; what does create a similar location is that they are in a position to experience the same events." For example, as Elder (1974) notes, within a particular historical location, there can be differential experiences, structured by way of class, race, and gender, as well as geographical location and other factors. Thus, while the focus of this book is on young adults nineteen to thirty-five, we conceptualize the boomerang age as somewhat akin to a "free-floating generation." It is characteristic of modern times and comprised of a diverse set of young people (thereby extending beyond generational concepts such as "Generation X"), rather than a distinct generation or group of cohorts confined to a specific time period.

## The Life Course Perspective

One of the most exciting areas of theoretical development to gain prominence recently has been in the advancement of life course theorizing. Life course theory, or more commonly referred to as the life course perspective, refers to a multidisciplinary paradigm for the study of people's lives, structural contexts and social change. Encompassing ideas and observations from an array of disciplines, notably sociology, demography, history, developmental psychology, biology and economics, initial applications of life course theorizing can be traced back to the beginning decades of the twentieth century (see Bengston and Allen, 1993; Mitchell, 2002 for full discussion). This field was pioneered by distinguished scholars such as Matilda White Riley, whose "sociology of age" perspective developed during her graduate work at Harvard University in the 1930s (Giele and Elder, 1998). It is generally considered an emergent perspective in sociology of families, although it is the dominant perspective in social gerontology at the present time (Chappell, Gee, Macdonald, and Stone, 2003).

This perspective also has its roots in age stratification theory and the work of prominent American sociologist C. Wright Mills. Mills (1959) was instrumental in developing a theoretical perspective that encompasses individual biography and history within the social structure. This necessitates the development of a theory capable of linking macro (history, social structure) elements and the micro (individual level). A distinct field of life course studies, with a focus on the variability of age patterns, developmental effects, and the implications of historical change, however, did not gain much notoriety until the mid-1960s. At this time, researchers from divergent social science disciplines (e.g., Clausen, Easterlin, Elder, Ryder, Riley, Neugarten, and Hagestad) examined a number of themes, such as the significance of age and cohort in explaining the relationship between individuals and social change. By the 1990s, the life course approach became commonly referred to as an "emerging paradigm" (Bengston and Allen, 1993), with both a distinctive theory and methods.

Glen H. Elder Jr., in particular, is a major architect of this approach because he began to formally advance core principles of life course "theory," which he describes as defining "a common field of inquiry by providing a framework that guides research on matters of problem identification and conceptual development" (1998:4). This perspective has also been (and continues to be) synthesized with other theories or fields of study, such as family development (e.g., Bengston and Allen), human development (e.g., Elder), status attainment (e.g., Featherman, Blau, and Duncan), family history (e.g., Hareven), life span (e.g., Baltes), stress theory (e.g., Pearlin and Skaff) demography (e.g., Uhlenberg), gerontology (e.g., Neugarten) and Bronfenbrenner's ecological perspective (e.g., see Moen et al., 1995).

## Conceptualizing the Life Course

The life course is defined as "a sequence of socially defined events and roles that the individual enacts over time" (Giele and Elder, 1998:22). These events and roles do not necessarily proceed in a given sequence, but rather, constitute the sum total of the person's actual experience Thus, the concept of life course implies age-differentiated social phenomena distinct from uniform life cycle stages and the life span. The concept of life cycle generally refers to normative stages that are comprised of a set of ordered stages or "ideal" sequencing of events, such as marriage, parenthood, and child launching. Life span typically refers to duration of life and characteristics that are closely related to age but which are largely invariant across time and place.

In contrast, the life course perspective elaborates the importance of time, context, process, and meaning on human development and family life (Bengston and Allen, 1993). Families are perceived as a micro social group within a macro social context—a "collection of individuals with shared history who interact within ever-changing social contexts" (Bengston and Allen, 1993: 470). This definition avoids some of the limitations inherent in creating one arbitrary construct of "the" family (see Eichler, 1988:3-10 for a full discussion). Although some may find this conceptualization rather elusive, concepts will be clarified throughout the book by using specific terms such as "remarried families," or "single-parent families."

Aging and developmental change, therefore, are continuous processes that are experienced throughout life. As such, the life course reflects the intersection of social and historical factors with personal biography and development within which the study of family life and social change can ensue (Elder, 1985; Hareven, 1996).

*A Matter of Timing*

Three types of time are central to a life course perspective: *individual* time, *generational* time, and *historical* time (Price, McKenry, and Murphy, 2000). *Individual* or *ontogenetic* time refers to chronological age. It is assumed that periods of life, such as childhood, adolescence and old age influence positions, roles, and rights in society, and that these may be based on culturally shared age definitions (Hagestad and Neugarten, 1985). *Generational* time refers to the age groups or cohorts in which people are grouped, based upon their age. As previously noted, persons born between 1946 and 1964, for example, are often referred to as the "baby boom" generation. Finally, *historical* time refers to societal or macro-level changes or events and how these affect individuals and families, such as political and economic changes, war and technological innovations (e.g., information access through the Internet).

Furthermore, Elder (1991) observes that time can also be envisioned as a sequence of transitions that are enacted over time. A transition is a discrete life change or event within a trajectory (e.g., from a single to married state), while a trajectory is a sequence of linked states within a conceptually defined range of behavior or experience (e.g., education and occupational career). Transitions are often accompanied by socially shared ceremonies and rituals (e.g., a graduation or wedding ceremony), while a trajectory is a long-term pathway, with age-graded patterns of development in major social institutions such as education or family. In this way, the life course perspective emphasizes the ways in which transitions, pathways, and trajectories are socially organized. Moreover, transitions typically result in a change in status, social identity, and role involvement. Trajectories, however, are long-term patterns of stability and change and can include multiple transitions and can be defined as a "pathway defined by the aging process or by movement across the age structure" (1985:31). As Elder (1985) further notes, "transitions are always embedded in trajectories that give them distinctive form and meaning."

It is also noteworthy that progress along trajectories is generally age-graded such that some transitions can be viewed as more "age appropriate" while others violate normative social timetables by occurring "too early" or "too late" (Hagestad and Neugarten, 1985). This is because societies have expectations about the appropriate age for individuals to take on (or exit from) social roles. These social roles are often referred to as "social clocks" and expectations can be formal (e.g., retirement at age sixty-five) or more informal, but embedded in wider social and cultural norms (Chappell, Gee, McDonald, and Stones, 2003). For example, an informal "off age" transition might be leaving home at a very young age (e.g., age fifteen) or becoming a teenaged parent. Moreover, as observed by Settersten and Hagestad (1996), age norms have three characteristics: (1) they are prescriptions for behavior; (2) they are supported by widespread consensus in society; and (3) they are enforced through processes of social control.

The life course perspective also alerts us to the fact that there is also the possibility of countertransitions or transition reversals. Countertransitions refer to transitions that are reversed or are produced by the life changes of others (Hagestad, 1988). Many countertransitions are also experienced in the family (e.g., parenthood creates grandparenthood, divorce produces 'ex-relationships"). An example of a transition renewal or reversal is when a young adult returns home after homeleaving or experiences a union break-up. The timing of transitions can also decrease the chance of success in a particular trajectory, such as completing school.

## Examining Family Lives in Historical, Socio-Economic, and Geographic Context

The life course perspective directs our attention to the powerful connection between individual lives and the historical and socio-economic context in which these lives unfold. An individual's own developmental path is embedded in and transformed by conditions and events occurring during the historical period and geographical location in which the person lives. Geopolitical events (e.g., war), economic cycles (e.g., recessions) and social and cultural ideologies (e.g., patriarchy) can shape people's perceptions and choices and alter the course of human development. For example, Elder (1974) draws our attention to how eras of rapid and drastic change can generate problems of human dislocation and deprivation. This is illustrated by the massive effects of World War II on morbidity, mortality, and migration in Greater Europe, and the massive historical effects of the Great Depression that occurred in the United States during the 1930s. Moreover, Elder's research demonstrated that individuals who encountered economic deprivation earlier in life (e.g., in their teens) showed persistent effects of this experience in their adult lives.

Thus, behavior and decisions do not occur in a vacuum — people and families are subject to the constraints imposed within a distinct socio-historical location. In this way, the life course perspective offers a view of behavior that is temporal and contextual. People and family members are situated within a unique historical context that interlocks with economic and political environments that are constantly in flux. An understanding of the location of various cohorts in their respective historical contexts aids scholars and policy makers to identity circumstances that have differentially affected people's respective life histories.

## Adaptation and the Life Course

Another important component of the life course approach is recognition of processes of adaptation. Life course patterns are typically viewed as adaptations to circumstances or what Thomas and Znaniecki (1918-1920/1927) referred to as "the solution of a situation," in which individuals react to external conditions with pre-existing attitudes and define the situation accordingly. This corresponds to the ideas of contemporary life course theorists (e.g., Clausen, 1991) who emphasize how the life course is shaped by the interaction of cultural and social structural features with the physical and psychological attitudes of people. As well, individual's commitments and purposive efforts affect their ability to adapt to external conditions and environments. In a similar vein, Elder states (1991: 74) that, "adaptive responses are shaped by the requirements of the new situation, but they also depend on the social and psychological resources people bring to the newly changed situation." For example, individual and relational attributes, such as family coping styles, can affect how young people adapt to events or crises such as unemployment or personal loss.

It is also' recognized that rapid social change can produce a disparity between people's ability to adapt and their resources to achieve goals. This observation illustrates Elder's concepts of "control cycles," and "attenuation." The concept of control cycles illustrates how families and individuals modify their expectations and behavior in response to changes in either needs or resources. For example, Elder (1974) found that families in the Great Depression regained a measure of control over their economic hardship through expenditure reductions and multiple family earners. In this way, social change can result in a corresponding loss of control, followed by efforts to regain control through adaptation of one kind or another. "Attenuation" can also occur, which refers to the process by which the new situation magnifies selected attributes (e.g., weak family relationships shatter under stress).

Thus, in order to accomplish tasks and objectives, individuals and their families both respond to the timing of external events and undertake actions, using their available resources. In this way, the timing of life events can be understood as both passive and active adaptation for reaching goals (Giele and Elder, 1998). Prolonged coresidence with parents, for example, may represent an adaptive strategy for young adults that allow them to prepare themselves for successful independent living (Aquilino, 1996). Generally, life course choices and behavioral adaptations are affected by the particular situation or circumstance and the resources or dispositions people have at their disposal, a theme that will be discussed in further detail in the next section.

### Heterogeneity in Life Course Timing and Family-Related Life Course Events

Historically, families expected a certain sequencing of family-related events. Young people in the 1950s, for example, typically expected to complete schooling, marry before having children and would later become grandparents. Patterns were so predictable that scholars found "life cycle" depictions of family life to be relatively accurate. However, with recent changes, the timing and sequencing of events are too varied to warrant this linear model of family development. For example, families are often simultaneously involved in multiple stages, they may reverse stages, and not all families exactly fit into any one stage or model (e.g., see Aldous, 1996). Furthermore, critics have noted the white, middle-class bias of the family life cycle perspective (Hogan and Astone, 1986), although some have modified it to recognize racial/ethnic and other social variations, such as child-free unions, single parenthood (Rodgers and White, 1993) and gay or lesbian families (Slater, 1995).

The life course perspective, on the other hand, emphasizes heterogeneity or diversity in structures or processes. One must consider not only modal or average developmental and transitional trends, but also variability. One important source of diversity stems from geographical location (e.g., across societies, regions). Regional variations, for example, can reflect unique social or community contexts that can shape family relationships and opportunities for young adults. Region of residence can affect socialization processes (e.g., through dominant religious organizations), job opportunities, and the availability of educational institutions; factors that can play a significant role in family-related transitional behaviors, such as marital and employment patterns (e.g., see Goldscheider and Goldscheider, 1999).

Considerable diversity can also exist across and within families and generations. Consistent with many contemporary definitions of "family," we do not assume that there is "the" family but rather diversity in "families." Previous popular definitions (particularly those formulated in the 1940s to 1960s) tended to emphasize that 'the family' was the basic institution of society and that it was a social and economic unit consisting of two adults of the opposite sex who shared economic resources, sexual intimacy, labor, accommodations, reproduction, and childrearing (Murdock, 1949; Goode, 1963). However, most scholars today readily acknowledge that previous definitions and studies of the family were often idealized and ideologically based and not always relevant to the realities of modern family life.

Past definitions often presented the family as having two parents, with a breadwinner husband and homemaker wife, such as the stereotypical *Leave it to Beaver* style of family popularized on North American television in the 1950s (with re-runs commonly telecasted in the present time). This image is certainly at odds with the real lives and historical experiences of many North Americans and Europeans. Moreover, we often use the term family when we really mean household, which includes all those sharing a dwelling. Household members, however, may or may not be related by blood, marriage or adoption. Conversely, "family" can refer to a number of different social entities and a great variety of living arrangements (Baker, 1993:3). For example, most people consider an aunt or uncle "family" but probably do not share a household with these relatives. As Eichler (1988) suggests, it is more realistic and productive to view families as varying along several key dimensions. These dimensions include procreation, socialization, sexual relations, residence, economic co-operation, and emotional ties. Therefore, in this book, we prefer to use the term "families" in the plural form to reflect diversity and to appreciate the fact that there are many acceptable family structures and relationships.

Moreover, there can be considerable diversity within generations or age groups. Riley's (1987) extensive research supporting a model of age stratification—the different experiences of different cohorts – has helped to overcome the fallacy of cohort centrism, the notion that cohorts share perspectives simply because they share a common age group. Indeed, generations or cohorts are not homogeneous collections of people, but rather, differ in terms of influential dimensions such as gender, social class, family structure, ethnicity and religion. Moreover, as previously noted, the ability to adapt to life course change can vary according to the resources or supports inherent in families and individuals. These resources can take the form of economic or cultural capital (e.g., wealth, education) or social capital (e.g., family social support), and these are often socially structured by factors such as ethnicity/race and gender.

Indeed, social capital is a concept that has been increasingly synthesized with the life course perspective (e.g., Mitchell, in press). It was originally pioneered by French social theorist Pierre Bourdieu in the 1970s and it is defined as "social connections among individuals" such that it "inheres in the structure of relations" (Bourdieu, 1986; Coleman, 1988; 1990; Putnam, 2000). Unlike economic capital, which is more "tangible," access to social capital can generate normative structures and resources (i.e., social support). For example, social capital can be found in cultural groups that emphasize familistic or family-centred norms, values, and obligations. This can create culturally specific social timetables with regard to the appropriate timing and circumstances for homeleaving or marriage. Daughters, in particular, may face greater expectations to leave home at the time of marriage than sons in traditional ethnic groups (Mitchell, in press).

Another interrelated source of social capital found within families can stem from the quality of intergenerational relationships, which can be considered apart from ethnocultural membership. Indeed, Coleman (1988: S111) states that, "even if adults are physically present, there is a lack of social capital in the family if there are not strong relations between parents and children." This is crucial for the child to profit from access to other kinds of resources. He states:

> The social capital of the family is the relations between children and parents…That is, if the human capital possessed by parents is not complemented by social capital embodied in family relations, it is irrelevant to the child's educational growth that the parent has a great deal, or a small amount of human capital (p.S110).

For example, Mitchell's (2000) research demonstrates that young adults with weak family ties may not have to option to return home during difficult economic times, regardless of other types of capital (e.g., economic). Moreover, parents typically monitor and supervise the behavior of daughters more closely than sons, and this may make delayed coresidence less attractive to them. Linking social capital to the notion of life course transitions and transition reversals, therefore, represents a dynamic perspective that is well suited to frame family diversity and to elaborate the significance of intergenerational ties in shaping transitions to adulthood, a theme that we explore in the next section.

## Linked Lives: The Interdependence of Family Members' Lives

Another tenet of the life course approach emphasizes how human lives are interdependent and reciprocally connected on several levels. Societal and individual experience are "linked" thorough the family and its network of shared relationships (Elder, 1998). As a result, macro-level events (e.g., war) can affect individual behaviors (e.g., enrolling in military service) and this can significantly affect other familial relationships. For example, during times of war young adults may join the military, leave home to travel abroad, and then return once they have completed their military service (Goldscheider and Goldscheider, 1999). This event has obvious social-psychological and economic consequences for daily family life and family relationships (e.g., interactions and well-being).

Moreover, on a slightly different yet interrelated conceptual level, generational relations are interconnected with experiences and transitions from earlier life. "Middle age," for instance, is not an isolated stage or experience. Instead, life stages are viewed as part of an

overall process of generational interaction in the context of changing family development, relationships and historical events (Hareven,
1996). In this way, stages and transitions in the life course are inter-
locked across generations and can have short and long-term consequences. Stressful events, such as the death of a family member, for
example, can profoundly affect family relationships since these types
of occurrences can trigger patterns of stress and vulnerability. Conversely, they can promote adaptive behaviors and family "resiliency,"
as well as reunite family members and bring them closer together in
later life.

In addition, family members can also "synchronize" or coordinate their lives with regard to life planning and matters related to the
timing of life events. This can sometimes generate tensions and conflicts, particularly when individual goals are different than the needs
of the family as a collective unit. Hareven (1996), for instance, notes
that historically, the timing of adult children's individual transitions
(e.g., when to marry) could generate problems if it interfered with the
demands and needs of aging parents. Furthermore, personality attributes of individual family members can also affect family coping
styles, functioning, well-being and the timing of transitions. For example, intergenerational conflict (an example of a lack of "social capital") as a result of personality clashes can trigger a "premature" exit
out of the parental home in order for a young adult to escape a con-
flict-ridden home environment. Alternatively, close intergenerational
ties may manifest themselves in ways that show more reciprocity and
supportive behaviors across the life course for both generations.

## Chain Reactions: How Prior Transitions Shape
## Later Outcomes

Finally, another hallmark of this perspective is that early life course
decisions, opportunities and conditions affect later outcomes. The
past, therefore, has the potential to shape the present and the future,
which can be envisioned as a "ripple" or "domino effect." This can
occur on a cohort/generational-level and an individual/familial level.
For example, one generation can transmit to the next the "reverbera-
tions" of the historical circumstances that shaped its life history, such
as living through wars or the feminist movement.

The timing and conditions under which earlier life events and
behaviors occur (e.g., dropping out of school, witnessing domestic
abuse,) can also set up a "chain reaction" of experiences for indi-

viduals and their families (e.g., reproduction of poverty, a cycle of family violence). Events experienced earlier in life may continue to influence an individual's or a family's life path in different forms throughout the life course. Elder (1974), for example, showed the negative impact the Great Depression in North America had on young men and women, such as the delay of education and early commencement of work. The past, therefore, can significantly affect later life outcomes such as socio-economic status, mental health, physical functioning, and marital patterns. This long-term view, with its recognition of cumulative advantage or disadvantage, is particularly valuable for understanding social inequality in later life and for creating effective social policy and programs (O'Rand, 1996).

At the same time, it should be noted that although "negative" events can accumulate, they are not necessarily irreversible. Elder and Hareven, for instance, found that military service during World War II had a major role in reversing or mitigating the negative impact of the Great Depression on the lives of young men from disadvantaged backgrounds. Many of these men were able to rise above their class origins because military service prevented them from slipping below their parents' working class status. These differences were also linked to occupational structures in the communities in which these men lived. Thus, while past events do indeed shape the life course, human lives are also the products of the interaction of time and place (Elder and Hareven, 1992).

## Innovation and Human Agency in the Boomerang Age

Another distinguished feature of the life course approach is recognition of innovation and human agency in the life course. New behaviors, when routinized, can be created or alter pre-existing trends. This can occur during times of uncertainty in the form of uncontrollable or involuntary events, such as the terrorist attacks on the U.S. (Sept. 11, 2001), natural catastrophes (e.g., the recent 2004 tsunami disaster in Southern Asia), or family crises. These events destabilize established patterns and sometimes alter power relationships, which makes room for renegotiation and innovation (Giele, 1998). New behaviors can also be the result of small or large-scale social movements (e.g., the student protest movements of the 1960s in the U.S.), or widespread normative shifts as new behaviors become institutionalized. For example, many writers speculate that behaviors such as home returning and cohabitation have become increasingly popular life styles, in part because they have lost the social stigma that once existed when these behaviors were not as widely practiced.

Thus, individuals are active agents who not only mediate the effect of social structure, but can also make decisions and set goals that shape social structure. This important tenet reminds us that human lives are not fully shaped or determined by social circumstances, or for that matter, by biology (Marshall, 2000, cited in Marshall and Mueller, 2003). Therefore, micro-level phenomena should be interpreted in terms of macro-level contextual features, and conversely, macro-level phenomena should be viewed in light of their significance for and impact on micro-level phenomena (Marshall, 1987). Social forces not only "trickle down" from social structures to individuals' lives but also "percolate up" from individuals' action to modify existing social patterns and institutions and perhaps create new ones (Mayer and Tuma, 1990:5). In this way, individuals are assumed to have the capacity to engage in planful competence. This refers to the thoughtful, proactive, and self-controlled processes that underlie one's choices about institutional involvements and social relationships (Clausen, 1991).

In this book, we acknowledge the dialectical relationship between social organization and the personal construction of the life course as a complex sequence of reciprocal interactions. Young adults approach their lives with a given set of personal characteristics that are enmeshed with their individual and family resources against the backdrop of environmental constraints. What seems to be a purely individual decision, therefore, is viewed as shaped by a wider social context. As a result, the subjective construction of the life course is neither completely predetermined nor an entirely free creation (Kohli, 1986: 290). However, it is recognized that the possibilities for negotiation and innovation are more limited among those who lack financial power, education and complex social networks (Giele, 1998). Yet young adults are conceived as social actors who have the potential to navigate their lives to some degree, and instigate social change. This notion will be the dominant focus of Chapter 7, which will seek to further explore the theme of social action in the boomerang age.

## Questions for Discussion and Debate

1.  Why is the relationship between individual lives and social structure considered "dialectical" by life course theorists? Provide specific examples to illustrate.
2.  Why should family-related issues of social timing (e.g., when to marry) be considered in the context of changing socio-economic and historical realities *and* family-level resources.
3.  From a historical perspective, how might household living arrangements reflect adaptive responses to external conditions among specific family members?
4.  Discuss some of the potential implications of the early or late timing of family-related transitional events on individual biography, later-life outcomes and parent-of-origin and child relationships over the life course.
5.  To what extent can persons from disadvantaged backgrounds create more successful life course opportunities for themselves and affect institutionalized social change?

# 3

# Family Transitions in Historical Perspective

In keeping with a life course perspective, this chapter elaborates on the importance of examining family lives in historical, demographic, and socio-economic contexts. This objective is achieved by providing an overview of historical trends in intergenerational coresidence and homeleaving, non-marital cohabitation, marriage timing, age at first child, and divorce among young adults. Although it is beyond the scope of this book to provide an in-depth, comparative analysis of key trends from a historical and international perspective, a summary of major patterns will be provided. This is partly because of numerous data limitations, and also because the main focus of this work is to document changes in North America from our historical benchmark of the mid-twentieth century until the present time.

Providing a longer-range historical perspective with examples from specific countries, however, will allow us to identify some general themes of continuity and change. It will also illuminate the value in placing family life within its particular time, space and location. Transitional behaviors only take on meaning when they are placed in a particular social context. In this way, we can appreciate how young people's respective life histories and experiences are profoundly shaped by their historical conditions and circumstances. Moreover, while it is recognized that all countries have unique histories, it will be shown that many Westernized societies share similar processes of social and economic transformations (e.g., due to industrialization, urbanization). These macro contexts fuel family change and are instrumental in shaping contemporary family life and the transition to adulthood.

In this chapter, attention will initially be paid to debunking the "myth of family homogeneity" that is often assumed to have occurred prior to World War II. Emphasis is also placed on how the transition to adulthood has changed over time, especially since the mid to late nineteenth century, although trends previous to this time period will be highlighted if they have relevance. This will be followed by a closer examination of family-related patterns starting at the 1950s, which, despite popular perception, were not a continuation of all traditional family patterns purported to exist in the "good old days." Rather, this was the beginning of a relatively unique time period with respect to family stability, affluence, and much family-related transitional behavior such as marital timing and family formation. Indeed, for the first time in history, the vast majority of children could expect to live with their married biological parents until they left home. Finally, the chapter will summarize these major trends in light of wider socio-demographic, economic, and cultural shifts occurring in North American and many European societies.

### The Historical Backdrop—North American and European Family Life Prior to World War II

As many researchers point out (e.g., Coontz, 1992; Gee, 2000, Hareven, 1992), many of our opinions about contemporary family life are conditioned by beliefs about what families used to be like in the past. These ideas often form the basis for an ideology of the modern "ideal" family and often romanticize the past by assuming that there was once "a golden age of family life." One of these sets of beliefs centers on the assumption that families of the past were large, stable, and harmonious units. Concurrently, there is the popular perception (often based on media images and stereotypes) that young adults from this era grew up in extended or multigenerational family living structures. They are also depicted as leaving home at a relatively young age for marriage (and permanently), and that this marriage would last their lifetime. Similarly, they are also characterized as being very unlikely to have experienced unmarried cohabitation and/or divorce.

Implicit in these stereotypical images is the belief that youth transitions into adulthood were universal, standardized, and compressed into a relatively short period of time. Families are reputed to be virtually identical, that is, families were conceptualized as homogeneous or "monolithic" (Gee, 2000). In comparison, modern-day transitions to adulthood are commonly seen as more chaotic due to "the rise of the nuclear family" and the decline of "the" family as a result of the changes associated with socio-demographic, cultural and economic conditions (e.g., individualization, secularization, women's entry into the labor force). Moreover, the rise of the nuclear family is often depicted in a negative light since contemporary families are viewed as small, rather isolated units, characterized by isolation and disharmony.

While there may be some "half-truths" to some of these allegations, Coontz (1992:1) argues, "the actual complexity of our history —even of our own personal experience—gets buried under the weight of an idealized image." In short, assumptions about "traditional" families of the past are overly simplistic and not empirically valid (Gee, 2000). Indeed, many researchers document that there never was a "golden age" of family homogeneity, although it is recognized that there have been some important continuities, fluctuations and transformations in family life that have affected the transitional behaviors of young adults.

It is also interesting to note that throughout history, social scientists have always expressed concern over the demise of "the" family. For example, in the late nineteenth century, the *Boston Quarterly Review* issued a dire warning: "The family, in its old sense, is disappearing from our land, and not only are our institutions threatened, but the very existence of our society is endangered" (cited in Benokraitis, 1993). In a similar vein, a well-known author writing in the 1920s (Groves, 1928: vii, 33-38) asserted that marriages were in "extreme collapse," in addition to citing numerous other problems purported to plague families at the time, such as high divorce, hedonism, independence, and financial strain.

Let us take a brief critical look in more detail at some dominant assumptions of past family life. This will be done within the context of key historical changes in the family-related transitional behaviors of young adults that comprise the foci of this book: intergenerational coresidence and homeleaving, cohabitation, marital and family formation patterns, and divorce. This will be followed by a more detailed examination of these trends since the 1950s.

### Living Arrangements in the Past: The Myth of Multigenerational Living and Early Homeleaving for Marriage

As many social historians (e.g., Demos, 1970; Hareven, 1992; Laslett and Wall, 1972) note, research on the family in pre-industrial North American and European societies has dispelled the myth centered on the existence of three-generational families. While most families were rural, land-based and self-sufficient units, families were simple in their structure and not drastically different in their organization from contemporary families. Instead, the Western European family ideal, which later came to North America with the first European settlers, was nuclear family living (Laslett, 1979). For example, Laslett (1969) documented that in England between the mid-sixteenth and early nineteenth centuries, mean household size remained about constant at 4.75 persons and few households contained three or more generations. In general, this pervasive residential pattern of nuclear households prevailed throughout Europe and North American until the beginning decades of the twentieth century.

There are several reasons for a predominance of nuclear families rather than extended families both in North American and Europe. First, high mortality levels (adult and infant) created high levels of family "disorganization" such that many grandparents did not live long enough to get to know their grandchildren. For example, life expectancy at birth in the nineteenth century was well below sixty years old, which meant that the odds of three generations of a family being alive at the same time were quite low, regardless of cultural ideals. Also, although women born in 1860 bore, on average, 4.9 children, only 3.2 survived to the age of twenty years (Gee, 1990). In addition, neither available living space nor material resources would have been sufficient for most families, especially poor ones, to support more than a few dependents (Anderson, 1987). As a result, pre-industrial households were not filled with extended kin, but rather, were more likely to contain strangers who lived in the home as boarders, lodgers, apprentices, or servants. Many of these "strangers" were young adults who were not blood relatives of the primary householder.

Overall, intergenerational coresidence patterns have varied considerably over time and across societies. While many young adults remained in the parental homes until marriage, historical research on the living arrangements of young unmarried adults before the twentieth century in countries such as Canada, the United States and Britain (e.g., Anderson, 1971; Katz and Davey, 1978; Wall, 1978) indicates that large proportions of children lived away from their parents. Katz and Davey (1978) refer to this living arrangement as "semi-autonomous" because they primarily lived as servants, boarders, or lodgers in other family households. About one-third of men and women in their twenties and thirties in the late nineteenth-century American urban communities, for example, boarded with other families (Hareven, 1996). Moreover, Katz (1975) notes those provisional or semi-autonomous situations reflect a tendency for these youths to become more independent (i.e., by acquiring the resources to establish their own families).

Young adults also sometimes lived as boarders in the households of older people whose own children had left home. This practice enabled young people to stay in surrogate family arrangements while creating economies of scale. At the same time, it could provide old people with the chance to continue heading their own households without being isolated. For older widows in particular, it provided the extra income needed to maintain their own residence (Harevan, 1992). Moreover, even when young adults were in their late teens and twenties and therefore old enough to leave home, at least one child (usually the youngest daughter) remained at home to care for aging parents if no other assistance was available. Although home returning among young adults was relatively rare in Western societies at this time, married children would sometimes return to the parental home to care for aging parents if there was no one else and they did not take in boarders or lodgers (Goldscheider and Goldscheider, 1999; Hareven, 1996).

Hufton's (1981) research on young women in eighteenth- and nineteenth-century France provides an excellent example of young people's transitional behaviors in relation to living conditions that was common in many European countries and in North America. He observes that, "the largest category of women in eighteenth-century France was that of the daughters of smallholders or of agricultural laborers, village artisans and casual odd job men" (1981:187). These young women lived in a society where the majority of all farms and other artisanal enterprises were unable to provide the support of even two or three children. Under such circumstances, a young girl would most likely have started to work around the age of twelve as a domestic servant. Similarly, like many of their European counterparts, the majority of North American women of the eighteenth to nineteenth centuries were commonly employed in domestic service, and this generally entailed living with the employer. Only a minority of girls from "the most fortunate circumstances in the towns and cities" escaped this fate (Anderson, 1981; Nett, 1981:247). Even at later ages, many unmarried women worked as domestics. For example, in 1871, 47 percent of employed Canadian females aged twenty-one to twenty-five lived in other family's homes as servants (Katz and Davey, 1978).

With regard to multigenerational living, there was only one brief period of time prior to industrialization in which this type of living arrangement became more prevalent (Wall, 1983; Flandrin, 1979), although the highest figure for extended-family households ever recorded in American history is 20 percent. This high point occurred between 1850 and 1885 during the most intensive period of early industrialization. At this time, the Western family lost its function as a productive unit, and many families were forced to move to towns and cities where they took wage-paying jobs. Some formed extended families out of economic necessity, since most families of the time depended on the labor of children and this required them to remain at home for as long as possible (Coontz, 1992).

With the changes associated with a shift toward industrialization and urbanization, then, came many changes in the living arrangements of young adults. Relatively large industries made it possible for young people to find work near home and they may have found it cheaper to live with parents than in lodgings. Moreover, community leaders were becoming more paternalistic with respect to protecting and socializing the young and this meant keeping them in their families of origin for as long as possible (Katz and Davey, 1978). Public attitudes toward children working were also shifting and North American and many European countries began to adopt compulsory public schooling by the end of the nineteenth century. Also, shocked by the conditions in urban tenements and by the sight of young children working full-time, middle-class reformers also played a role in keeping children out of the labor force (Coontz, 1992).

Gutmann et al. (2002) further argue that the process of homeleaving for young adults is closely related to becoming an independent adult and they further distinguish between involuntary and voluntary homeleaving. Involuntary homeleaving occurs when both parents die and when poverty leads to the disintegration of the family household. In comparison, children may leave home voluntarily when they choose to attend school or work away from home, join the military, or when they marry or otherwise establish an independent household separate from that of their parents.

From a historical point of view, involuntary homeleaving has decreased, largely due to a decline in the likelihood of becoming an orphan between the ages of fifteen to twenty-nine. However, since

1880, changes in social conventions, family relationships and individual characteristics became increasingly more important as adult mortality began to decline. High rates of immigration into the U.S. up until the 1920s also affected the age at which young people left home, because young adults who immigrated by themselves during the peak years did not live with their parents. Finally, as previously mentioned, social change that led to decreased child labour and increased schooling in the first decades of the century also led to later homeleaving.

As a result of these transformations, at the turn of the twentieth century there was a steady increase in the average age of homeleaving in North America and in many European countries. It is has been estimated, for example, that in Canada, the average homeleaving age was about twenty-four for men born between 1910 and 1920 (leaving 1930-40) and about twenty-two for women (Ravanera, Rajulton, and Burch, 1992). Similarly, Gutmann, Pullum-Pinon, and Pullum (2002) document that in the United States, the age at which young people ceased to live with their parents rose from 1880 until 1940 for males and 1950 for females. Led by men in 1940, the generation of the Second World War experienced a sharp decline in the age at which young people left home, a trend that continued until 1960. The percentage of young adults living with their parents reached a peak during the Great Depression of the 1930s. This was probably because these young people could not afford to live independently of their parents (Elder, 1974). Some parents may also have depended on their children's earnings in order to survive, since there was a complete absence of state supports to look after aging parents.

Moreover, historical research by Gutmann, Pullum-Pinon, and Pullum (2002) finds that the age at which young men and women left home varied by race and across the regions of the United States. For white men and women, a consistent pattern emerges. Young men left home earliest in the West and latest in the Northeast, although young people in all four regions exhibit the same relative changes in homeleaving over time. One exception is the low age at leaving home for Western young men in 1880, which can be attributed to westward migration and employment opportunities for the very young. However, the median ages at leaving home by region for black males and females show very different results in that for every region, the age that black men (and to a lesser extent women) left home varied considerably over time. This suggests that these groups were more sensitive to social and economic changes than were whites.

Farm residence is another important factor that affected the timing of homeleaving for young people in the U.S. According to Florey and Guest (1988), the strongest predictor that a late nineteenth-century American farm boy would remain in the parental home was the likelihood that he would inherit the family farm. Generally, for all groups (black and white, male and female), farm residents left home later than non farm-residents until at least 1940 (Gutmann et al., 2002).

Finally, while the average age of homeleaving increased in the early part of the twentieth century, "intimacy at a distance" continued to be the preferred formula for married adult children's living arrangements. For example, in 1900 only 9.4 percent of married U.S. white males and 4.9 percent of married white females lived with parents. For married black males and females the percentages were slightly lower at 4.3 percent and 4.6 percent, respectively. Percentages living with parents while married increased to their highest level in 1950 at 14.2 percent for white males and 15.5 percent for white females, and a striking 22.9 percent for black males and 24.1 percent for black females (Gutmann et al., 2002). It is also important to note that the older generation rarely resided with their married adult children in the same household. Also, when newlywed children or young families lived in their parents' home, it was usually for a short period time and they typically found housing nearby and often received assistance from their parents. This would help them to establish a new household or to care for their young children (Chudacoff and Hareven, 1979).

## Cohabitation in the Past

Although non-marital romantic cohabitation is commonly viewed as a "new" phenomenon, it has actually existed long enough to pre-date marriage. Until the mid-eighteenth century, the difference between marriage and cohabitation was fluid in many countries. In England, for instance, the distinction between these two unions was not always officially recognized until Lord Hardwick codified marriage in 1753 (Wu and Schimmele, 2003). This was done largely to prevent "clandestine" marriages and to ensure that the Church kept accurate and complete registers of all marriages. Despite his attempts, however, common-law marriage continued to remain popular until the Registration Act of 1836, which gave the supervision of marriages to civil, rather than ecclesiastical authorities (Haskey, 1987).

Similarly, in many other countries, due to a lack of officials to oversee formal marriages, marriage did not develop into the institution that we know until the nineteenth century. During this time period, marriage transformed from a religious practice to one commonly formalized under civil law. Thus, from this perspective, it is somewhat inaccurate to assert that cohabitation is "aberrant" because this implies that legal marriage has always been the norm (Wu and Schimmele, 2003).

Despite the fact that cohabitation has existed throughout history, we do know that it was relatively rare among North American couples born before 1940 and that it was largely confined to those with limited education (Kamerman and Kahn, 1997). Starting in the 1940s, cohabitation began to increase among young adults regardless of their educational background (Cherlin, 1992). Thus, it is fair to say that modern trends are qualitatively different from those of the past—although Sweden is an important exception. Yet it is important to reiterate that cohabitation has dramatically increased in a context in which conventional marriage is a clearly defined and dominant institution.

### The Myth of Early Universal Marriage and Early Family Formation

Contrary to popular assumption, the work of several researchers, extending back for several centuries, shows that not all North American and European men and women legally married, and of those who did marry, they did so later than is commonly imagined. For example, in table 3.1 we observe that the proportion of women who never married by age forty-five to forty-nine in 1900 was not that dissimilar from the percentage who never married in 2000. Notably, in the U.S., 8 percent of women never married in 1900 compared to 9 percent in 2000. Similar patterns are found in Canada and many European countries, with the exception of Sweden which shows a much higher proportion of never married women in 2000 (27 percent) compared with 1900 (19 percent), most likely due to the popularity of unmarried cohabitation. Also, Britain exhibits a much higher percentage of never married in 1900 (17 percent) compared to only 8 percent in 2000.

**Table 3.1**
**Percentage of Women Never Married by the Age of 45-49**
**(as percentage of age group), Selected Countries, 1900 and 2000**

|               | 1900 | 2000[a] |
|---------------|------|---------|
| Britain       | 17   | 8       |
| Canada        | 10b  | 10c     |
| France        | 12   | 14      |
| Germany       | 10   | 13      |
| Italy         | 11   | 6       |
| Netherlands   | 14   | 12      |
| Sweden        | 19   | 27      |
| United States | 8    | 9       |

Sources: 1900 data from Hajnal (1965: 102); 2000 data from Eurostat (2000a: Table F11), as cited in Therborn (2004).

Notes: a = the proportion never married by 1999 in the age cohort born in 1955, b=based upon 1891 data from Gee (1982), c=author's tabulation from Statistics Canada, 2001 GSS.

Moreover, in a landmark essay on historical demography, Hajnal (1965) showed that the historic pattern of marital timing in Western Europe differed dramatically from that of other parts of Europe and from the rest of the world. Coined "the European Marriage Pattern," this term was used to characterize very late marriage for both men and women and high proportions of individuals never marrying. Notably, Hajnal documented the mean age at first marriage prior to 1850 for Western-European women varied from twenty-four to twenty-seven, and for men from twenty-six to thirty.

Similar patterns of relatively later ages of marriage are exhibited in many Western and Northern European countries, largely gleaned from the European Fertility Project monographs. The trend toward late marriage persisted after 1850 in Western Europe and was later exhibited in the U.S. (Fitch and Ruggles, 2000). For example, after 1880, the age at first marriage in the U.S. rose from 26.5 years for males and 23.0 for males to a peak in 1890 at 27.6 for males and 23.6 for females, at which time it began to decline.

Overall, in the late nineteenth and early twentieth centuries the United States most closely resembled France within Western and Northern Europe in terms of age of marriage. However, relatively high ages of marriage are also observed in other countries, particularly for males. For example, the average age of marriage in 1900 in Germany for males was 27.8 and 25.5 for females, compared to

27.6 in the U.S. for white males and 23.9 for white females (Haines, 1996).

Age at first marriage began to rise again during the difficult economic times of the 1930s and the 1940s, a trend common throughout Western societies. In 1941, the average age of an American bride was 23.5, while the average age of a groom was approximately 26.5. This trend generally declined until a low point in 1960 at the peak of the baby boom, although ages of marriage for black were less than those for whites, a trend that remained until about 1950 (Haines, 1996).

Explanations accounting for historical fluctuations in marriage rates show that over the past century, marriage rates relating all marriages to the total population have varied widely under the influence of wars, changing economic conditions, the sex ratio of the marriageable population and the number of potential brides and grooms. Marriage rates have generally risen at the outset of a major war, declined during the course of the conflict, and increased sharply in the immediate postwar years (Cherlin, 1992). For example, the average age of first marriage increased during the Depression.

With regard to parenthood, in earlier times conception was most likely to occur very shortly after marriage. This combination of a later age at marriage and higher fertility provided little opportunity for a family to experience an empty nest stage. Prior to the decline in mortality among the young at the beginning of the twentieth century, marriage frequently ended with the death of a spouse before the end of the child-rearing period. As a result of higher fertility, children were spread out over a wider age range. For example, the youngest child might be entering school as the oldest was preparing for marriage. The combination of later marriage, higher fertility, and widely dispersed childbearing resulted in a different timing of family transitions. Individuals married and become parents later, but they typically carried child-rearing responsibilities almost until the end of their lives (Hareven, 1992).

In 1910, more than half the wives twenty to twenty-four years old married less than three years (with an average marriage duration of eighteen months) had borne a child. Changes began after 1910 until 1940, probably indicating a more widespread knowledge of contraception. Many couples also waited to have children because of the uncertain economic setting that was created by the depression

(Cherlin, 1992). Beginning in the 1940s, a rapid shortening of the interval between marriage and first birth took place, similar to the patterns set in 1910. While part of this shift can be accounted for by rising rates of premarital pregnancy, changing preferences seemed to dictate the rest (Wu and Schimmele, 2003).

## Divorce Rare

Divorce was also relatively infrequent prior to the twentieth century, although it became more prevalent throughout the twentieth century as divorce laws in many Western countries gradually liberalized. In North America, divorce laws were heavily influenced by English traditions. Divorce, in the modern sense of a judicial decree dissolving a valid marriage, and allowing one or both partners to remarry during the life of the other, did not exist in England until 1857 (Callan, 2005). The Ecclesiastical Courts retained their exclusive jurisdiction over marriage and divorce in England until 1857. As a result, civil divorce in England was impossible without a private act of Parliament. In 1858, divorce jurisdiction was transferred to the Civil Court System, and divorces were authorized for adultery. However, the underlying premise of divorce law remained the same and was based on the premise that marriage was a permanent and cherished union within the Church and one that state would have to protect and preserve (see Weitzman and Dixon, 1992 for full discussion).

Successive legislation in North America and many European countries has slowly broadened its availability in terms of grounds and access. Each of these measures has stimulated at least a temporary rise in frequency. In general, though, the increase in divorce has not depended on legislative steps but has occurred in response to demand within most divorce law regimes, especially in the turbulent times during and after both world wars. After reaching peaks following each war, divorce declined following the Civil War, rose in 1919 and 1920 following World War I, and sharply increased after World War II. The Depression temporarily lowered the divorce rate in the 1930s (with jobs and housing scarce), a time in which family stability and levels of illegitimate births also dropped (Cherlin, 1992). Also, with the reduced probability of dissolution by death, marriages enjoyed stability during this time without precedence in history (Kamerman and Kahn, 1997).

Divorce rates in the United States have been among the highest in advanced industrialized countries. Rates have increased since at least 1860, the earliest year for which data are available. However, rates were still very low in the first decades of the twentieth century. For example, in 1900 only 3 percent of all brides—including both the never and previously-married—were divorced, and this rose to 9 percent in 1930 (Cherlin, 1992). These rates reached a first peak in 1945-47, at which time they began to steadily rise.

## Our Focal Point: The Post-World War II Years

Based on the preceding discussion, it becomes clear that family-related transitions to adulthood have fluctuated over time and that diversity has always been the norm. Yet there remains continuity in many family-related transitions and there have been many dramatic transformations in family-related behaviors. For example, similar to the past, most young adults eventually "couple" and have children, although rates of divorce are extremely high from a historical perspective. In this section, we begin by providing a focus on changes in key family-related events of young adults, beginning with an overview of family life (with a focus on North America) during the 1950s. This is followed by a closer examination of how these trends differ and have changed within a comparative context. A focus on diversity in contemporary patterns and their implications for "linked lives" —namely midlife family intergenerational relations—will comprise the basis for the next two chapters.

## The Postwar North American Family—A Historic Fluke?

It is important to note that only for a short period of history—the post-World War II "baby boom" years (circa 1946-64) did North American families approach near uniformity. This time period was somewhat anomalous from a larger historical perspective in that many of the trends characterizing the rest of the twentieth century reversed themselves. The age when young people left home in the U.S. began to fall in conjunction with the fall in the age of marriage in the 1940s and 1950s. For example, at the time of the 1940 census, 63 percent of young adults aged eighteen to twenty-four were living at home, and this decreased to 42 percent by 1960, a drop of 21 percentage points. This marked a low point in the proportions of young adults living with their parents or the high point in the speed with which they departed parental homes (Goldscheider and Goldscheider, 1999).

Marriage also became the predominant route of the parental home at this time. For the first time in 100 years the age for marriage and motherhood dropped, there was near universal marriage and parenthood, family "intactness" (and the divorce rate stabilized) and highly differentiated gender roles. During the 1950s, all but 5 percent eventually married, and this was a time in which half of all women married by age twenty and half of all men by about age twenty-three, which brought average ages of marriage to an historic low (Bachrach, Hindin and Thomson, 2000; Glick, 1992). Indeed, getting married within weeks of graduation was a symbol of success for many American college-educated women in the 1950s and 1960s, a time in which the saying "Ring by spring or your money back" was a popular saying among coeds (Cherlin, 1992). In fact, by the mid-1950s, 60 percent of female undergraduates were dropping out of college to marry (Banner, 1984).

The 1950s nuclear family was considered by many to be a new cultural ideal, based on a unique and temporary conjuncture of economic, social, and political factors (Coontz, 1992). Cherlin (1992) asserts that after the turbulence and uncertainty of the Depression and World War II, people sought security and predictability in home and family life. This was made possible by rising economic prosperity, which made it possible for people to pursue these goals by purchasing homes and raising families in the suburbs of American cities. Indeed, suburbs mushroomed between 1950 and 1960 as nearly 66 percent of the population increase occurred in the suburbs and the ranch house became the architectural embodiment of "the good life" (Coontz, 1992). The federal government, fearful of a return to depression conditions, underwrote the construction of homes in the suburbs. Massive highway construction programs also enabled people to commute from the city to the suburbs with relative ease (Benokraitis, 1993).

This postwar economic expansion also increased opportunities for young men, especially in contrast with their Depression-era childhood (Easterlin, 1980). Real wages increased by more than they had in the entire previous half-century. Also, during the war Americans had saved at a rate more than three times higher than that in the decades before which helped to fuel consumer spending (Coontz, 1992). Economic prosperity was also magnified by the role of government, which could afford to be generous with respect to education benefits, guaranteed mortgages and housing loans, and job training. This allowed the majority of middle-class North Americans and a large number of working-class families to adopt family values and strategies that assumed the availability of low-interest home loans, expanding educational and occupational opportunities, and steady employment.

The impact of such prosperity encouraged early marriage, followed by childbearing. In fact, men and women born between 1920 and 1945 married at earlier ages than any other cohort in the twentieth century (Cherlin, 1992). As a result, couples bore their children earlier and closer together, completed their families by the time they were in their late twenties, and experienced a longer period living together as a couple after their children left home. The suburban way of life also added a new dimension to the traditional role of women. For example, the duties of childrearing underwent expansion, since suburban mothers often volunteered, took part in PTA activities, and were expected to make the family home an oasis of comfort and serenity for harried husbands (Chafe, 1972).

The mass media also played a significant role in reinforcing family values and celebrating the rise of suburbia and this greatly affected young people's family-related behavior and the adoption of highly differentiated gender roles. Coontz (1992), for example, documents how public images of Hollywood stars were consciously manipulated to show their commitment to marriage and stability. This was evidenced when after 1947, the Screen Actors' Guild organized "a series of unprecedented speeches...to be given to civic groups around the country, emphasizing that the stars now embodies the rejuvenated family life unfolding in the suburbs."

Moreover, as Betty Friedan (1963: 38) argued in her critique of American women's magazines, "fulfillment as a woman had only definition for American women after 1949—the housewife mother." Popular writing also reflected a concern for the consequences of maternal employment and the problems associated with nonmaternal care. Expert directives were simple—women were advised to enter and withdrawal from the job market in accordance with the family life cycle; part-time work was preferred to full-time employment, and under no circumstances should the demands of a career with a woman's primary responsibility to her children (Margolis, 1984).

Generally, motherhood was defined as "biological destiny," and women who did not embrace marriage or motherhood were thought to be unnatural (Wilson, 1991). Similarly, men were also pressured into "acceptable" family roles, since lack of a suitable wife could mean the loss of a job or promotion. Bachelors were routinely stigmatized with unflattering labels such as "immature," "narcissistic," or even "pathological." These views are reflected in the opinion of family advice expert Paul Landis (cited by Coontz, 1992:33) who argued: "Except for the sick, the badly crippled, the deformed, the emotionally warped and the mentally defective, almost everyone has an opportunity [and, by clear implication, a duty] to marry."

It is also important to note that despite the fact that the dominant family configuration of that time was that of a male breadwinner and a full-time housewife living with several children, millions of North American people did not conform to the suburban family model. Notably, the poor, blacks, immigrants, and working people introduced a level of diversity that was rarely acknowledged by the mass media and by social scientists. For example, a full 25 percent of Americans, forty to fifty million people were poor in the mid-1950s, and in the absence of food stamps and housing programs, the effects of poverty were searing. Also, African Americans in the South (including slave children) faced systematic, legally sanctioned segregation and pervasive brutality, while those in the North were excluded from many of the benefits that their labor helped sustain (Coontz, 1992, Newman and Grauerbolz, 2002).

In the next section, we will make a closer examination of the family-related changes of young adults that have occurred in North America and selected European countries since the 1950s, beginning with trends in intergenerational living arrangements and unmarried cohabitation. Focus will then turn to trends in legal marriage and the transition to parenthood, and finally, to patterns in divorce.

## Trends in Living Arrangements, 1950s to 2000s

Since the 1950s, there have been some noticeable shifts in patterns of homeleaving and intergenerational coresidence. In most countries between 1950 and 1970, there were generally low median ages by which young people left the parental home compared to earlier decades. This is particularly evident in the U.S. and Canada. For example, in the U.S. and Canada for young women born in the 1930s (and leaving in the 1950s) the median age of homeleaving was approximately nineteen years of age. Prior to the Great Depression, it was common to find a substantial group of American young adults aged twenty-four or older who had never left the parental home. However, by the Vietnam cohort (1966-1972), three-quarters had left home shortly after the age of twenty (Goldscheider and Goldscheider, 1999).

In the U.S., Goldscheider and Goldscheider (1999) found that the baby boom cohorts, increasingly freed of the pressure to join the armed forces, generated a spike in leaving home for marriage (which was occurring at relatively young age), and this remained high through the Vietnam years. These researchers document that these young adults continued the early nest leaving of the war period. In doing so, young people changed the process of leaving home through their early marriages and childbearing. Yet this trend of early homeleaving contrasted with that of their parents, most of whom entered adulthood during the Depression.

In 1970s and 1980s this process of early homeleaving was reversed. This was driven by a strong economic "push" to remain home, given the problems that many young adults of the late 1970s and 1980s experienced in a difficult job market and an increasingly expensive housing market. Moreover, the increasing importance of higher education delayed full economic "adulthood" well beyond its legal attainment. Remaining at home, therefore, provided young adults with a stronger family "safety net" because their parents usually did not share their levels of poverty and unemployment (Goldscheider, St. Clair and Hodges, 1999).

As a result, young adults began to delay their first departure from the parental home from the 1970s until the turn of the twenty-first century. In the U.S., for example, 51.6 percent of males aged twenty to twenty-four lived at home in 1994 compared with 49.5 percent in 1986. Among U.S. women, this percentage grew from 36.3 percent to 37.3 percent in the same period. Similarly, in Canada, about 41 percent of the 3.8 million young adults aged twenty to twenty-nine lived with their parents in 2001, up from 27 percent in 1981 (Statistics Canada, 2002a). Rates also generally increased in many European countries. However, compared to the U.S., in West Germany and the Netherlands, the percentages were even greater (around 65 percent for males aged twenty to twenty-four and 43 percent for females), but there was little change between 1986 and 1994 (Hooimejijer and Mulder, 1998). Moreover, there has been a general tendency for young adults over the age of twenty-five to remain at home until later ages, a phenomenon known as "mature coresidencey" (Mitchell, Wister, and Gee, 2002). Italy has a particularly pronounced pattern of mature coresidency among sons, a phenomenon known as *"mammoni"* (see chapter 4). Also, Britain follows the North American pattern, in that a Social Trends survey found that nearly a third of men aged between thirty to thirty-four lived with their parents in 2001, compared with only one in four in 1977/8 (Furedi, 2003).

While recent high rates of intergenerational coresidence have been deemed one of the few "profamilistic" socio-demographic trends of the late twentieth century (Alwin, 1996), it is also significant that there has also been a rapid expansion of the numbers of young people living alone and maintaining their own household. The U.S. Bureau of the Census first made it possible to study this phenomenon in 1947 when it created the category "one-person families." Primary individuals are those who live alone as heads of households, as well as the small proportion whom head households containing non-relatives. The increase in primary individuals began after 1950, rose between 1960 and 1970, and has continued, despite the counter tendency of young adults to remain at home until later ages, relative to earlier decades.

In Canada, for instance, the size of households has dropped in the last two decades, as fewer people live in large households and more people live alone. In 2001, there were as many one-person households as there were households with four or more people, although many of these are formed in later life (Statistics Canada, 2002a).

## Changing Pathways Out of (and Back Into) the Parental Home

Changes in living arrangement patterns can also be attributed to changes in the pathways taken out of the parental home. One important change is the decreased likelihood that young adults leave home for marriage. The phenomenon of living on one's own before marriage, sometimes termed "premarital residential independence" (Kobrin, 1976) refers to the tendency for youths to seek independence in their living arrangements. Accelerating between 1960 and 1970, a trend emerged whereby young adults tended to set up their own apartments or lived with their friends before marriage. This trend is partly explained by later ages of marriage and an increase in individualism. Kobrin (1976) suggests several other reasons for this change. For example, she postulates that the growth of separate housing may have been the result of a rise in affluence and the availability of housing. People have been able to buy privacy and independence.

Moreover, it is important to note that rising rates of intergenerational coresidence reflect not only those who have remained at home (having never left), but also those who have left home, but have returned to refill the parental nest as "boomerang kids." As previously mentioned, there has been a dramatic increase over time in rates of returning home over the twentieth century in North American society. Much of the change occurred between the 1920s and World War II, and there was a major jump in the odds of returning home for the Vietnam cohort, who came of age between 1966 and 1972. This trend has persisted, and contributes to the current high rates of intergenerational coresidence. Currently, it is estimated that approximately 40 percent of American young adults have returned home at least once (Goldscheider and Goldscheider, 1999) and multiple returning is not that uncommon. In Canada, we observe slightly lower levels of home returning than the U.S., possibly because there is less homeleaving for college or military service. Recent Statistics Canada data (2002a) reveal that 28 percent of young women aged 33 percent of young men aged twenty to twenty-nine have returned home at least once after an initial departure. These levels appear unprecedented from a historical perspective (Beaupré et al., 2003) and will be discussed in further detail in chapter 4. Generally, explanations for high rates of returning focus on changing economic opportunities, the increased need for higher education and delayed marriage. In short, home returning represents an adaptive response to current social and economic conditions that can ease the transition to adulthood. In addition, as this trend has become more prevalent, the stigma that was once associated with returning has considerably lessened, which further contributes to its popularity (Mitchell, 2000).

Unfortunately, historical European data on home returning is lacking, making it difficult to provide cross-national comparisons. However, available evidence documents that this "boomerang" phenomenon is also increasingly likely to occur in many industrialized countries throughout the world (e.g., Britain, France, Germany, Australia, Japan), although there is considerable variability across societies. Similar to North America, many Westernized European countries appear to be experiencing an increase in this transition reversal, although in highly traditional, familistic European countries (e.g., Italy) there is little evidence to suggest similar patterns to North America and Britain.

## Cohabitation—Heterosexual and Homosexual

Although there have been marked improvements in the collection of cohabitation data, historical data prior to the 1970s is largely non-existent, making it difficult to make cross-national comparisons. Not only are cohabitation data scarce, but when available, definitions, sample sizes, and representativeness can vary across countries and historical time (Kiernan, 2000; Wu, 2000). Despite these limitations, there is ample evidence to suggest that non-marital heterosexual cohabitation has become a very popular lifestyle choice for many young people in Westernized countries. Although relatively uncommon before the 1970s, there were subgroups that were probably more prone to cohabitation than others: the very poor; those whose marriages had broken up but were unable to obtain a divorce; certain rural dwellers; and groups ideologically opposed to marriage. In the early 1960s, marriage continued to be a normative prerequisite before couples could live together in North America and Europe. A notable exception is Sweden, a country where cohabitation has old roots (Hoem, 1995).

During the 1970s, the form of cohabitation that came to the forefront in North America and many Northern and Western European countries has been aptly termed "nubile cohabitation." This refers to the trend whereby young people, predominantly in their twenties and early thirties, live together either as a prelude to, or as an alternative to, marriage. Additionally, with the rise in divorce, "postmarital cohabitation" is also likely to have become more prevalent to, or as a prelude to remarriage. Although many data sources do not distinguish between the two types, the increased prevalence of cohabiting unions is likely to lie behind much of the decline in first marriage and remarriage rates that have occurred in many countries in recent decades (Kiernan, 2000).

Between 1970s and 2000, there were some interesting differences in the cohabitation rates among the countries of interest in this book. Overall, rates have generally increased in all countries. In the United States, the number of unmarried couples living together has increased tenfold between 1960 and 2000 (U.S. Bureau of the Census, 2000). With regard to Canada, the Canadian census did not begin collecting information on cohabitation (more commonly referred to as "common-law" unions) until 1981. At this time, common-law families accounted for 6 percent of all families, and this has increased to 14 percent of all families in 2001 (Statistics Canada, 2002b). Moreover, Wu (2000) found that the number of people in cohabiting unions increased by 158 percent from 1981 to 1996, and that the increase in Quebec is particularly striking, despite its history of strict Catholicism. Indeed, the Quebec rate of cohabitation is now equal to that of the Scandinavian countries (Statistics Canada, 2002b), and this is why the Canadian rate of cohabitation is about twice as high as in the United States.

There is also evidence that there is a good deal of diversity across European countries in the incidence of cohabitation and the trend to increased cohabitation had already appeared by the end of World War II (Kamerman and Kahn, 1997). The Netherlands is the first country in Europe to formalize heterosexual cohabitation (Kiernan, 2000)—a country with intermediate levels of cohabitation and low rates on non-marital childbearing. This country instituted the formal registration of partnerships for both heterosexual and homosexual couples. This made legally registered cohabitation functionally equivalent to marriage, except that cohabiters do not have the right to adopt children.

Why has cohabitation increased so dramatically from the 1970s? A number of explanations have been offered by researchers (e.g., see Bianchi and Casper, 2000; Wu, 2000). These include: increased uncertainty about the stability of marriage, the increasing social acceptance of this lifestyle and sexual relations outside of legal marriage, the wider availability of reliable birth control, and increased individualism and secularization (Bianchi and Casper, 2000). The rise in cohabitation is also often viewed as a response to changing gender roles. Economist Gary Becker (1981), for example, argued that men and women marry only if both will gain from marriage. As women become more like men in terms of labor market participation, the incentive to marry declines. Moreover, over the past two decades, young adults have also experienced more divorce than any other generation before them. Cohabitation can offer many benefits, such as pooling resources and the opportunity to live together in an intimate relationship without the commitment of marriage (Bianchi and Casper, 2000; Wu, 2000).

Meyer and Schulze (1985) compared several European countries and the United States and argue that the most important reason for the increase in cohabitation was the growth in female labor force participation. This is because women with strong commitments to employment are less committed to marriage and family life and more receptive to alternate living arrangements. Moreover, women in cohabiting relationships are more educated than the average and are materially less dependent on their partners than less educated women. This represents a significant change over the past when it was the less educated who were more likely to cohabit. Overall, the rise in cohabitation suggests that people want intimate relations that are more flexible and less socially binding than legal marriage (Mills, 2000). This can offer many of the usual benefits of marriage with fewer socially imposed expectations and fewer legal obligations.

Finally, although cross-national data are relatively scarce, there is some evidence to suggest that same-sex cohabitation is an important trend to consider in light of recent media attention and increasing social acceptance. However, while gay and lesbians have formed and lived in couples since the beginning of families, it is a challenge to know how many there are in the population. For example, a recent U.S. study (Black et al., 2000) that examines national data from the U.S. Census and from other national datasets concludes that these couples are considerably underestimated and that only one-third self-report as such. In Canada, the 2001 Census of Canada provided data on same-sex partnerships for the first time in this country. A total of 34,200 same-sex couples were counted, representing .5 percent of all couples in the country and male couples outnumbered female couples (Statistics Canada, 2002b). Many European countries have acknowledged gay and lesbian couples, although data on its prevalence are generally lacking. Denmark legally accepted gay couples since 1989, and since then, all Scandinavian countries, Switzerland, the Netherlands, and Belgium have legally recognized these unions. Germany, Italy and Spain also have jurisdictions in which same-sex couples are legally recognized (McDaniel and Tepperman, 2004).

### Trends in Age at Marriage, 1950s to 2000s

Table 3.2 presents the mean age at first marriage in North America and selected European countries from 1951 to 2000. In the U.S., we observe that the average age of marriage was relatively low throughout the 1950s and 1970s For example, in 1951, males married, on average at age twenty-four and females married, on average at age 21.5, a trend that persists until 1980, at which time average ages begin to rise. In virtually every other country, average ages do not reach their lowest points until the 1960s (Canada, Britain, Sweden, France, Italy, Netherlands) or the 1970s-1980s for Germany. In the mid-1970s the average age of most first time brides was clustered in the twenty-two-to-twenty-four-year range, whereas, similar to the U.S., by the mid-1990s it became clustered in the later twenties, in the range twenty-six to twenty-nine years (Kiernan, 2000). In fact, all countries display increasing ages of first marriage throughout the 1980s, and reach their highest levels in history at the turn of the twenty-first century.

It is also interesting that there is remarkable similarity throughout all countries in average age at first marriage—approximately age thirty for males, twenty-eight for females at the turn of the twenty-first century. Ages of first marriage are slightly lower in the U.S.; however, it is difficult to make accurate comparisons based on U.S. data, which provide only median levels. Moreover, it is important to recognize that there are important differences in average age of first marriage by ethnic/racial group in the U.S., a topic that will be further explored in chapter 4. Finally, Sweden displays the highest average ages of all countries. Based upon 2000 data, the average age at first marriage in Sweden is 32.4 for males and 30.1 for females. The widespread popularity of cohabitation no doubt contributes to these late ages of first (legal) marriage.

Another important pattern with regard to patterns in "marriage entry" in all countries is that women continue to marry at younger ages than men. However, these age differentials have generally narrowed over time. For example, in 1951, women married at the earliest ages in the United States at 21.5, while men married, on average, at age 24.2, which constitutes approximately a three-year age difference. Over time, the age difference has decreased to approximately a two-year age difference between the sexes, on average. This trend has occurred in not only the U.S., but in all other countries, with the exception of Germany and Italy. These countries continue to display a three-year age gap in mean age at marriage between males and females, although there have been some fluctuations over time, particularly in Germany.

## Table 3.2
## Mean Age at First Marriage for Selected Countries, Males and Females, 1951 - 2000

| Year | Britain[n] | | Canada | | France | | Germany[o] | | Italy | | Netherlands | | Sweden | | USA | |
|------|------|------|------|------|------|------|------|------|------|------|------|------|------|------|------|------|
| | M | F | M | F | M | F | M | F | M | F | M | F | M | F | M | F |
| 1951 | b 26.6 | b 24.2 | 26.6 | 23.8 | ----- | a 23.3 | a 26.4 | a 24.7 | b 28.6 | b 24.9 | a 28.0 | a 25.6 | b 28.0 | a 25.8 | c 24.2 | c 21.5 |
| 1955 | b 26.6 | b 24.2 | 26.2 | 23.5 | ----- | 23.2 | 25.9 | 23.8 | b 28.6 | b 24.9 | ----- | 25.1 | b 28.0 | 25.3 | d 24.0 | d 21.3 |
| 1960 | e 25.9 | e 23.5 | 25.8 | 23.0 | 26.1 | 23.5 | 25.9 | 23.7 | 28.6 | 24.8 | 26.8 | 24.5 | 27.3 | 24.3 | f 24.1 | f 21.4 |
| 1965 | 25.4 | 22.9 | 25.3 | 22.6 | 25.1 | 22.6 | 26.0 | 23.7 | 28.2 | 24.5 | 25.8 | 23.5 | 26.1 | 23.3 | 24.0 | 21.6 |
| 1970 | 24.9 | 22.4 | g 24.9 | g 22.6 | 24.4 | 22.4 | 24.8 | 22.5 | 27.5 | 24.1 | 24.8 | 22.9 | 26.2 | 24.0 | 23.8 | 21.6 |
| 1975 | 25.0 | 22.7 | 24.9 | 22.5 | 24.6 | 22.5 | 24.3 | 22.0 | 27.2 | 24.0 | 24.8 | 22.7 | 27.5 | 25.1 | 24.0 | 21.9 |
| 1980 | 25.5 | 23.0 | 25.5 | 23.3 | 26.2 | 23.0 | 24.8 | 22.4 | h 26.8 | 24.1 | 25.5 | 23.2 | 29.0 | 26.4 | 24.8 | 22.7 |
| 1985 | 26.0 | 23.8 | 26.7 | 24.6 | 26.4 | 24.3 | i 26.9 | 24.6 | i 27.3 | 24.5 | i 26.3 | 24.4 | i 30.0 | 27.5 | 24.8 | 24.0 |
| 1990 | 27.2 | 25.2 | j 27.6 | 26.0 | 27.8 | 25.7 | k 28.5 | 25.2 | 29.6 | 25.6 | 28.2 | 25.9 | k 30.4 | 27.6 | 27.0 | 25.0 |
| 1995 | 28.5 | 26.3 | l 28.8 | l 26.9 | 29.2 | 27.2 | l 29.4 | 27.3 | 29.6 | 26.9 | 29.7 | 27.4 | 31.2 | 28.7 | p 26.9 | p 24.5 |
| 2000 | 30.4 | 28.3 | 29.6 | 27.6 | 29.7 | 27.7 | 31.2 | 28.4 | m 30.0 | m 27.0 | 30.0 | 29.1 | 32.4 | 30.1 | p 26.8 | p 25.1 |

a) 1950  
b) 1951-55 average  
c) 1950-54 average  
d) 1955-59 average  
e) 1956-60 average  
f) 1960-64 average  
g) 1971  
h) 1979  
i) 1984  
j) 1988  
k) 1992  
l) 1994  
m) 1997  
n) 1951 - 1990 data refers to England & Wales; 1995 & 1999 data refers to the United Kingdom  
o) 1951-55 and 1970-80: separate mean ages for West Germany (FRG) and the East Germany (GDR) were averaged;  
    1960-65 and 1985: West Germany (FRG); 1990-99: unified Germany  
p) median age

Sources: 1951-1990 British data from Office of Population Censuses and Surveys (1982, 1992); 1951, 1955, 1960, 1965 Canadian data from Dominion Bureau of Statistics (1954, 1958, 1962, 1968); 1951 and 1955 French, German, Swedish data from UNECE (2003), except for Swedish males from Official Statistics of Sweden (1992) and German males from Dorbritz and Hohn (1999); 1951-1955 Italian data from Livi-Bacci (1977); 1951 Netherlands data from Statistics Netherlands (2003); 1951, 1955, 1960 U.S. data from Kreider and Fields (2001); 1960-1980 Italian data, females, from Council of Europe (1991) and 1960-1985, males, from Council of Europe (1991), 1985 and 1990 Italian data, females, from Council of Europe (1994) and males, 1990 from UN (1995); 1970, 1975, 1980, 1985 Canadian data from Statistics Canada (1973, 1978, 1985, 1990); 1960 to 1980 French data from Council of Europe (1991); 1970-1985 U.S. data from National Centre for Health Statistics (1996); 1985-1995 French data from Institut national d'etudes demographiques (2002); 1960-1985 German, Netherlands, Swedish data from Council of Europe (1991); 1990 and 1995 Swedish data from Council of Europe (1994, 1999); except for Swedish males 1990 from UNECE (1995); 1990 Netherlands data, females, from Council of Europe (1991) and males from Statistics Netherlands (2003); 1990 U.S. data from UN (1997); 1995 British, Canadian, Italian, German, Netherlands, Swedish data from UN (1999), and UNECE (2003); 1995 U.S. data from U.S. Bureau of the Census (2001); 2000 European and Canadian data from UNECE (2003); 2000 U.S. data from U.S. Census (2001a).

## Trends in Maternal Age at First Birth, 1950s to 2000s

Data are presented on mean maternal age at first birth in table 3.3. Here, we observe the lowest average ages of first material birth generally occur earlier in the U.S. compared to other countries. From 1950 until 1970, we observe the lowest ages of mean maternal age at first birth in the U.S. at approximately twenty-one to twenty-two years of age, whereas, the average ages are considerably higher in all other countries, except for Canada. Here, the lowest point is reached in 1965 (22.1). In other countries, lowest ages are exhibited during the 1970s, but all countries reach their highest ages in at the turn of the twenty-first century. For example, the average age of first birth for U.S. mothers rose from 22.5 in 1950 to 25.0 in 2001 and for Canadian mothers from 23.4 in 1950 to 29.5 in 2001. In 2001, the latest ages of first birth in Europe are seen in both Italy and the Netherlands at 30.3, followed by Sweden (30.0), France (29.4), Germany (28.8) and Britain (28.6), although it is important to note that these ages are remarkably similar to one another, since they all generally occur between the ages of twenty-eight and thirty.

## Divorce—How Common?

Table 3.4 displays divorce rates, which are calculated as the number of divorces in a given year, divided by the mid-year population, multiplied by 100,000. This rate is deemed "crude" because it generally yields relatively low rates. This is because the denominator includes everyone in the population, many of whom are not at risk of divorce, since they are children, single, or already divorced. This estimate can be improved by standardizing for age and other social characteristics that are deemed to affect people's propensity to divorce. Nonetheless, other measures of divorce rates are rarely available, such that we have to rely on crude rates as a general indication of divorce rates.

A cross-national comparison of crude divorce rates reveals a general tendency for divorce to remain relatively low from the 1950s, reaching its highest levels by the mid-to-late1980s, at which time it tends to generally stabilize and decline (with the exception of France, which showed no significant decrease relative to other countries). The U.S. displays the highest rates of marital dissolution throughout this time period of all countries, reaching its peak in 1980 at 5.19. Many other countries also reached their highest rates in the 1980s,

Table 3.3

Mean Maternal Age at First Birth for Selected Countries, 1951 - 2001

| Year | Britain | Canada | France | Germany [e] | Italy | Netherlands | Sweden | USA |
|------|---------|--------|--------|-------------|-------|-------------|--------|-----|
| 1951 | 25.7 | 23.4 | ---- | d 24.6 | 25.9 | d 26.4 | ---- | c ,e 22.5 |
| 1955 | 25.3 | a 24.0 | ---- | ---- | a 25.7 | 26.1 | ---- | ---- |
| 1960 | 24.8 | b 22.5 | 24.8 | 23.9 | 25.8 | 25.7 | 25.5 | e21.8 |
| 1965 | 24.1 | 22.1 | 24.4 | 24.1 | 25.4 | 25.2 | 25.2 | e 21.9 |
| 1970 | 23.8 | 22.6 | 24.4 | 23.4 | 25.1 | 24.8 | 25.9 | 21.4 |
| 1975 | 24.6 | 23.5 | 24.5 | 23.7 | 24.7 | 25.2 | 24.4 | 21.8 |
| 1980 | 25.0 | 24.3 | 25.0 | 23.8 | 25.0 | 25.7 | 25.3 | 22.7 |
| 1985 | 24.8 | 25.4 | 25.9 | 24.3 | 25.9 | 26.6 | 26.1 | 23.7 |
| 1990 | 25.5 | 26.4 | 27.0 | 26.6 | 26.9 | 27.6 | 26.3 | 24.2 |
| 1995 | 26.7 | 26.9 | 28.1 | 27.5 | 28.1 | 28.4 | 27.2 | 24.5 |
| 2001 | 28.6 | 29.5 | 29.4 | 28.8 | 30.3 | 30.3 | 30.0 | 25.0 |

a) 1956
b) 1961
c) 1950

d) 1951, 1960, 1970 - 1985: separate mean ages for the West
Germany (FRG) and East Germany (GDR) were averaged; 1955,
1965: West Germany (FRG); 1990-99: unified Germany

e) median age

Sources: 1950-1980 British data from Office of Population Censuses and Surveys (1982); 1960-1995 European data from Council of Europe (1994, 1998, 1999, 2000, 2002); French 1951 and 1955 data from Sardon (1990); German 1951, 1960, 1970-85 data from UNECE (2003); 1955 German data from Sardon (1990); 1990-1995 German data from OECD (2002), Canadian; Italian and Netherlands 1951 and 1955 data from OECD (2002); 2001 European data from Eurostat (2004); 2001 Canadian data from Statistics Canada (2004a); 1951-1995 U.S. data from Mathews and Hamilton (2002), 2001 U.S. data from Martin et al. (2003).

Table 3.4
Crude Divorce Rate (# of divorces per 1,000 population) for Selected Countries, 1951 - 2001

| Year | Britain [a] | Canada | France | Germany [d] | Italy [f] | Netherlands | Sweden | USA [g] |
|------|---------|--------|--------|---------|-------|-------------|--------|------|
| 1951 | 0.64 | b 0.38 | 0.80 | 1.49 | -- | 0.59 | 1.19 | 2.48 |
| 1955 | 0.60 | b 0.38 | 0.67 | 1.10 | -- | 0.51 | 1.21 | 2.29 |
| 1960 | 0.51 | c 0.39 | 0.66 | 2.17 | -- | 0.49 | 1.20 | 2.18 |
| 1965 | 0.78 | 0.46 | 0.72 | 1.19 | -- | 0.50 | 1.24 | 2.47 |
| 1970 | 1.18 | 1.37 | 0.79 | 1.44 | -- | 0.79 | 1.61 | 3.45 |
| 1975 | 2.43 | 2.23 | 1.16 | 2.10 | 0.19 | 1.47 | 3.14 | 4.75 |
| 1980 | 2.99 | 2.59 | 1.50 | 2.12 | 0.21 | 1.82 | 2.39 | 5.19 |
| 1985 | 3.08 | 2.46 | 1.95 | 2.59 | 0.27 | 2.35 | 2.37 | 4.99 |
| 1990 | 2.88 | 2.94 | 1.86 | e 1.70 | 0.48 | 1.91 | 2.26 | 4.70 |
| 1995 | 2.89 | 2.62 | 2.01 | 2.07 | 0.47 | 2.21 | 2.54 | 4.45 |
| 2001 | 2.60 | h2.30 | 1.90 | 2.40 | 0.70 | 2.30 | 2.40 | 4.00 |

a) 1951 – 1980 data refers to England & Wales; 1985 & 1999 data refers to the United Kingdom
b) excludes the Yukon and Northwest Territories
c) excludes the Yukon
d) 1951- 1985: separate mean rates for West Germany (FRG) and East Germany (GDR) were averaged
e) 1991
f) 1951 – 1970: there is no legal provision for 'divorce' during this time
g) 1951 – 1985: data are estimates based on divorces reported by a varying number of States
h)2000 data

Sources: All countries 1951-1995 UN (1969, 1975, 1984, 1992, 1995, 1999, 2002); 2001 European data from Eurostat (2003); 2000 Canadian data from Statistics Canada (2004b); 2001 U.S. data from U.S. Bureau of the Census (2003).

with the exception of Sweden, which shows its highest rate in 1975 at 3.14, at which time rates generally declined until 1999. Italy is the only county that actually shows increasing rates over this time period, although it should be recognized that data do not exist until 1975 (because divorce was not legal), at which time the rate is reported as .19. It is also important to note that divorce is still limited in Italy, and only in 1987 did the period of separation necessary to obtain a divorce drop from three to five years. In addition, in spite of the growing secularization of society, catholic values continue to exist, which strongly prohibit divorce (Onagaro, 2001).

In 2001, the U.S. shows the highest divorce rate of 4.0, with the lowest rate displayed in Italy at .70. This is not surprising given that nearly 50 percent of all first marriages in the U.S. end in divorce (Cherlin, 1999). Rates in other countries in 2001, in order of highest to lowest rates are: Britain (2.60), Germany (2.40), Sweden (2.40), Canada (2.30), the Netherlands (2.30) and France (1.9) although it is interesting to observe that these countries exhibit remarkably similar rates of divorce.

Many explanations have been offered to account for the dramatic increase in divorce since the 1950s, which usually center on how decisions to divorce are strongly affected by large processes in the structure of society. This would include macro-level factors and trends such as wars and migration, economic cycles, gender expectations and cultural values. For example, sharp increases in divorce rates usually follow wars, possibly because war separates couples for long periods of time. Moreover, many researchers argue that the postwar shift in cultural values from an emphasis on community and the institution of marriage to the primacy of the individual has contributed to the sharp increase in divorce (McDaniel and Tepperman, 2004).

## Summary of Major Trends and Explanations

This chapter has examined family-related transitions to adulthood using a life-course perspective. The emphasis has been on situating family behavior and social change within a historical context. This approach provides a way of understanding how people's lives are profoundly shaped by their social and historical circumstances, such as industrialization, urbanization, economic conditions, migration, wars, and educational opportunities. Moreover, it was recognized that while families have changed in significant ways, many of our current behaviors are reminiscent of those evidenced over a century ago. For example, similar to the past, most young people "couple" and have children, and many are delaying marriage and parenthood until much later ages. Indeed, there has always been diversity in family life and fluctuations in the timing of family-related transitional behaviors are the norm rather than the exception. This idea supports our "boomerang age" metaphor in a broader sense that family life does not display a linear pattern of development, and in fact, can sometimes revert to patterns very similar to "bygone days."

Similarly, compared to our primary historical benchmark of the 1950s, we have also observed continuity in many family-related behaviors. Yet profound transformation in the family-related transitional behaviors of young adults in many Westernized societies have occurred at the same time. It was emphasized that the "traditional" family of the 1950s was a qualitatively new phenomenon and actually represented a "historical fluke" based on a unique and temporary conjuncture of economic, social, and political forces. For example, for the first time in over a hundred years, the age of marriage and motherhood fell, fertility increased, and divorce rates declined. Since that time, however, young adults have been remaining at home until later ages, are staying in school longer, and are marrying and having children at later ages. They are also increasingly likely to return to refill the midlife parental nest.

Young adults commonly experiment with non-traditional living arrangements, formed by non-marital heterosexual and homosexual partnership unions. Divorce rates have also skyrocketed, although they have declined somewhat in most countries under study over the past ten to fifteen years. One notable exception to these patterns is Italy, which exhibits stronger traditional or "familistic" behaviors, such as remaining at home until marriage and relatively low divorce rates. Thus, despite continuity and some minor exceptions to broader patterns, these widespread changes, especially since the 1950s, further converge to produce a unique socio-historical location. In short, unlike the post-World War II family, current living arrangement patterns and family-related transitional behaviors of young adults are characterized by greater flexibility, reversibility, and impermanence.

There are many macro-level factors that contribute to evolving family behaviors. As noted by Liefbroer (1999), the economy and social structure of Western societies have undergone dramatic changes since the 1950s. One major change has been in the area of educational expansion. Although this process began more than a century ago, increases became more apparent during the second half of the twentieth century. Now, young women are as likely to go to college as young men, and this prolonged participation in the educational system has had profound consequences for the process of family formation. For example, in the U.S. in 1950, among people twenty-five to twenty-nine years of age, 53 percent were high school graduates and 8 percent were college graduates. This rose to 74 percent and 16 percent, respectively, by 1970, and this rise continued for decades. Among African Americans the increase was even more striking, with the gap in educational attainment narrowing substantially (See U.S. Bureau of the Census, 1992, table 219). Marriage and children can be an impediment to one's studies, particularly for women. Moreover, in virtually all Western countries, women have increasingly been likely to participate in the labor force. Young adults also typically have fewer resources than older-aged adults (especially students), such that living with parents can be an attractive way to maximize economic and social resources.

The transition to adulthood has also influenced by economic developments in Western society. In the 1960s and 1970s, Western countries experienced a boom, which resulted in a sharp rise in income. Despite rising educational levels during the 1970s, the postwar period of economic security and relative affluence did not last. The economic well-being of North American families began to drop during the recessions of the 1970s and the early 1980s. Unemployment reached a high of almost 10 percent of the labor force in 1982, the highest rate since the Great Depression of the 1930s (U.S. Bureau of the Census, 1993, table 608). Despite the increased labor force participation of women, the poverty rate for families began to increase in the second half of the 1970s, from a low of 8.8 percent in 1974 to 12.2 percent in 1982 (U.S. Bureau of the Census, 1993, table 744).

This economic climate deteriorated in the 1980s and 1990s, and this may have contributed to the postponement of adult roles and the increasing likelihood of coresidence. Moreover, increasing immigration in North America from countries contributes to higher rates of intergenerational doubling-up, since cultural preferences for family living predominate in many ethnic families. This factor is also illustrated by the fact that many young adults in familistic European societies (e.g., Italy) exhibit the highest coresidence rates and the latest ages of homeleaving.

Cultural and technological changes have also played a major role in affecting the timing and nature of family-related transitions to adulthood. First, there has been steady erosion in the authority of existing normative institutions. In particular, many young adults, as a result of secularization, have increasingly been likely to question traditional "family values," which include earlier family formation and a tendency to shun non-marital cohabitation and divorce. One important consequences of this individualization process is that young adults structure their intimate relationships in different ways. Living together in "trial marriages," for example, is an increasingly popular union formation that reflects a trend toward secularization and a break away from traditional family practices and values. Furthermore, more egalitarian gender roles as a result of the feminist movement have resulted in women giving more priority to their education and careers, which leads them to postpone marriage and divorce.

Technological innovations have also been instrumental for the changes in family formations, which have occurred in Western societies. One of most significant was the sexual revolution, spurred by the introduction and widespread distribution of reliable contraceptives, such as the pill, IUD, and condoms. These contraceptives have increased opportunities for family planning, and enabled people to postpone having children. Moreover, as observed by Liefbroer (1999), the general availability of contraceptives has also changed the values of young adults about family formation—namely, it brought about the separation of sex and reproduction.

Finally, the mass media and consumerism has also played a role in affecting the transition to adulthood. Generally, many young adults have become enthusiastic consumers of mass media products and services, such as magazines, movies, television, advertising, music, consumer goods, and financial services. Therefore, delaying adult transitions (e.g., getting married and having children) and remaining at home until later ages, allows many economic benefits. However, being able to purchase these goods and services requires young adults to have relatively high disposable incomes. Young people living at home, for example, can save money and purchase luxury goods, since many do not have to full pay rent or room/board. Homeward-bound college grads, for example, can not only pay back student loans and save money, but can also invest their entry-level earnings and begin to make long-term financial investments (Paul, 2001).

Indeed, in the U.S., many business people actively target the "boomerang kid" market (Furedi, 2003).

In summary, it is important to consider that when we compare today's families to earlier times in history, we must be careful not to overestimate familial change and trends related to diversity. This does not mean that young adults and their families have not experienced dramatic changes that have profoundly affected transitions to adulthood and created a "boomerang age." Rather, it means that we must be cognizant of the fact that the life courses of young adults and their families continue to evolve in ways that reflect innovation and adaptation to changing economic and social contexts.

## Questions for Discussion and Debate

1.  Social historians argue that family relationships reflect the socio-demographic, political and economic context in which families live. What major factors have affected family life courses over the past century in North American and/or specific European countries? How have these factors affected intergenerational relations and patterns of support?

2.  How have technological advances (medical and non-medical) impacted the family-related life courses of aging families? Are factors such as gender, race, socio-economic status and geographical region important to consider?

3.  "The past is said to be a window into the future." Critically evaluate this statement with respect to one family-related aspect of the transition to adulthood (e.g., such as gender roles in relation to employment or marital patterns).

4.  Provide an argument for and against the following statement: "Today's young adults have more choice with regard to their marital and family formation patterns compared to young adults 100 years ago."

5.  Discuss how changes to state policies and programs (e.g., in education, housing, labour market) may have affected family-related transitions to adulthood over the last century? Provide examples to illustrate.

# 4

# Leaving the Parental Home: Homeleavers, Mature Coresiders, and Boomerang Kids

Moving out of the parental home and into a separate residence is a significant and meaningful milestone for most young people in navigating their way to adulthood. As previously noted, we have witnessed dramatic transformations in the timing, as well as in the circumstances underlying this transitional event. Compared to earlier decades, today's young adults in the United States, Canada, and many European countries are increasingly leaving home at later ages, and tend to leave to form non-family households (e.g., see Aquilino, 1999; Cherlin et al., 1997; Galland, 1997; Goldscheider and Goldscheider, 1999). Moreover, young adults are less likely to leave home to form legal, heterosexual marital unions, which was a dominant pathway out of the parental home in many industrialized countries during the 1950s and 1960s (Goldscheider and Goldscheider, 1999).

Extended intergenerational coresidence involving young adults can be formed by either delayed homeleaving or when young adults return home. Not only are young people postponing their final departures from the parental home without ever having left, but they are increasingly likely to refill parental nests as "boomerang kids," particularly in the United States, Canada and in many European countries such as Britain and France.

Indeed, this trend of home returning has become an expectable transitional event during midlife family development and is regularly reflected in popular culture. For example, American consumer trend expert Faith Popcorn recently coined a new term, "B2B" or "Back to Bedroom," which she describes as "the phenomenon of jobless Gen Xers and Gen Yers returning to their parents' homes." Additionally, NBC's 2004 fall lineup included a new show called

Happy Family, a sitcom about a middle-aged couple living with their adult children.

This high rate of home returning is unprecedented from a histori-cal perspective and contributes to the pattern of later homeleaving. It also sensitizes us to the fact that life course and living arrange-ment transitions are not always permanent and are highly fluid in modern society. In this case, the transitional event of homeleaving can become "reversed." It is also understood that reverting back to a previous state can bring with it new experiences, expecta-tions, roles, and statuses. Thus, home returning is important to consider as an emergent and distinct transitional behavior because it has unique demographic, economic, and sociological causal structures and implications.

In light of these trends, the purpose of this chapter is to present contemporary North American and European research on homeleaving, parent-child coresidence, and home returning. This will entail consideration of how socio-demographic, family background and individual-level factors, within the context of broader macro-level patterns, are linked to the timing and nature of homeleaving and re-turning. Moreover, since patterns of intergenerational coresidence have profound implications for other family members (notably parents), attention will also be paid to examining intergenerational relations. For example, Hareven (1996) notes that the task of synchronizing individual transitions with familial ones can sometimes generate intergenerational tensions and conflicts, especially when a young adult's individual goals are at odds with the needs of aging parents during this phase of family development.

Before we turn to contemporary homeleaving trends and their explanations, it is important to first consider a number of conceptual and methodological issues relevant to the launching phase of young adults' lives. A review of research on the timing and pathways out of (and back into) the parental home will follow. This will lead to a discussion of how the timing and nature of these events affect "linked lives," with a focus on midlife parent-adult child relationships.

## Who is a Homeleaver? A Mature Coresider?
## A Boomerang Kid?

It is commonly recognized that leaving the parental home is a transitional behavior that entails a *process of separation*. Young adults can physically separate from the parental home, although they can continue to be financially or social-psychologically dependent upon their families and/or on parental household resources. For example, a young adult may move into an apartment with a roommate, but continue to have daily, emotional contact and support from one or both parents, receive food, money, or gifts, and continue to rely on many of their parent's household utilities (e.g., to do laundry, use the family car). Indeed, some research suggests that parents are more likely than children to report them still living at home (Young, 1987).

In addition, some young adults leave home but live in group quarters (e.g., barracks, dorms) or family settings, illustrating Goldscheider and DaVanzo's (1985) concept of "semi-autonomous" living arrangements. The two most commonly identified routes out of the home that lead to semi-autonomous living arrangements are leaving to attend school and military service, although both of these pathways have changed substantially over the past century. For example, in chapter 3 it was shown that the dominance of the military in the early lives of American men during the middle of the last century should not be underestimated. Nearly half (47 percent) of the young men in the nest-leaving cohort of 1938 to 1944 first left home to go to war as their first "family role hiatus." The importance of military service continued even after World War II, although sharp declines occurred. Yet still more than a quarter of young men in the later years of the baby boom first moved out of the parental home and into the military (Goldscheider and Goldscheider, 1999: 31).

Ideally, homeleaving should be conceptualized as a multi-dimensional behavior that entails physical as well as non-physical dimensions of separation and autonomy. However, researchers usually measure it as a discrete transitional event in the form of a physical residential move from the parental home. Typically, young adults must be absent from the parental home for spells of at least four months or more to constitute a separation. Researchers also tend to collect data on the first and last departure, since counting only the "last" departure as "true" nest-leaving would miss home returning. Moreover, remaining at home past the usual age of approximately nineteen is generally conceptualized as "home staying" or intergenerational coresidence, while coresidence past the age of twenty-five has been deemed "mature coresidency" (e.g. see Mitchell, Wister, and Gee, 2002). Similar to the measurement of homeleaving spells, home returning as a "boomerang kid" is usually measured as a return that consists of a stay of at least four months, after a duration away for at least four months. This time frame is widely adopted in order to prevent the inclusion of returns that are of a very short or temporary nature (e.g., returning for summer break), since these types of returns are qualitatively very different from a more definite return.

Another important measurement issue relates to how estimates of homeleaving behavior are calculated. Researchers commonly employ two methods and each approach has its unique strengths and weaknesses. One method is to provide median (or sometimes mean) ages of leaving home in a particular year for all young adults of a particular age. The other method is to calculate age at leaving home by following specific birth cohorts over time (either using panel data or retrospective event-history questionnaires in which an individual is asked to recall dates of housing moves, etc.). While the former method provides a rough estimate of homeleaving timing in a given year, a key limitation of this approach is that some people in the population have not been exposed to the full risk of homeleaving. In other words, if the rate is changing, there will be error in using cross-sectional data. The problem can be mitigated by using a particular age group, such as young adults aged twenty-five to twenty-nine, since exposure is less variable. The strength of the latter approach lies its ability to capture the probability of young adults leaving home over time. This method is sensitive to the changing rates and differential exposure to those rates. However, cohort-based research on homeleaving is usually dated because of the time lag between data collection periods.

In chapter 3 it was demonstrated that, from a socio-historical macro-perspective, broad fluctuations in homeleaving patterns can be traced to changing economic times and employment opportunity structures, as well as to alterations in marriage and family patterns, such as later ages of marriage. However, in keeping with the life course perspective's concept of heterogeneity in life course transitional behaviors, it is acknowledged that considerable diversity at both the macro and micro level characterizes the homeleaving process. As we have already shown, not all Westernized industrialized countries exhibit identical patterns of homeleaving and intergenerational coresidence, despite some similarity in economic conditions and in family formation trends.

In fact, studies on this topic reveal considerable diversity in homeleaving or home staying processes within countries. In other words, there is not a singular institutionalized life course. Also, the trajectories followed during young adulthood are shaped by the unique characteristics of the individual, their families, and the broader ecological environment. For example, at the level of the individual and their families within a given country, one's gender, cultural heritage (race/ethnicity), and personal resources are qualities that influence opportunities, constraints, and behaviors. In the next section, a review of literature on the theme of heterogeneity of the life course will be examined in order to appreciate diversity in nestleaving trends within the countries constituting the focus of this book. This will be followed by a more detailed explanation of reasons for variability in these patterns as well as their general implications for intergenerational relations.

## The Timing of Homeleaving and Pathways Out of the Parental Home

Recent statistics document that a large proportion of young adults aged eighteen and over reside in parental homes. Furthermore, there is also an increasing propensity for older-aged young people to live at home in North America as "mature coresiders." According to the 2001 Current Population Survey (CPS), 50.2 percent of U.S. young adults aged eighteen to twenty-four and 10.6 percent of those aged twenty-five to thirty-four were coresiding in a parental household. It should be noted that the U.S. Census included unmarried students living in college dorms as "living at home," which may slightly inflate coresidence rates. Yet a similar pattern is revealed for Canada in 2001, although rates for the identical age groups are not available. In Canada, 58 percent of young adults aged twenty to twenty-four and 23.7 percent of those aged twenty-five to twenty-nine were living in a parental home (Statistics Canada, 2001). Moreover, these rates of coresidence have risen over the last few decades. For instance, 41 percent of Canadian young adults aged twenty to twenty-nine lived with their parents in 2001, a jump from 27 percent in 1981 (Statistics Canada, 2002).

European data on intergenerational coresidence also demonstrates a general tendency for young adults to remain at home until later ages. However, variations in the age at leaving home show a geographical gradient. Generally, the median age at leaving home is lowest in Northern Europe, similar to the U.S. In Southern Europe, leaving home occurs much later than in Northern and Western

Europe. In figure 4.1, we observe that the median age at which young adults leave home is approximately nineteen to twenty in the U.S. and Canada for females and males, respectively. In Europe, there is considerable variation in the median age at homeleaving. Italy displays the latest median ages by which 50 percent of young adults leave home at approximately thirty-one for males and twenty-eight for females, while Sweden exhibits the lowest median ages, which are similar to North American patterns. The European Datamonitor also highlights the Italian experience—at least 90 percent of young Italian men and women aged eighteen to twenty-four lived with their parents in 2002. This compares to only about 45-60 percent in countries such as Britain, France, Germany and the Netherlands (BBC News, 2002).

With regard to mature co-residency in Europe, it is interesting to note that while this trend is also evident in many countries, living at home past the age of twenty-five is not as common in the Netherlands and Sweden while it is particularly pronounced in Italy. In Italy, it is especially prevalent among older males and is known as

**Figure 4.1**
**Median Age at Leaving Home Estimates for Selected Countries,**
**Males and Females, 2000**

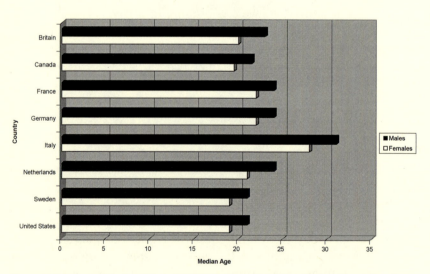

Sources: European data from Eurostat (2002). Canadian data calculated by author from Stats Canada, 2001 GSS; U.S. female data from Andersson and Philipov (21002), male data estimated by author. All estimates are based on life table survival analysis.

the "mammoni phenomenon." Between 1995 and 2000, for example, the proportion of Italian men aged thirty to thirty-four rose from 20 to 27 percent. Indeed, other studies show that seven of ten single Italian men over the age of thirty-five still live in the parental home, and it is considered normal for a man to live at home into his thirties or even forties (Pike and Allen, 2002). Conversely, in Germany and France only about 10 percent of young adults have not left their parents by age thirty (Corijn and Klijzing, 2001).

Yet even with the same country, young adults display considerable diversity in homeleaving. Generally, researchers find that characteristics such as gender, family structure, socio-economic status, race/ethnicity, intergenerational relationship quality, school attendance, labor force activity, personal income and region/community size can profoundly shape the timing and nature of this life course event. Next, we summarize research that documents the relative importance of these factors, first by reviewing North American research, followed by an overview of European research on this topic.

Consistent with its life course location in late adolescence and early adulthood, patterns of leaving home among women and men are quite marked. Overall, young women tend to leave home earlier than young men in both the United States and Canada, although overall timing conceals wide gender differences in the likelihood of leaving home by a given pathway. Women tend to marry at earlier ages than men and are also more likely to begin a nontraditional family, either through cohabitation or single parenthood. At the other extreme of gender role specialization, nearly all those who left home in the U.S. to join the military are men. In fact, women were only 3 percent as likely to leave home in conjunction with military service as men during the twentieth century (Goldscheider and Goldscheider, 1999).

A variety of family background factors are also found to affect homeleaving. Family structure has an important influence on the timing and pathways out of the parental household. Living in non-intact households is found to lead to early homeleaving. In particular, exposure to a stepfamily is found to lead to early homeleaving and more often due to conflict (Aquilino, 1991; Zhao et al., 1995; Mitchell, 1994). Moreover, there may be a positive selection factor in the propensity to remain home until later ages; that is, adult children who get along better with their parents are more likely to do so (Aquilino, 1990; Mitchell, Wister, and Gee, 2000), after controlling

for other factors. Thus, "social capital" in the form of close, supportive family bonds can make the family home a very comfortable "feathered nest" and decrease the probability of early homeleaving.

Parental socio-economic status, number of siblings and parental
financial support are additional family background factors found to
affect the timing and pathways of homeleaving (Beaupré et al., 2003;
Goldscheider and Goldscheider, 1999; Mitchell, Wister and Gee,
2004). More highly educated parents generally expect their children
to complete their high school education and attend college, which
can reduce the probability of delayed homeleaving. Moreover, parental financial resources may be influential in homeleaving transitions. Avery, Goldscheider, (1992), Ermisch (1997) and Garasky and
Speare (2002) find that greater parental resources (i.e., income,
wealth) accelerate homeleaving processes. It is speculated that this
allows these families to purchase privacy and independence in their
living arrangements. Number of siblings is also found to affect the
probability of remaining at home until later ages because of limits to
and competition over parental resources or because of household
crowding (Avery et al., 1992, Ward et al., 1992).

Race/ethnicity are factors also found to significantly affect the
timing and routes out of the parental household. Goldscheider and
Goldscheider (1999) assert that this occurs because ethnicity often
implies both restricted access to opportunities and some particular
norms and preferences. These authors find that in the U.S., blacks
and Hispanics, compared to non-Hispanic whites tend to leave home
more slowly. However, ethnic differences in timing obscure even
larger differences in routes out of the home. Notably, leaving for
marriage or for employment show some of the strongest differences
by race/ethnicity. Whites have increasingly been leaving home to
cohabit, and both blacks and non-Hispanic whites are less likely to
marry than Hispanics. This finding is supported in a recent national
survey which found that 78 percent of Latinos agreed with the statement, "it is better for children to live in their parents' home until they
get married" (Paul, 2003).

Leaving home to attend college has become a popular route out
of the home. Although there has been sign of slight convergence
among all groups, it is less likely among blacks and Hispanics than
non-Hispanic whites. With regard to leaving home to take a job, few
black Americans in the 1980s and 1990s left home to establish a
new home in conjunction with getting a first job or changing jobs.

This finding is attributed to differences in employment opportunities between blacks and whites and may also reflect suggests stronger intergenerational ties in the black community. However, Hispanics often leave home to find a job, partly because many are recent immigrants. Finally, there is evidence of convergence in the likelihood of leaving home for the military between blacks and whites. Interestingly, the convergence in leaving home for military service occurred when it stopped being an important pathway out of the home and to a secure career.

Moreover, Goldscheider and Goldscheider (1999) further assert that:

> Our understanding of the ethnic differential in leaving home suggests that only when ethnic communities retain some aspects of language or live in residentially dense ethnic areas do their family patterns remain distinctive. In short, the structural basis of ethnicity that indicates community and shared values reinforces ethnic distinctiveness. When assimilation occurs, there are few supports to ethnic family continuities; ethnic groups lose their distinctive family traits, including their distinctive patterns of when young adults leave home and the context that pulls them from the parental home or pushes them out of the home. Exposure to the culture of the United States and the increasing use of English as a daily language appear to be important factors in their loss of distinctive family patterns.

These researchers observe that outside of larger residential enclaves (which may have a counter-assimilatory tendency), Hispanics (and the ethnic diversity within the Hispanic population) are moving toward the white model of family patterns. Conversely, the continuing racial divide between blacks and whites profoundly affect racism and discrimination. This perpetuates the distinctive family patterns of blacks, particularly in ways that are disruptive to family life among the current generational and can limit family formation and the economic activities of black young adults. Unfortunately, very little data on other racial/ethnic groups (such as Asian Americans) is available.

In Canada, Boyd (2000) using census data shows that ethnic origin is one of the strongest demographic factors related to intergenerational doubling-up. Notably, those from Southern European, South Asian, and Asian countries display high rates of coresidence. Moreover, many young adults from familistic backgrounds report that they are more likely to leave home for marriage rather than individualistic pursuits, such as "to seek independence" or to "cohabit," Indo-Canadian young adults display late ages of homeleaving and often leave home at the time of marriage (particularly daughters), and this often entails some type of arranged marriage. In contrast, those identifying with British cultural backgrounds are the most likely to report leaving home to "seek independence," while Chinese young adults commonly leave for educational pursuits. Those identifying with Southern-European origins also show later ages of homeleaving, but reveal more "mixed" routes out of the parental home (Mitchell, Wister, and Gee, 2003).

Other research on this topic also reveals that young adults perceive greater parental involvement in their decision to leave home, depending upon a young adult's ethnic identity. In particular, Indo-Canadians report a very high level of parental input in their decision to leave home, while those identifying with British backgrounds are more likely to perceive their decision in individualistic terms, unless they left home under conditions of strained or conflictual intergenerational relations (Mitchell, 2003).

With regard to other characteristics of young adults, researchers find that in both the United States and Canada, youths with greater financial resources and those who are employed generally leave home earlier than those with less income and the unemployed (Boyd, 1998; Boyd and Norris, 1999). Higher personal income enables young adults to support residential independence since they have the income necessary to maintain an independent lifestyle (Card and Lemieux, 2000; Rosenweig and Wolpin, 1993). Conversely, young adults who are looking for work have a tendency to remain at home longer than those who are attending post-secondary school or are in the paid labor force (Goldscheider and Goldscheider, 1999; Mitchell, Wister, and Gee, 2004).

It is also important to consider geographic factors in addition to individual and family-level characteristics, since where one resides can greatly affect opportunities related to employment and the location of educational institutions. "Local culture" can also affect family-related norms and preferences, as well as expectations related to dependency and autonomy. In short, regional variations can be viewed as an important social or community context that can shape family relationships and family behaviors. The American West, for example, has long been characterized as an area of strong "individualism," with early marriage and independence from parents and high levels of divorce (Castleton and Goldscheider, 1989). Conversely, the South has historically exhibited earlier and more stable marriages (Goldscheider and Waite, 1991), and these trends have persisted over time. The regional pattern of leaving home for employment reasons resembles that of leaving home for independence, although the patterns are less strong. With regard to leaving home for college, those growing up in New England are the most likely to leave home for this reason. For example, those living in the Mid-Atlantic/Midwest area display only about three-quarters the likelihood of taking this pathway out of the home at a given age (Goldscheider and Goldscheider, 1999).

Moreover, there are also large regional differences in military service out of the home. Young people growing up in the traditional core area (the South and Western portions of the Midwest) as well as the area to its immediate north and east (the Mid-Atlantic/Midwest regions) have the lowest likelihood of leaving home to the military. By way of contrast, both New England and the Mountain regions exhibit higher levels of leaving to the military, with the Pacific region at a somewhat intermediate level (Goldscheider and Goldscheider, 1999).

In Canada, there are also some striking differences by region, especially by province/territory in the propensity of young adults aged twenty to twenty-nine to live in parental homes. Notably, about half of young adults from Newfoundland and Ontario were living with their parents in 2001 compared to less than one-third in provinces such as Saskatchewan, Alberta and the Yukon. Moreover, the proportion of young adults in the parental home is highest in metropolitan areas such as Toronto (54 percent) and Vancouver (45.7 percent) (Statistics Canada, 2001), urban centers that also have very high housings costs. Unfortunately data are not available on how pathways out of the parental home vary by regional factors in Canada.

European research on the timing and pathways of homeleaving usually focuses on the same sets of factors as North American researchers and generally finds similar influences. For example, women in the European countries of interest in this book tend to leave home earlier and are less likely to coreside with parents than men (e.g., Corijn, 2001). Married young adults rarely live at home, and higher parental and personal income is negatively related to the propensity to coreside. Employment status is also found to affect intergenerational household living arrangements. Yet this fact is not as influential in the decision to leave home in Northern Europe, while being unemployed in Italy is positively associated with staying home (Giannelli and Monfardini, 2000).

Family background factors and the quality of intergenerational relations are also influential in homeleaving timing and the routes taken out of the parental home. French researchers Bozon and Villeneuve-Gokalp (1994), for instance, show that when relationships are difficult, children tend to leave the parental home to form a union about one year earlier than those with good relations, and that parental divorce results in children leaving the parental home earlier than those whose parents remained together.

Finally, geographical variations in homeleaving are also found within European countries, often due to the availability of jobs, accessibility to post-secondary institutions, and the cost of housing. For example, in Italy, many young adults face dim job prospects after a university education, since unemployment is above 9 percent nationally. In southern Italy, unemployment rates are up to 18 percent (Pike and Allen, 2002). Housing costs also tend to be higher in urban areas, which can make extended home staying attractive to many young people.

### Premature or Postponed Passages: Factors Contributing to Early or Late Homeleaving

Research has also focused on factors that contribute to early or "premature leaving" and "mature coresidency." These patterns of homeleaving are important to consider separately because they have the potential to significantly affect the life courses of young people and their families in profound ways. Transitions occurring "too early" or "too late" can also reflect levels of social capital embedded within the intergenerational relationship, as well as to set up a chain reaction of consequences for parent-child relations and interactions that can reverberate over the life course. Early homeleaving, particularly when not in conjunction with attending a residential school away from home (e.g., under the age of under the age eighteen), has been shown to have a host of negative repercussions for the trajectory of young people into successful career patterns and stable families (Goldscheider and Goldscheider, 1999). For example, these early leavers tend to have lower educational attainment and are at a higher risk of homelessness, prostitution, and other problems, which can seriously limit their life chances and opportunities. Moreover, many of these young people do not have the option to return home because of a history of problematic intergenerational relations and this can place them at a distinct disadvantage. This is because they are unable to draw upon parental household resources during times of crisis or need.

At the other end of this age spectrum, living at home well past the "normal" age of emancipation (e.g., past age twenty-five) as a "mature coresider" is viewed as a living arrangement that can have important consequences for both adult children and their families. For example, late homeleaving can delay the empty nest period for parents, while providing the potential to provide a myriad of benefits to young adults that can make the "complete" transition to adulthood much easier. These young adults can use the resources of the parental household to expand their educational training, save money, and acquire consumer goods while continuing to live in a supportive family setting.

What factors promote early or late nestleaving? One of the strongest sets of findings is that family disruption in the parental household can promote premature homeleaving. In particular, children who have experienced a great deal of household change while growing up or are exposed to stepfamilies have a high risk of early home leaving due to "conflict at home" (Goldscheider and Goldscheider, 1999; Mitchell, 1994; Zhao, Rajulton, and Ravanera, 1995). Young people will often try to escape these stressful environments or move because they feel abandoned by their parents. Moreover, very young leavers are particularly likely to be girls from poor families. Yet contrary to stereotypes, young people from both black and Hispanic families are generally less likely than non-Hispanic whites to leave the parental home at very early ages, such as at age fifteen or sixteen (Goldscheider and Goldscheider, 1999).

Turning to late homeleaving, research on "mature coresidency" also finds that there are a number of factors that increase the likelihood of remaining at home until later ages. Not surprising, those with more social capital in the form of supportive intergenerational ties (especially with moms) are more likely to remain at home past the age of twenty-five. For example, a recent national Canadian study by Mitchell, Wister, and Gee (2002) find that emotional closeness to parents (while growing up) plays a strong role in the determination of living at home as "mature coresiders," controlling for other factors such as the child's level of educational attainment or their employment status. Other key predictors include: younger age (twenty-five to twenty-nine vs. thirty to thirty-four), being male, unemployment, having higher levels of education, and being unmarried.

Overall, this body of research reveals some dominant themes when trying to summarize and explain current trends in homeleaving. First, it is clear that family-related contexts shape nestleaving on a variety of levels. The timing of marriage, as previously outlined, is often linked with leaving home and may be affected by a young adults' gender, cultural background, and family history. In addition, the emergence of alternates to marriage, particularly cohabitation, nonfamily living arrangements, and unmarried parenthood have been clearly linked to the timing and pathways out of the parental and the propensity to adopt these behaviors is affected by family norms, expectations, and preferences. Moreover, the family context of the parental home with respect to the quality of intergenerational relations is also crucial; whether or not young adults can be provided with a supportive environment has a significant impact on whether or not a young adult will remain at home for a longer period of time (Mitchell, Wister, and Gee, 2004).

Economic conditions are also highly important in understanding the timing of leaving home and the paths taken out of the parental household. As noted by Goldscheider and Goldscheider (1999), independence requires a set of economic conditions conducive to residential independence. This can include resources that parents can use to support the independent residence of their children and/or the ability of children to sustain their independence through steady employment.

It is also recognized that family-related and economic circumstances can widely vary among the countries of interest in this book. For example, there are considerably higher levels of cohabitation outside of marital unions for Canada (particularly Quebec), Britain, Sweden, France, Germany, the Netherlands than for United States or Italy. These countries also differ in employment policies. Sweden, France, Germany, and Italy, similar to many other European countries with a strong social safety net, protect the jobs and wages of the currently employed and tolerate high levels of unemployment. The Netherlands, in contrast, like the United States, Canada, and Britain, has cut benefits and encouraged employment growth, if often mostly of "lousy jobs" with the result that its unemployment rate is barely half of these other countries. The lower-unemployment economies of the Netherlands and the United States may provide jobs that, although unlikely to be "career" opportunities and thus not the basis for making long-term plans and commitments, are more likely to allow young people to move out of the parental home into shared apartments with roommates and/or cohabiting partners.

Moreover, the United States has the highest proportion of young adults who attend college and is also the only country where such a high proportion attends while living away from home. This trend has been associated with particularly American patterns of semiautonomous living arrangements among very young adults, similar to the military experience of generations past. However, this residential college pattern is more common among both young women and men whereas military service has largely been the domain of young men (Goldscheider and Goldscheider, 1999).

## Home Again: Contemporary Patterns of Home Returning

It has been noted that the phenomenon of adult children moving back to the parental home has been rising since the 1970s, and also contributes to the dramatic increase in the number of young adults who live with their parents. In table 4.1, it is estimated that about 40 percent of American young adults return home, and it is observed that sons are more likely to return than daughters (Goldscheider and Goldscheider, 1999). In Canada, recent census data (2002a) reveal that 28 percent of young women aged 33 percent of young men aged twenty to twenty-nine have returned home at least once after an initial departure. Indeed, Goldscheider and Goldscheider (1999) document that, "The leaving home transition has become more renewable, less of a one-way street and more like a circular migration."

With regard to home returning trends in Europe, the scant research that is available to date is mainly based on Britain (e.g., see Berrington, 2001), although it is documented that there is an increasing likelihood that young people, especially in Northern Europe, "boomerang" home (BBC News, 2002). In July 2001, for example, a British study commissioned by Abbey National showed that the proportion of young adults who return home had nearly doubled from 25 percent in 1950 to 46 percent in 2003, however, some researchers maintain that this is an inflated estimate. More similar to Canadian trends, another British survey commissioned by Btopenworld in 2002 claimed that 27 percent of first-time home leavers return home at least once, and that one in ten newly independent young adults move out and are back again (up to four times) before they leave for good. Many of these young adults originally

left home "to seek independence," or for reasons related to employ-
ment/education, rather than for a union formation, a finding that
was replicated in another large-scale British study, known as the
National Child Development Study. This is one of the few national
data sources of reasons for leaving home and the probability of returning (Jones, 1995).

Likewise, in countries whereby marriage is not a primary pathway out of the parental home, returning has become more commonplace. It is estimated that more than one fifth of young adults in
France return home (Villeneuve-Gokalp, 2002), and there is some
evidence to suggest that home returning rates are similar in Germany (Corijn and Klijzing, 2001). Although exact estimates are unavailable in the Netherlands and Italy, home returning in the Netherlands is purported to similar to Sweden, since both countries have
more favorable economic conditions and housing policies conducive to residential independence. While unemployment is high in
Italy, home returning is probably the least common here because
children tend to depart at relatively late ages for marriage and have

**Figure 4.2**
**Home Returning Estimates Among Young Adults**
**for Selected Countries, 1995-2001**

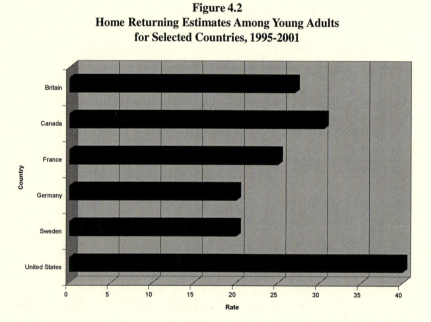

Data Sources: Britain (Btopenworld, 2002); Canada (Statistics Canada, 2002); Germany
(Corijn and Kilzing, 2001); France (Villeneuve-Gokalp, 2002); Sweden (Lieberg, 1997);
U.S. (Goldscheider and Goldscheider, 1999).

a very low divorce rate. Italian young adults also tend to move very close to the parental home, which can facilitate exchanges of support when needed (Mazzuco, 2003).

Why are young adults increasingly likely to flock back to the parental nest? At a macro-level, researchers usually emphasize economic factors which in turn affect opportunity structures and delay adult transitions and statuses. In this way, family-related change in union formation among young adults has also helped to fuel the trend of home returning. Transitions out of the parental home have become increasingly unstable since the 1950s, when leaving home for marriage during an era of low divorce was generally fairly permanent. In North America and Britain, one-third to one-half of all first marriages are expected to end in divorce, and young adults are marrying and having children at later ages. This can make the parental home a convenient "home base" when one is single and during "transitional periods" or to save money, for example. Cohabitation has also become a popular living arrangement for many young adults, yet this type of union is considerably more fragile than legal marital partnership.

The need for post-secondary attendance has also increased, with enrollment levels skyrocketing in the 1990s in North America and many European countries. Rising tuition costs and the growth of nonresidential colleges have made it more attractive for students to attend colleges part-time, or to take a break after school to save resources before professional or graduate school. Moreover, fewer women return from college bearing an "MRS" degree (Paul, 2001). Robbins, co-author of *Quarterlife Crisis: The Unique Challenges of Life in Your Twenties*, adds another perspective, stating that, "Particularly after losing the structure of academic life, coming home recreates the boundaries that help twentysomethings feel sheltered and anchored." He further adds that this is "a product of the Internet age—there is so much more uncertainty now."

This theme is further echoed by other commentators who assert that young adults may want to return to the safety of their family homes during periods of political and economic instability and upheaval. A notable example is "9/11" (referring to the events of September 11, 2002), when the U.S. was attacked by terrorists by four hijacked jetliners. These planes hit the World Trade Center in New York City, the Pentagon outside of Washington, and one plane crashed into a field in Pennsylvania. Over 3,000 people were killed in a matter of hours, trading on Wall Street stopped, and the U.S. military was placed on high alert. In short, countless lives were significantly changed forever. And although only anecdotal evidence is available at the present time, many observed that in the wake of this horrible devastation, many young people flocked back to the security and comforts of their parents' homes for at least a short period of time.

Moreover, according to Paul (2001), the rise in the homeward bound signifies not only the changing transition to adulthood, but also a fundamental shift in how parents and adult children view their roles within the family. Prior to the mid- to late 1990s, having an adult child back at home was not generally perceived as a desirable living arrangement. This is because it was assumed to violate parental (and Western cultural) expectations for independence and autonomy. This theme was reflected by the North American media and the scholarly literature on the subject by books such as *Boomerang Kids: How to Live with Adult Children who Return Home* (Okimoto and Stegall, 1987). This book counseled parents about thorny issues like charging children rent, the move toward eventual eviction, and negotiating household chores and the general tone was that parents should work hard to "let the children move on."

However, with changing times, parental roles have shifted such that some point the finger at the older generation for facilitating longer periods of residential stays and their children's "bouncing back and forth" from the parental home. For example, a recent (and controversial) article in *Psychology Today* entitled, "The PermaParent Trap" (Paul, 2003) discusses how many parents in today's society are unable to "let go when they ought to" and that this is partly to blame for the high numbers of boomerang kids. Whereas previous generations emphasized educational and financial independence, baby boomer parents (born between 1946 and 1964) are the first generation for whom their children's emotional fulfillment is a primary goal. As a result, some suggest that there is more of a tendency to "hyper-invest" in children and one manifestation of this is the reluctance of some parents to want to empty the nest during midlife.

Moreover, over the past several decades, returning home has become a popular and expectable lifestyle choice for many young adults, especially after college because of low starting salaries in expensive housing markets, to repay student loans and to save money during transitional periods. Research also documents increasing destigmatization and acceptance of intergenerational coresidence, particularly among younger cohorts (Alwin, 1996) and that the majority of college students expect to move back home after completing their education. For example, an on-line job-listing service called Jobtrak.com polled 1,500 American college students and found that 62 percent of them planned to live with their parents after graduation (Franklin, 2003). Moreover, as this living arrangement continues to become more widespread, young adults have become less likely to report feelings of stigmatization by their friends, family, and members of their cultural group (Mitchell, Wister, and Gee, 2004). Therefore, reduced stigma and increased social acceptance can further perpetuate and fuels the popularity of home returning.

With regard to the personal reasons provided by young adults themselves for returning home, young adults usually report that they typically return home for economic reasons, although not necessarily dire economic circumstances. For example, a recent Canadian study conducted by Mitchell (2004) shows that 85.7 percent of all reasons provided by a sample of 1,907 young adults fall into an economic category. A majority (45.1 percent) cites transitional or temporary reasons (e.g., just finished school or travel and need a temporary home base). Other commonly cited economic reasons for home returning are: to save money (e.g., to become residentially independent, to purchase a car, or for a down payment on a condo or house), school-related reasons, financial problems (e.g., business failure, credit card debt), because a relationship ended, or due to high housing costs (especially in urban areas). Moreover, many young adults indicate that they could afford to live on their own, although it would be more difficult to make ends meet. However, they were willing to sacrifice some independence to maintain their parents' standard of living, a phenomenon that has been called an "intergenerational taste effect," whereby the luxuries of one generation become the necessity of the next generation (Crimmins et al., 1991).

To a lesser extent but also noteworthy is the fact that many young adults cited non-economic reasons for returning (14.3 percent fell into this category). Common explanations focused on the following three themes in descending order of preponderance: (1) parents needed help at home because of health issues, aging, separation/ divorce, or death of a spouse; (2) psychological reasons, such as "needed emotional support from parents" or "wanted companionship of parents"; and (3) personal health problems, such as due to substance abuse problems, accident, injury or illness (Mitchell, 2004).

Studies have also been conducted at a multivariate level on how individual-level and family background factors affect the propensity to return home in North America. Generally, in the United States and Canada, sons are slightly more likely to return than females (Aquilino, 1996; Buck and Scott, 1993; Mitchell, Wister, and Gee, 2004). This trend is partly explained by the fact that females tend to marry at younger ages. Also, Boyd and Pryor (1989) postulate that females may be less likely to reside at home at later ages because they are typically subjected to higher levels of intergenerational monitoring and supervision. They also generally face greater expectations with regard to their contributions to domestic labor. Marital status also affects the propensity of young adults to return. Generally, the vast majority of returnees are single, although a small percentage is divorced/separated and married. However, race/ethnicity is not found to affect the likelihood of returning home (Goldscheider and Goldscheider, 1999; Mitchell, Wister, and Gee, 2004).

Another basic tenet of the life course perspective is that early transitions may have significant effects on later transitions. Earlier age at first homeleaving is found to decrease the probability of a return since premature homeleaving may be indicative of a problematic family environment (Mitchell, 1994). Moreover, the pathway taken out of the home at the time of leaving is found to affect the probability of a return. For example, educational and employment transitions at the time of homeleaving are associated with a greater chance of a return, whereas the marriage transition reduces the probability of a boomerang home (Aquilino, 1996; Goldscheider and Goldscheider, 1999; Gee, Mitchell, and Wister, 1995). Leaving home for independence or to cohabit is also strongly associated with home returning, and these pathways are found to be more predictive of a home return that leaving to attend school (Goldscheider and Goldscheider, 1999). Young adults with higher personal incomes are found to be less likely to return home (Mitchell, Wister, and Gee, 2004). Thus, the parental home can act as an important safety net for young adults unable to obtain the income necessary to maintain an independent lifestyle (Card and Lemieux, 2000; Rosenweig and Wolpin, 1993).

With regard to family background factors, findings are mixed with regard to the influence of higher parental socio-economic and family structure on the likelihood of returning home. On the one hand, higher parental socio-economic status is associated with indepen-

dent living because parents are able to purchase privacy and independence in their living arrangements (Ermisch, 1997; Garasky,
2002). On the other hand, more highly educated parents may expect
children to complete their high school and attend college, which
translates to a higher probability of a return once students complete
their schooling (Goldscheider and Goldscheider, 1999). With regard
to family structure, some research finds that lower intergenerational
closeness in stepfamilies or the potential for greater intergenerational
monitoring in lone-parent households may act to deter returning to
these family environments (Gee, Mitchell, and Wister, 1995). However, other research does not find any strong effects related to family structure.

Greater number of siblings is found to decrease the likelihood
of a return due to limits to and competition over parental resources
or because of household crowding. Moreover, research has established that there may be a positive selection factor in the propensity to return home (Aquilino, 1990; Mitchell, 1998); that is,
adult children who get along better with their parents are more
likely to do so. Unfortunately, European research on this topic is
virtually non-existent, although researchers speculate that individual and family-related factors such as gender, marital status,
and family background characteristics (e.g., family structure) have
similar influence on the propensity to return home after an initial
launch.

## Linked Lives: Implications for Intergenerational Relations

Although much remains to be learned about how young adults'
homeleaving decisions affect the life course of other family members, there is some research that highlights how family ties are affected when children leave or return home. In particular, there is a
growing body of literature that documents how nest leaving and
intergenerational coresidence (as a result of delayed homeleaving
or home returning) affects parental experiences and parent-child relations in midlife, a topic to which we now turn.

## Empty Nest Syndrome—Fact or Fiction?

One pervasive belief is that middle- and older-aged parents—
particularly stay-at-home mothers—suffer severe emotional crises
when all their children grow up and leave home (Newman and
Grauerholz, 2002). Commonly dubbed "the empty nest syndrome,"

some psychiatrists claim that this syndrome is a clinically diagnosable condition, and medical journals used to run full-page advertisements for anti-depressants that can be prescribed as treatment (Harkins, 1978).

Why should parents experience the empty nest syndrome? Many theorize that during middle-age and the transition to old age, individuals experience "loss" events. These loss events include the loss of work, the departure of children, the death of partner and the loss of autonomy, or the so-called *cathexis-objects* (Mazzuco, 2003). In order to avoid the emotional suffering from the absence of these persons or activities (or objects), the aging individual needs to have the capacity to shift their emotional investment from one person or activity to another, or to have what Peck (1968) calls "emotional flexibility." Therefore, if one is not able to reinvest one's emotions into another person or activity, these loss events will cause some distress in the form of physical and psychological benefits. Moreover, the psychological consequences depend not only on the number of other roles occupied, but on the nature of the particular role and whether it's loss will result in decreased benefits, privileges, status, and self-esteem.

On one level, the empty nest syndrome makes some intuitive sense, since the roles people occupy provide meaning and behavioral guidance in their lives. And since most women have devoted a significant portion of their lives to raising children, one might expect women to suffer when their children leave because an important part of their identity and motherhood role has gone. Yet according to many researchers, such an explanation rests on some dubious assumptions. Notably, it assumes that being a parent is the individual's only pertinent social role; that when children are gone, they are gone for good, and that when children leave, parenting abruptly stops (Newman and Grauerholz, 2002).

In reality, and contrary to popular belief, research on the "empty nest syndrome" finds that, for most parents, the departure of children is a positive experience. Parents can find freedom, relief from responsibilities, and time for themselves. For example, sociologist Lillian Rubin (1992) found that the stereotype of the painful empty nest is largely a myth. In fact, many of the mothers that she interviewed experienced feelings of accomplishments that they had done their "job" well and were ready to move on the next stage of life. Moreover, many seemed guilty about feeling happy. Such guilt illustrates the pervasiveness of gender-based expectations in parenting and the stereotype that women are supposed to be unhappy when their children leave. However, Rubin did notice some class differences in the way mothers respond to their children leaving home which related to the predictability of the of the "departure date." Notably, working-class parents could not take for granted that their children would attend college, and this made preparation for the empty nest more difficult. Yet, the difficulty is generally brief and does not constitute clinical depression.

Although North American research has not examined ethno-cultural variations on this topic, there is some European research on intergenerational relations in relation to the "empty nest syndrome" which highlights how cultural factors can affect intergenerational relations during homeleaving. For example, Bonifazi et al. (1999) found that many Italian young adults are worried about how their homeleaving will affect their parents because Italy is a country well known for its "familistic" orientations. This includes late departures from the parental home and the strong affective bonds it creates between parents and children. A recent comparative analysis by Mazzuco (2003) on the effect of children's leaving home on parental well-being in France and Italy reveals some distinct differences. Italian mothers show a negative effect of the event, especially when the homeleaver is the last child to leave. Conversely, French mothers report higher levels of well-being since they become more satisfied with their leisure time. Italian fathers, however, do not exhibit a significant negative reaction to their last child's departure while French fathers become less satisfied with their housing situation, but increased satisfaction with their financial situation.

In order to interpret these results, Mazzuco (2003) argues that we need to consider cultural differences in parent-child relations as well as the nature of child launching. Italian society is strongly family-oriented with greater parent-child dependence. For example, the highest percentage in Europe of old individuals having contacts with family every day is registered in Italy at 70 percent (EC Commision, 1993). Whereas in France, the parent-child relationship is more conflictual, especially for girls (Bozon and Villeneuve-Gokalp, 1994). Departures by Italian adults children are also more definitive, whereas departures by young French people are unstable and so the likelihood of returning is higher. Therefore, parents may be aware of this and their reactions are affected by these differences. Italian mothers (who are often homemakers) may also be highly conscious that their day-to-day maternal role has come to an end and that there is a low probability that their children will return. Many French mothers, however, expect that the separation is only temporary, which makes them appreciate the higher disposable leisure time that they have. Also, Italian mothers tend to be much older (aged fifty-seven, on average) when the last child leave home compared to French mothers who are generally much younger (aged fifty-one, on average), such that age differences can also affect reactions (Mazzuco, 2003).

Furthermore, it should be recognized that relationships with parents usually continue long past the time when children leave home, and most young adults find that parents are a continuing source of companionship and support. Yet some young people, after leaving home, have little contact with parents; and others can harbor feelings of resentment toward parents from childhoods that were less than idyllic (Amato and Booth, 2000). Generally, then, the nature of these relationships has important implications, as feelings of affection facilitate exchanges of assistance between parents and adult children (Hogan, Eggebeen, and Clogg, 1993).

## Effects of Staying at Home and Returning Home—Too Close for Comfort?

While research documents the effect of homeleaving on parent-child relations, there is a growing body of literature that highlights the effects of staying home on the parent-child dyad. On a broad level, the trend toward delayed intergenerational coresidence suggests that parental roles and responsibilities have become restructured and more protracted due to social change (Buck and Scott, 1993). Now, many parents must modify prior expectations and resume their day-to-day "in house" parental roles to facilitate their children's transition to adulthood. This has led researchers to comment that parenthood has become a more unpredictable and complex role and experience (Ambert, 1994). In fact, Ambert (1994) urges us to discard outdated notions of parenthood and to recast the construct, including its rights and duties. This is important, she argues, given new social conditions and because of the strong likelihood that parents will continue to be held accountable for their children's survival and well-being. This issue is particularly salient for mothers, who in general are more bound to the parenting role.

However, as previously discussed, recent changes are not uniformly experienced across all social groups. Thus, some families are more likely to be confronted with the extended stay of children or the renewed task of parenting than are other groups.

In a similar vein, the trend of home returning has several distinct implications for intergenerational relations and socialization over the life course. When adult children return, mid- and later-life parents are confronted with carrying out "additional" socialization. This occurs, in part, because parents must continue to impart the expertise, skills and knowledge necessary for their children to become independent adults. It has also been suggested that young adults living at home may adopt their parents' behavior more thoroughly (Boyd and Pryor, 1989). Since "co-residency is an experience lived through a network of family relationships" (Lee and Levy, 1997: 3), it follows that there are unique processes of reciprocal socialization that occur during home returns. One outcome of mutual influence may be greater intergenerational monitoring, whereby parents monitor adult children and children monitor middle-aged and elderly parents (Boyd and Pryor, 1989). It is also possible that parents and their children develop more peer-like orientations toward each other at this time. All of these elements introduce new dimensions into lifelong family socialization.

Moreover, staying at home until later ages or returning home has the potential to either increase intergenerational solidarity or to weaken it (e.g., create intergenerational conflict). While traditional life course theory predicts general dissatisfaction with "mature coresidence" or the return of an adult child, Elder (1994) emphasizes the interplay of human lives and socio-historical context. Given changing social and economic times and the diminishing stigma associated with delayed departures, transition expectations may be redefined in the face of specific parent-child circumstances of adult children and their parents.

During the postwar period between the 1950 and 1990s, social scientists and the popular press usually portrayed home-returning (or mature coresidency more generally) as something aberrant or abnormal. Home returning was assumed to signal family dysfunction or individual pathology, and social scientists frequently offered conceptualizations fraught with negative connotations such as "the returning adult syndrome" and the "cluttered nest" (Boyd and Norris, 1989; Schnaiberg and Goldberg, 1989). Indeed, it was not uncommon for researchers to assume that when young adults return home "everybody loses" (Bibby and Posterski, 1992: 221).

In addition, media images of "boomerang kid" families tended to be sympathetic to a middle-aged, middle-class readership. Parents were often portrayed in newspapers and magazines or on daytime talk shows as victims of greedy or lazy children (Hartung and Sweeney, 1991) afflicted with what has been termed the "Peter Pan Syndrome" (Goldscheider, 1997). Young men, in particular, have been depicted by the media as immature adults (Mamma's boys) or "Scrubs" (a hit song by TLC) who are unable or unwilling to let go of "the apron strings" (Gross, 1991). One article, for instance, urged parents to "cut the cord" before sharing the parental home once again (Tennant, 1992). Taken together, it was typically assumed that mature coresidency or a return to the parental home could only present serious problems for the midlife family.

A growing body of literature provides empirical evidence of the effects of home returning on the social-psychological well-being of parents and their children. These studies generally find that the vast majority of parents and their children are highly satisfied with the living arrangement (Aquilino, 1996; Mitchell, 2001). For example, only a minority of "boomerang kid" families report significant conflict and stress. This is possibly due to a "positive selection factors." Close families tend to stick together, such that unhappy coresident living arrangements would likely dissolve before the typical four-month spell needed to be considered a home returner. This selection process can also inhibit the formation of boomerang living arrangements among less compatible family members.

What are some of the direct effects on intergenerational relations when young adults return to live with their parents? As previously noted, in the past, it was assumed that the presence of boomerang kids in the household because it can create intrafamilial conflict and tensions (Clemens and Axelson, 1985; Schnaiberg and Goldenberg, 1989; Umberson, 1992). Mid-life parents, faced with the day-to-day presence of returnee children were speculated to experience disruption and to think that this situation reflects badly on their childrearing skills (Aldous, 1996). Similarly, children were assumed to feel like social and economic failures due to their inability to maintain residential independence and adult roles and responsibilities. As a result, stress associated with a mutual intergenerational mindset of "where did I go wrong," combined with the extra dependency and responsibility, was speculated to create a host of negative side effects for family functioning and well-being.

Despite these alleged negative effects for intergenerational relations, research shows that over all, both generations are fairly satisfied with the boomerang living arrangement and they do not generally experience high levels of intergenerational combat. Rather, intergenerational relations are characterized by mutual interdependence and reciprocity. Although children tend to receive more instrumental and financial support than parents, children attempt to maintain reciprocity by exchanging a variety of helping behaviors. Some of these exchanges are non-tangible, yet may be perceived as an adequate "reward" for instrumental and financial contributions. Parents, for example, commonly report that they receive a multitude of benefits such as companionships and emotional benefits (Veevers and Mitchell, 1998). That being said, parents are the most satisfied with boomerang home when their children show definitive signs of moving toward adult roles and statuses (Mitchell, 1998). It is also important to note that many parents report that they enjoy helping their children establish themselves as adults, although they do not want this to be a permanent situation. Thus, parents may perceive (and accept) resource imbalances, as well as concomitant "irreplaceable losses" (Berman, 1987) because they feel an obligation and derive fulfillment in providing a home and in continuing support to their children during coresidence.

Young adults also reveal that they enjoy the day-to-day companionship and emotional support of their parents, in addition to the "comforts of home." However, children are more likely than their parents to report economic benefits (e.g., "it is cheaper to live at home, I can save money"), while parents sometimes complain that they feel "taken advantage of" with regard to their domestic labor and financial help.

It is also not surprising that while both generations report that they are mainly satisfied with the return home, the vast majority is able to cite several aspects that they don't like about the living arrangements. These negative consequences have the potential to weaken intergenerational solidarity and create conflict. From the parental perspective, the most commonly cited problem includes a lack of privacy/independence. This finding is hardly surprising, given the long-standing Western cultural ideal of "intimacy at a distance"

(Rosenmayr and Kockeis, 1963). That is, most aging parents want to maintain close contact with their adult children but they generally do not want to live with them. Parents also complain about the following aspects: child messy/does not help out, child's personality/ attitude or lifestyle, child's dependence (Mitchell, 2000). Additional research on this topic finds that while home returners do not negatively affect midlife marriages, returning home multiple times is found to negatively affect the marital relationship (Mitchell and Gee, 1996a), which can spill over to parent-child relationships and create resentment and stress.

Moreover, adult children coresiders also commonly cite a "lack of privacy and independence" as a negative drawback to coresidence (Mitchell, 2003). Other negative aspects of coresidence commonly reported by young people include: conflict and stress, parental rules and regulations, feelings of dependency and having to subject themselves to the parental dictum: "As long as you are under my roof you'll do what I say." This can be difficult for young people after having lived on their own for a period of time prior to their report (Mitchell, 2000).

Finally, although there is an absence of research on the long-term effects of extended coresidence on intergenerational relations, Norris and Tindale (1994) emphasize the need to consider reciprocity in exchange relations in aging family relations in "global" rather than immediate terms. According to Webster, Benson, and Spray (1994: 135) "from a broader sociological perspective, when two individuals enter into a relationship...they make an implicit agreement to give and receive future assistance from one another." Indeed, some research suggests that a return home can result in greater intergenerational sharing and closeness that may affect exchange relations in later life. Notably, young adult coresiders may want to provide more help to parents in later life (i.e., in old age) than non-coresiders in an attempt to "repay" parents for providing them with a home base and burdening them with extra household responsibilities in their time of need (e.g., see Veevers and Mitchell, 1998). In this way, extended coresidence has the potential to enhance intergenerational solidarity and facilitate the continuation of supportive relations across the life courses of parents and their children.

## Summary and Conclusions

This chapter has focused on contemporary patterns in homeleaving as a major family-related transition to adulthood in modern societies. Definitional and measurement issues related to homeleaving were presented, with an emphasis on how homeleaving should ideally be conceptualized as a multi-dimensional transition with both physical and non-physical dimensions. In other words, young adults can physically leave the parental nest although they can continue to have frequent contact with their parents and draw upon parental household resources. Similarity and diversity in the homeleaving process in North America and the selected European countries were also discussed. Generally, departures have become delayed in most Westernized countries due to significant transformations in economic and family-related realms, such as the prolongation of educational enrolment and the related postponement of entry into the labor market and family formation. However, as noted in chapter 3, within a historical or cross-cultural perspective, it is important to consider that parent-child coresidence is not something "new." For example, high rates of coresidence between an aging parent and unmarried adult child were observed in earlier parts of the twenty-first century, particularly during recessionary periods (White, 1994). Some important differences in homeleaving and intergenerational coresidence across and within countries were also noted.

It was also recognized that leaving home is not necessarily a one-time event, and that current high rates of home returning (which do appear unprecedented from a historical perspective) in many countries suggest that this trend is here to stay, a theme that will be revisited in chapter 7. Home returning has become a popular strategy for young adults to maximize their economic and social well-being during the transition to adulthood. This trend also highlights the fact that transitions to adulthood are flexible and subject to reversibility.

Implications of the timing and nature of homeleaving (as well as intergenerational coresidence) for linked lives or intergenerational relations were also explored. It was noted that extended coresidence is generally a positive experience for midlife families. However, parental experiences during midlife can be significantly altered when children remain or return at home, although research suggests that the "empty nest" syndrome is largely mythical. That being said, parental or young adults' reactions to homeleaving may depend upon cultural context and expectations as well as to other related issues such as role loss and identity.

In the next chapter, we will turn our attention to another key family-related transition to adulthood-partnership formation and parenthood. This will include a focus on: unmarried cohabitation and legal marital unions, the timing of first birth, and divorce/union dissolution. Cognizant of the fact that similar to homeleaving these transitions can also become reversed, we will also consider trends in union dissolution such as separation and divorce. And since these transitions can also have profound effects on other family members, we will also consider how union formation/dissolution can affect intergenerational ties.

## Questions for Discussion and Debate

1. Relate notions of individual volition or "free choice" in family-related transitional behaviors to contemporary patterns in homeleaving and home returning.

2. Many researchers argue that "mature coresidency," or living at home past the age of twenty-five carries less stigma now than it did in previous decades. However, the mass media and the general public continue to stereotype older, single males living at home as social and economic failures. Present an argument for and against this negative image and consider how the timing of homeleaving is affected by age norms and social timetables. Also consider why this stereotype is not as prominent in Italy (a phenomenon known as "*mammoni*").

3. Returning to the parental home can also occur in mid or later life (i.e., after the age of thirty-five). Do you think that the reasons for returning are different at later ages compared to the reasons commonly reported by young adults between nineteen and thirty-five? Also, discuss the implications of returning home in mid or later life for individual and family well-being as well as for intergenerational relationships.

4. Generally, early homeleavers are found to experience many negative consequences later in life as a result of their early departures. There is also growing concern over high rates of homelessness among young adults.What kinds of government or community programs and services could assist families and their children to diminish these problems?

5.  Discuss how globalization, technological change, and population aging will affect homeleaving and home returning processes and intergenerational relations in the future.

# 5

## Partners and Parenthood: Family Formation and Dissolution Transitions of Young Adults

The establishment and maintenance of long-term intimate partnerships and the creation of one's own family are often considered key challenges of young adulthood. The life course perspective provides a dynamic and flexible framework for understanding the formation of young people's intimate partnerships and their fertility behavior. It also underscores the importance of situating family-related transitions within their unique historical, socio-economic, and cultural contexts. Whereas the "boomerang age" generation has grown up in an era of sharp social change, their parents grew up in their own distinct historical period—a time when young people left home relatively young to get married and have children, families were relatively prosperous, the "intact" nuclear family was the norm, men were the main breadwinners, and most marriages lasted a lifetime. In other words, most of the parents of the current generation experienced a standard "package of transitions" to adulthood that was fairly stable and predictable.

Since our historical benchmark of the 1950s, however, significant transformations have occurred in the timing and nature of union formation, dissolution, and childbearing activity among young people. Today, most young adults in Western, industrialized societies do not remain at home until they get married and have children, and they are delaying these events until later ages than ever before in history. They are also more likely to have fewer children, and more are born outside of legal, traditional marriage. It has also become commonplace for young adults to begin conjugal life in nonmarital romantic cohabiting relationships. For example, there were about 1.6 million unmarried-partner households in 1980 in the U.S., and this rose to 3.8 in 2000 (Fields and Casper, 2001). Indeed, at least one-half of adult women in the U.S. are expected to experience cohabitation at least once between the ages fifteen and forty-five and one third of children are expected to experience maternal co-habitation by age sixteen (Heuveline and Timberlake, 2004). Yet cohabitation is subject to higher rates of dissolution than marriage, and it tends to be of a shorter duration (Smock and Gupta, 2002).

Despite widespread changes in partnership formation and fertility behavior, there is considerable diversity in the timing and nature of these family-related transitions, both across countries and within societies. In light of these patterns, the purpose of this chapter is to present an overview of contemporary trends in partnership formation and dissolution and the transitions to parenthood with a focus on North America. Comparisons in the timing and pre-dictors of these events will also be made with our selected Euro-pean countries of interest (Britain, France, Germany, Italy, the Netherlands, and Sweden). This will include a focus on non-marital cohabiting living arrangements (both heterosexual and homosexual), legal marital unions, the timing of motherhood, and divorce. And consistent with a major theme of this book—namely, that the timing and nature of young people's transitional behaviors are intertwined with parental lives in significant ways, we will also consider how these events affect, and are affected by, aging family intergenerational relationships.

## "Living Together"—Contemporary Trends in Non-Marital Cohabitation

As noted in previous chapters, the increasing prevalence of un-married heterosexual cohabitation over the past several decades has significantly altered family patterns in the United States, Canada, and many Western European countries. By 1981, only about 4 per-cent of all American couples cohabited (Spanier 1983). More re-cently, the 2000 U.S. Census indicated that 7.6 million men and women were cohabiting, which represents 3.8 million unmarried-partner households and approximately 9 percent of all unions in the United States (Fields and Casper, 2001; U.S. Census Bureau, 2001b). Indeed, the U.S. Bureau of the Census projects that the number of cohabiting couples will reach approximately 6.5 million by 2006 (Shaw Crouse, 1999). Furthermore, although marriage is the modal type of living arrangement for young people aged twenty-five to thirty-four, the majority of American couples marrying today have lived together first (Bumpass and Lu, 2000, U.S. Bureau of the Census, 2000).

The 2001 Canadian Census also reveals that an increasing proportion of couples choose to cohabit (more commonly referred to as "common-law" unions in Canada). From 1981 to 2001, the proportion of common-law families increased from 5.6 percent to 14 percent, and an estimated 56 percent of young adults aged twenty to twenty-four now live common-law (Vanier Institute of the Family, 2000). Thus, similar to the U.S., it is not surprising that for young adults in their twenties, unmarried cohabitation is likely to be their first conjugal union. The Census counted a total of 1,158,410 common-law families in 2001, although the trend toward common-law is most common in Quebec. In this province, there were 508,520 common-law families, which represented 30 percent of all couple families in that province. Interestingly, the prevalence of cohabitation in Quebec is higher than in many Western European countries and in the U.S., and is very similar to Sweden, a country often referred to as having one of the highest incidence of non-marital unions in the world (Statistics Canada, 2002b).

With regard to European patterns in heterosexual cohabitation, there is diversity in the propensity for young adults to share a household with a romantic partner, similar to other family-related transitions to adulthood. As previously noted, cohabitation is high in Sweden (with almost 30 percent of all couples cohabiting). It is suggested that social reforms have eliminated many of the traditional incentives to marry. For example, marital-type property rights of married couples were extended to cohabiting couples in 1987 and there are no direct economic policy benefits to Swedish women or men for being married (Seccombe and Warner, 2004:294). France also has relatively high proportions cohabiting, with 17.5 percent of all couples reporting this living arrangement. There is also an intermediate group of countries, which includes the Netherlands, Great Britain, and Germany, somewhat similar to the U.S. rates at 8.2 percent of all couples. At the other end of the extreme is Italy, where only a small minority of couples cohabit, although rates have been increasing at a faster rate than in other countries (Kiernan, 2002). For example, in Italy, even among the youngest birth cohorts, no more than 10 percent of women have adopted cohabitation before eventually entering into first marriage (Nazio and Blossfeld, 2003).

Figure 5.1 also provides the percentage of young people aged twenty-five to thirty-four currently cohabiting for our selected countries in 2000-1. This age range was selected because it is during this time period that most young people will have left home and finished their full-time education. They are also more likely to be establishing partnerships and contemplating or having children (Kiernan, 2002). Not surprising, 39 percent of Swedish young people report living in non-martial partnerships, while only 8 percent of Italians in this age group cohabit. Cohabitation is also popular in France (31 percent), whereas intermediate levels are found in the Netherlands (22 percent), East Germany (21 percent), Britain (18 percent), West Germany (15 percent), and Canada (18.5 percent). Interestingly, the lowest proportion of unmarried heterosexual cohabitators is found in the United States at 7.2 percent. However, Fields and Casper (2001: 12) caution that this estimate may underrepresent the true number of cohabiting couples. This is because only householders and their partners are tabulated, rather than all unmarried couples present in the household. Moreover, respondents may be reluctant to classify themselves as such in a personal

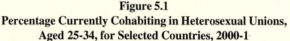

**Figure 5.1**
**Percentage Currently Cohabiting in Heterosexual Unions,**
**Aged 25-34, for Selected Countries, 2000-1**

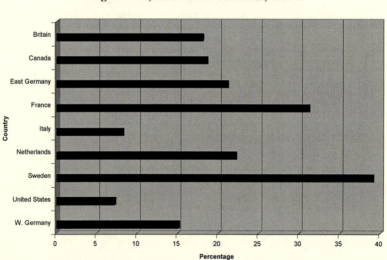

Source: European data from Kiernan's (2002) Eurobarometer tabulations; Canadian data based upon author's tabulations from Statistics Canada, 2001 GSS; U.S. data calculated from 2000 Census Bureau data in Fields and Casper (2001).

interview situation and may describe themselves as roommates, housemates, or friends not related to each other.

Furthermore, these cross-sectional rates may underestimate the prevalence of cohabitation in some countries because of relatively low duration rates. A recent study by Heuveline and Timberlake (2004) document substantial variation in duration rates based on international data from eleven countries using life tables. This analytic tool provides a general class of demographic models that describe the transition over time of a cohort of individuals from one life state to another (Preston, Heuveline, and Guillot, 2001). With respect to the U.S., these researchers show that the median duration of premarital cohabitations is distinctly shorter at 1.17 than in other countries. Conversely, other societies such as France, Sweden, and Canada exhibit median durations of three or more years (4.28, 3.44, and 3.32 years, respectively), whereas Germans display duration rates of 2.24 years. Unfortunately, they do not provide data for Italy (due to an insufficient sample of cohabitation spells) and Britain. However, one would assume that median durations are higher in these countries than in the U.S. based upon similar studies (e.g., see Kiernan, 2001). It is also interesting to note that Heuveline and Guillot (2001) find high rates of cohabitation dissolution, particularly in Canada (63.9 percent), the U.S. (52 percent), France (53.7 percent), and Germany (46.7 percent), although the proportion separating is relatively low in Sweden at 38.8 percent.

Why is cohabitation so popular in North America and many European countries? The two most salient features of most Western cultures include a movement toward secularization and individuation. Secularization reduces formalized religious commitment and thus the strength of the moral values derived from religious theology and is accompanied by a shift towards individualistic, self-oriented pursuits (Lesthaeghe and Surkyn, 1988). Also fuelled by the growth of the global capitalist system and increased affluence, the rise of individualism is characterized by self-fulfillment, a growing demand for gender equality, and the emergence of the ideology of materialism (Shorter, 1975). This change erodes old social norms because they are incompatible with values such as freedom and autonomy, companionship, and self-gratification (Burch and Matthews, 1987). Thus, non-marital cohabitation is compatible with this cultural value system, since there has been a weakening of social constraints that would deter the formation of informal marital structures (Hall, 1996; also see Giddens, 1991, 1991a, 1991b).

Yet, as previously noted, despite the broad ideational trend toward individualization and the rising acceptability of cohabitation in many Western countries, cohabiting unions are generally more unstable than marital unions. This illustrates how contemporary transitional events into adulthood are subject to reversibility and contributes to our "boomerang age" metaphor. Moreover, it is recognized that there is considerable diversity across and within countries with regard to the propensity of young adults to cohabit and this can be related to a number of individual and family background factors, as well as the geographical and community context in which one lives, a topic to which we now turn.

## Who Lives Together?

Research identifies several sets of factors that characterize those individuals most prone to heterosexual cohabitation. These relate to characteristics of the individual, their family background, and "local culture" or geographical location. With regard to personal characteristics, cohabitors are primarily selected from younger groups. Recent 2000 U.S. Census data shows that 35 percent of all cohabitors were between the ages of eighteen and thirty-four. A larger proportion were between the ages of thirty-five and forty-four, and it is relatively rarer in older age groups (Fields and Casper, 2001). Males are more likely to cohabit than females, possibly because they are selected into cohabitation at a greater rate. In other words, males remain unmarried longer and this places them at a greater risk for cohabitation (Wu, 2000).

Smock and Gupta (2002) also document that cohabitation tends to be selective of people who are more liberal, less religious, and more supportive of egalitarian gender roles and nontraditional family roles. For example, women in unmarried-partner households are less likely to be in a traditional homemaking role than their married counterparts. Unmarried partners are also more egalitarian in terms of their labor force participation. Sixty-five percent of unmarried partners had both partners working in 2000, compared with only 54 percent of married couples. It is also interesting to note that 28 percent of women in unmarried-partner households had higher levels of education than their partners, compared with 21 percent of wives in married-couple households (Fields and Casper, 2001).

The educational and income level of young adults and their race is also related to the propensity to coreside, although the education effect is much stronger in the U.S. than in Canada. Generally, cohabitors have slightly less educational achievement and income than the married, although cohabitation is still quite common among people of all levels of education. For instance, recent American data reveal that among nineteen to forty-four-year-old women, nearly 60 percent of high school dropouts have cohabited compared to approximately 37 percent for college-educated women (Bumpas and Lu, 2000). Also, median household income for cohabiting young adults was roughly 85 percent that of their married counterparts in the United States in 1998, and Canadian cohabitors experienced a similar income shortfall (Smock and Gupta, 2002).

With regard to the effects of religion, some religious groups are less likely to cohabit than others. For example, in the U.S., Mormons continue to be the least likely to cohabit, and in Canada, and traditional religious groups such as those found within the Indo-Canadian community have extremely low rates of common-law unions (Lehrer, 1999, Mitchell, 2001). Turning to racial differences, greater proportions of Hispanics and blacks than whites in the U.S. select cohabitation as their first union (Clarkberg, 1999). It is also interesting to note that the vast majority of cohabiting partners are of the same race, although unmarried partners are about twice as likely to be of different races as married couples (13 percent compared with 5 percent). Moreover, about half of interracial cohabiting couples are made up of a white woman and a man of another race (Casper and Bianchi, 2002).

There also appears to be some intergenerational effects linking cohabitation to family background. For example, a U.S. data set that followed a cohort of children and their mothers over time revealed that children whose parents divorced and whose mothers expressed favorable approval were more likely to cohabit as young adults than other children (Axinn and Thonton, 1993; Thornton et al., 1992). Similarly, In Canada, Turcotte and Bélanger (1997) find that dissolution of parents' marriages before age fifteen substantially increases the likelihood of cohabitation. Moreover, there appears to be a family background, social class dimension (i.e., economic standing and educational attainment), since cohabitation has always been more common in lower than higher socioeconomic groups. Part of the reason for this association may be that high-resource parents discourage their children from cohabiting. However, it should be noted that the effects of family background have greatly diminished over time as this living arrangement becomes highly prevalent (e.g., see Lehrer, 1999).

Finally, there are geographical or regional variations in rates of cohabitation. In the U.S., cohabitation is most likely for those who grew up in Western regions than Eastern ones (Lehrer, 1999). Unmarried partners are also more likely than married couples to live in metropolitan areas (Simmons and O'Connell, 2003). In Canada, the most striking regional disparity in cohabitation is between Quebec and the rest of Canada, with cohabitation a much more prominent feature of family life in the former. Similar to Sweden, this region has "retreated" from marriage and embraced cohabitation (see Smock and Gupta, 2002 and Le Bourdais and Juby, 2002, for a full discussion). Moreover, the Yukon Territory of Canada has one of the nation's highest proportions of common-law families, whereas common-law families are less prevalent in provinces such as Saskatchewan (Statistics Canada, 2002b).

Many similar predictors of those prone to cohabitation are also found in Europe. For example, the more secular members of society and those who have experienced parental divorce during childhood are more likely to cohabit. A recent study shows that among twenty to thirty-nine-year-old women who had been in a union, church attendees were somewhat more likely to marry without cohabiting than women who had never attended church (Kiernan, 2000). Being in full-time education also inhibits this type of union formation, although the association between level of education and employment status is less clear cut and tends to vary across nations (Kiernan, 2002). There is also evidence to suggest that cohabitation is more common for those residing in metropolitan areas, or in the case of Italy, living in the northern parts of the country (Prinz, 1995).

Additionally, there are large differences in the extent and meaning of cohabitation among the countries of interest in this book. In Italy, cohabitation is generally rare and not socially supported, unlike North American and many European countries such as West Germany and the Netherlands whereby cohabitation has become a kind of socially accepted, short-term prelude to marriage. In these countries, cohabitation is typically transformed into marriage when couples have a child (Blossfeld and Mills, 2001). In other countries, such as France and Great Britain, cohabitation has evolved into an accepted alternative to marriage connected with high rates of extra-marital births (Kiernan, 1999). And in Sweden and the province of Quebec in Canada, cohabitation and marital unions seem to have normatively and legally converged. Now, for many young couples, the choice between formal marriage and informal cohabitation seems to be solely a matter of personal preference, even when children are involved (Duvander, 2000; Nazio and Blossfeld, 2003).

## Gay and Lesbian Cohabitation

Research has also begun to acknowledge and document same-sex cohabitation. In the U.S., it is estimated that about 4 percent of cohabiting couples are in same-sex relationships (Casper and Bianchi, 2002). However, it is very difficult to know exactly how many gay and lesbian cohabiting couples there are in the country. Black et al. (2000) examined data from the U.S. Census and from other national data sets and concluded that the number of these couples is considerably underestimated, with perhaps only one-third identifying themselves as such. In addition, most nationally based surveys with questions regarding sexual orientation are too small to provide reliable estimates of the numbers of cohabiting same-sex couples (Casper and Bianchi, 2002).

In Canada, the 2001 Census was the first to provide data on same-sex partnerships. In this survey, same-sex couples reflect people who identified themselves as living in a same-sex common-law union. A total of 10,360 same-sex couples fell into this category, representing 0.5 percent of all couples (married and unmarried). Unfortunately, these data have not been broken down by age group and sex and comparable estimates of same-sex cohabitation are unavailable among the European countries of interest in this book.

It is also intriguing to acknowledge that many homosexual couples in North America and some European countries are registering as "domestic partners" or as "civil unions." Many Scandinavian countries, the Netherlands, and France have created registered partnerships for both gay/lesbian and heterosexual unions. For example, in 1994 Sweden introduced legislation that ensures similar rights and benefits for cohabitors as for households headed by a married couple, regardless of sexual orientation. However, partners are not allowed to adopt children, similar to domestic partnerships in the Netherlands (Rigaux, 2003). More recently, France has introduced PACS (Pacte civil de solidarité, or civil solidarity pact), which began as an effort to legalize gay and lesbian unions. This legislation was instituted into law only in 2000, after intense debate and public protests. Interestingly, in the first four months, 14,000 couples had made PACS, and they included both homosexual and heterosexual couples (McDaniel and Tepperman, 2004). In Germany, however, the protection of the family enshrined in the constitution applies only to marriage and not "marriage-like partnerships" (Ditch, Barnes, and Bradshaw, 1996).

Registering as domestic unions is also increasingly becoming an option offered by some U.S. cites and counties, mainly with gay and lesbian couples in mind. Domestic partnership ordinances have been implemented in three states: Hawaii in 1997; California in 1999 (same-sex only); and Vermont in 2000 (same-sex only, referred to as civil unions; Willetts, 2003). Like other countries, many homosexual couples are choosing to license their cohabiting unions for practical reasons or to show their solidarity as a gay/lesbian couple. However, statistics on the number of registered domestic gay/lesbian partners are not available, since some municipalities don not track domestic partners' gender or make their registries public (Irvine, 2004).

In Canada, only heterosexual couples could legally marry until 2003. Shortly after that time, many other provinces and the Yukon passed legislation to permit gay and lesbian couples to enter civil unions (Moore, 2003). On July 20, 2005, the same-sex marriage bill (Bill C-38) was passed, making same-sex marriage a federal law. Yet public opinion continues to remain divided on this issue. For example, Alberta premier Ralph Klein has vowed to draft legal protections for civil marriage commissioners who don't want to officiate gay unions because they oppose them for religious or cultural reasons.

With regard to characteristics of gay and lesbian cohabiting couples, there are slightly more male same-sex common-law couples than females in both the United States and Canada. For example, the Canadian census counted about 19,000 male same-sex couples, or 55 percent of the total. Most of these couples have higher educational attainment than either heterosexual unmarried partners or married couples. Gay cohabiting partners generally earn less money than other men, whereas lesbian cohabiting couples tend to earn more than other women (Black et al., 2000). Also, the rate of home ownership is lower for gay and lesbian cohabiting couples than for married-couple families (Casper and Bianchi, 2002).

Most gay and lesbian cohabitors also tend to be urban dwellers in both the United States and Canada. In the U.S., Black et al. (2000) found that most same-sex cohabiting couples were concentrated in only twenty cities, with greatest proportions residing in San Francisco, Washington, D.C., Los Angeles, Atlanta and New York. In Canada, 6,455 lived in the census metropolitan area of Montreal, while an additional 1,140 lived in the Quebec census metropolitan area. Ontario has the largest number of same-sex partners (12,505), while Newfoundland and Labrador had the lowest proportion of same-sex couples (0.1 percent of all couples). Male couples are more likely to live in census metropolitan areas; 85 percent live in the larger urban areas of Canada, compared with 76 percent of female couples (Statistics Canada, 2002b).

## The Consequences of Cohabitation
## for Intergenerational Relations

The vast majority of studies pertaining to romantic heterosexual or homosexual cohabitation and intergenerational issues focus on the cohabiting relationship and their children, rather than on the couple and their parents (e.g., see Manning, 2000). The few studies that have been conducted, however, support the notion that intergenerational relations and exchanges of support affect a young adult's transition to cohabitation in many ways. Parental characteristics in the family-of-origin and family histories can affect not only the propensity of some young adults to coreside (as previously discussed), but can also influence intergenerational relations on a number of levels.

In particular, parental reactions to their child's (heterosexual) cohabitation are found to affect the quality of intergenerational relations and exchanges of support. While many parents support and approve of their child's living with someone as an unmarried couple, studies show that parental acceptance of non-marital cohabitation is dependent upon a number of factors. These include aspects such as: parental religiosity, race/ethnicity, liberalism, and socio-economic status. Highly religious or "traditional" parents may disapprove of this living arrangement, for example, because it is viewed as immoral or as "living in sin" (Mitchell, 2001). Conversely, parents with non-traditional views are more likely to approve of cohabitation (Axinn and Thornton, 1993).

Also, although cohabitation is more socially acceptable now than in the past, high status parents have more to lose than low-status parents if their children engage in controversial (and disreputable) behavior. As a result, high-resource parents may not only disapprove of cohabitation, but they may pressure cohabiting offspring either to marry or to break up (Amato and Booth, 2000). Finally, it is also interesting to note that, in general, cohabiting couples generally receive less support from their parents than married couples (Nock, 1995).

In comparison with opposite-sex cohabitation, research suggests that families experience more ambivalence with regard to gay and lesbian cohabitation (e.g., see Mackey, O'Brien and Mackey, 1997). Indeed, the concept of "intergenerational ambivalence," defined as "the experience of contradictory emotions toward the same object" (Weigert, 1991), has utility in furthering our understanding of aging parent-child relationships across the life course. This line of thinking suggests that because contemporary family life is characterized by a multiplicity of forms, such as cohabitation, divorce, marriage, or blended families, family relationships may be characterized by "intergenerational ambivalence" (Luescher, 2000).

Generally, the concept of intergenerational ambivalence can be conceptualized as structurally created contradictions that are experienced by individuals with others and it reflects contradictions in relations between parents and adult offspring (Lowenstein et al., 2003). It also highlights how intergenerational solidarity is not a one-dimensional concept (Bengtson et al., 2002) because ambivalence is both a variable feature of structured sets of social relationships and a catalyst for social action, since actors can negotiate and renegotiate relationships over time. In this way, ambivalence represents a valuable "bridging concept" because it allows a conceptual link between social structure and individual agency (Connidis and McMullin, 2002).

With regard to the impact of cohabitation among gay and lesbian partners on linked family lives, there is ample evidence to suggest that families can experience more ambivalence in their attitude toward same-sex cohabitation than heterosexual cohabitation. This may be partly due to a general lack of social acceptance toward this type of union (because of homophobic ideologies), and this in turn can make family acceptance more challenging. As a result, there may be more resistance from family members than in heterosexual partnerships (Aquilino, 1997; Nock, 1998). Some young adults may be led to conceal the "true" nature of their partnership from their parents and other family members, in an effort to avoid conflict and stress.

However, similar to the research on heterosexual cohabitation, the reactions and support from family members (particularly parents) is shown to vary according to a number of factors such as: religion, race and ethnicity, parental education, and pre-existing relationship quality. For example, many religious orientations support only heterosexual unions, and some racial/ethnic groups, such as some Hispanic groups, are less supportive in their attitudes (Morales, 1990). Ambivalent or negative reactions are also more evident among older parents, those with less education, and those who had strained relationships with their children prior to learning of their gay or lesbian identity (Cohen and Savin-Williams, 1996; Savin-Williams, 2001).

Yet, research shows that over time, family members who initially disapproved often become more accepting and supportive of the relationship over time (Bernstein, 1995). This lends support to the idea that familial ties can involve more or less ambivalence at different points in the life course (Connidis and McMullin, 2001). However, in general, gay and lesbian cohabiting couples are found to receive more social support than nongay couples from friends and subculture than from their parents and their family of origin (Kurdek, 1988).

Unfortunately, European research on the effects of non-marital cohabitation on intergenerational relations is sparse. However, there is evidence to suggest that intergenerational ties can be affected by many of the same factors reviewed above. Yet, it is important to recognize that some countries more readily embrace unmarried cohabitation as a normative lifestyle choice (i.e., Sweden), whereas it may be more heavily stigmatized in countries such as Italy. Also, homophobic ideologies against gay/lesbian cohabitation may also have a cultural basis and this can also affect parent-child relations. Now that we have examined cohabitation trends and their implications for intergenerational relations, we will now turn our attention to more formalized unions—getting married.

## Getting Married

Marriage can traditionally be defined as a socially and legally recognized relationship between a woman and a man that includes sexual, economic, and social rights and responsibilities. This definition draws our attention to the fact that marriage is a matter of public concern and that society maintains norms and sanctions for appropriate behavior related to marriage (Seccombe and Warner, 2004). Moreover, researchers (e.g., McDaniel and Tepperman, 2004) observe that two trends characterize contemporary marriage: decline in marriage rates and the continuing popularity of marriage. And although these trends appear contradictory, they actually are not. From a historical perspective, more people now marry at some point in their lives than they did in the 1910s. But at the same time, there has been a decline in marriage rates since the 1970s. Furthermore, despite the ever-increasing popularity of cohabitation, the institution of marriage remains highly valued in contemporary society and the vast majority of young people in Western countries eventually marry. Notably, an estimated 88 percent of American young women are likely to marry eventually (Raley, 2000).

With regard to contemporary patterns, it is clear that people tend to marry later now than they did in previous times, especially since our historical benchmark of the 1950s. Yet, in some ways young adults are reverting back to behaviors characteristic of young people a century ago, since average ages of marriage were also quite high at that time, albeit for different reasons. Part of the reason for the recent postponement of marriage compared to the 1950s, for example, relates to the increase in heterosexual cohabitation, but also because of shifting economic and social conditions outlined in chapter 3. Figure 5.2 shows that the median age of marriage in 2000 for American men is 26.8 and 25.1 for women (U.S. Bureau of the Census, 2001a). In Canada, comparable data indicate that women were 27.6 years of age, on average at first marriage, and men 29.6 (Statistics Canada, 2003a). It should be reiterated that American data commonly use median rather than mean ages, making it difficult for cross-national comparisons. Generally, the mean is more sensitive to the distribution of marriages than the median, the latter of which is the middle point of the age distribution.

In European countries, there is diversity in average age of marriage. Specifically, in 2000, the oldest mean age at first marriage for males occurs in Sweden (32.4), followed by Germany (31.2), Britain (30.4), Italy and the Netherlands (30.0), and France (29.7). For women, the oldest mean age at first marriage is evidenced in Sweden (30.1), followed by the Netherlands (29.1), Britain (28.3), Germany (28.4),

**Figure 5.2**
**Mean Age at First Marriage for Selected Countries, Males and Females, 2000**

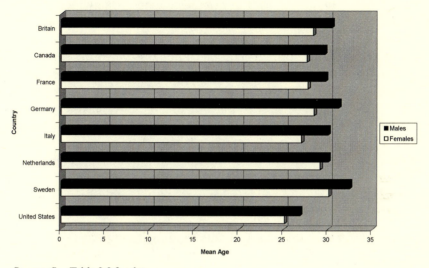

Source: See Table 3.2 for data sources.
Note: U.S. data based on median ages.

France (27.7), and Italy (27.0). Overall, these data reveal some interesting variations in mean age at first marriage, although all average ages tend to cluster within a three-year age span between the
ages twenty-nine to thirty-two for men and twenty-seven to thirty for
women. As well, these data reveal important gender differences in
the timing of first marriage, a topic to which we briefly address.

## Age Differences between Bride and Groom
## and Implications for the Life Course

It is well established that men tend to marry women younger than
themselves. Similar to many Western, industrialized countries, in the
U.S., only about 12 percent of all marriages consist of wives who
are two or more years older than their husbands (U.S. Bureau of the
Census, 2000). This phenomenon is known as "the mating gradient," which was first discovered by well-known sociologist Jessie
Bernard in the 1970s. However, in chapter 3 it was noted that while
this gap persists, it has declined steadily throughout the twentieth
century, such that the current gender disparity is generally about

two years, as shown in table 5.2 (with the exception of Germany and Italy, which display three-year age gaps). Yet the fact that women continue to marry younger than men has important implications for women over the life course. The younger spouse (the wife) typically starts marriage with fewer assets, such as less schooling, less job experience, and lower income.

Over time, this disadvantage accumulates, since the husband's job will be given priority because it is deemed more important to the overall economic situation of the family. A woman will also usually be the one who quits her job (which is usually lower paid) to care for young children. In this way, the initially small economic difference becomes a substantial gap. Women's "choice" to marry at a younger age, therefore, in addition to other structural economic inequities that exist, contributes to their economic dependency and illustrates how gendered marital patterns have economic implications that operate in rather subtle but potent ways (Gee, 1995).

## Social Timetables and "Early" versus "Late" Marriage

Despite the long-term trend toward later ages of marriage, the near universality of marriage in young adulthood, and the narrowing of age differences between men and women, research documents diversity in marital timing within the countries of interest in this book. These patterns also highlight the need to consider two levels of social context relevant to marital timing—societal and familial/individual. On a societal level, most transitions in Western countries are age-graded in that they generally occur during predictable times in the life span. For example, most individuals marry during young adulthood and it is estimated that the vast majority of American men (89 percent) and women (92 percent) age thirty-five and over in 1998 have married at least once (Casper and Bianchi, 2002).

However, within the broad age range of young adulthood, there may be culturally embedded expectations that dictate whether one marries "too early" or "too late," and which vary according to one's social location. Indeed, Hogan (1981, 1986) suggests that social clocks and transition patterns are, to an important degree, shaped in primary groups and significant others. On this level, sub-cultural and familial norms, available resources and interdependent lives also mold individual trajectories within boundaries set by social institutions. For example, young adults from wealthier families are generally discouraged from marrying "too early," and these families usually have the resources to support a priority on other pathways to adulthood, such as going to college and career development before marriage.

In this next section, we will build upon this theme of "social timetables" by considering marital timing in relation to the concepts of "on time" and "off time" transitions—that is, the predictors of early versus later marriage. This emphasis is warranted given that the timing of marriage has enormous ramifications for the life course of young adults. In particular, marrying at an early age (especially teenage marriage) has been shown to be associated with a number of negative long-term effects, such as a higher risk of divorce, and poorer educational and career outcomes (e.g., Bumpass, Martin, and Sweet, 1991; South, 1995). Conversely, marrying later during the young adult years tends to be less risky behavior and is associated with fewer disadvantages. Moreover, the timing of marriage has the potential to significantly affect intergenerational bonds in the family of origin, a topic which will be explored in greater detail below.

### Who Marries Early? Who Marries Late?

As previously noted, women tend to marry at earlier ages than men. In addition, young adults with higher levels of education marry later than those with less education (e.g., Bramlett and Mosher, 2002; Raley, 2000). Religious effects are also found in relation to marital timing. For example, in the U.S., compared to mainline Protestants, fundamentalist Protestants and Mormons have a pattern of earlier marriage, and Jews tend to delay marriage. For Catholics, there is a tendency to enter marriage at an intermediate age, avoiding both early and late entry (Lehrer, 1999).

With regard to intergenerational influences on marital timing, inconsistent findings are reached on the effects of parental divorce and the timing of children's marriage. Some children from divorced families marry relatively early, possibly to escape an unhappy home environment. However, other studies (e.g., Goldscheider and Goldscheider, 1993; Li and Wojtkiewicz, 1994) find that children from divorced families marry relatively late, consistent with the idea that children of divorce develop a more cautious attitude toward marriage (e.g., see Amato and Booth, 2000). A mother's preferred age for the child to marry, on the other hand, is shown to have a strong effect on children's marital timing. For example, a recent study by Axinn et al. (1999) shows that the children of mothers who prefer that their child marries at age twenty are twice as likely to marry early than those whose mothers prefer that they marry at age thirty.

Social class differences are also found with regard to marital timing. Generally, children parents' socioeconomic resources "slow down" children's formation of intimate relationships (Amato and Booth, 2000). This is revealed by the fact that children from lower and middle-class families marry earlier than those from well-educated or privileged families. This segment of the population usually marries in their late twenties and rarely marries before the graduate school years (Furstenberg, 2003). This is because high resource parents can encourage their children to obtain education and plan for careers (Goldscheider and Goldscheider, 1993). Also, the role models provided by mothers in professional occupations may reduce daughters' interest for early marriage and increase their labor force attachment (Amato and Booth, 2000).

There are also racial and cultural variations in the propensity to marry early or late. For example, among American Hispanic women, affiliation with either fundamentalist Protestant or other Protestant faiths is associated with early marriage, and these individuals have a higher probability of first marriage by age eighteen than non-Hispanic blacks, whites, or Asians (Bramlett and Mosher, 2002). Overall, early marriage is more likely for Hispanic women, followed by white women, and is less likely for black women and Asian women. It is also interesting to observe that there are significant differences in the proportions never married by race. According to the 2000 Census, about four out of every ten black men and black women over the age of fifteen had never been married, the highest proportion of any racial category. Asians, on the other hand, had one of the highest percentages married at 60 percent for men and 61 percent for women (Kreider and Simmons, 2003). As a result, marriage by age thirty is considerably lower for non-Hispanic Black women, with virtually no differences among other racial groups (Bramlett and Mosher, 2002).

Geographical or regional variations are also found in marital timing. Entry into marriage appears to be slowest for individuals who at age sixteen lived in the Northcentral and Northeastern regions of the United States (Lehrer, 1999). Also, early marriage is more common in less affluent communities. Notably, marriage by age eighteen is more likely in communities with higher male unemployment, lower median family income, higher poverty, and higher receipt of public assistance. Moreover, marriage by age thirty is less likely in metropolitan areas than nonmetropolitan areas (Bramlett and Mosher, 2002). Similarly, in Canada, later marriage is evident in metropolitan areas compared to residents living in small cities and rural areas (Lapierre-Adamcyk and Charvet, 2000).

European research on marital timing reveals similar predictors. Highly educated young adults typically delay marriage, while more religious young people usually marry earlier (Jansen and Liefbroer, 2001). Male unemployment leads to a postponement of marriage in many countries, such as Germany and Italy (Corijn and Klijzing, 2001). More privileged socioeconomic backgrounds are associated with a delay into marriage in virtually all countries (Berrington, 2001). Family structure factors reveal more mixed findings. British research, for example, shows that parental separation is associated with teenage marriage among women, while the experience of a parental separation appears to delay marriage among young adults in countries such as France (Corijn, 2001). Regional factors are also evident. For example, Berrington (2001) finds a persistent tendency for men and women who were living at age sixteen in London and the Southeast to have lower rates of marriage, and Hullen (2001) finds that in Germany, first marriages take place earlier in the East than the West (Hullen, 2001).

## Implications of Marriage for Intergenerational Relations

Continuing with our theme of interdependent lives, the transition to marriage begets change in family-of-origin intergenerational relations. Until the wedding, the young adult's family of origin usually has greater claim to their loyalties than their spouse-to-be (Strong and DeVault, 1992). Once the ceremony is completed, however, the newlyweds must establish their own families independent of their families of orientation. Therefore, the couple usually negotiates a different relationship with their parents and each generation establishes its own boundaries. For example, young adults decide how much interaction is desirable and couples need to consider how much influence their families of orientation will have in their lives. Indeed, Lawton, Silverstein, and Bengtson (1994) assert that distance, contacts, and affection between adult children and their parents are strongly interrelated and can affect intergenerational relations and exchanges of support when one marries.

Generally, when young people marry they usually have strong ties to their parents. However, there is some evidence to suggest that marriage can actually strengthen and solidify intergenerational bonds. For example, studies show that from a parent's perspective, getting married improves a daughter's relationships with her parents (Kaufman and Uhlenberg, 1998). Both generations also perceive that they have fulfilled normative expectations and their "developmental tasks" as individuals at this stage of the life course (Aldous, 1996). Interestingly, research also shows that married individuals report being closer to their parents than do cohabiting couples (Nock, 1995)

Conversely, stress and conflict can occur in the parent-child relations if the marriage occurs under less than optimal conditions, such as due to an unwanted pregnancy, or because a young person marries an "undesirable partner." Intergenerational conflict can also occur if the marriage violates social timetables or parental expectations of "appropriate" timing. In particular, if a marriage occurs "too early" it can bring tremendous psychological hazards for both generations. For instance, if a young man or woman uses marriage as a means of breaking away from overly possessive parents, the complexities and subtleties of the parent-child battle will reflect themselves in the marriage itself (Bernard, cited in Strong and Devault, 1992).

Intergenerational ties are also affected because the transition to marriage also produces an expanded kin network through "in-laws." Notably, young adults experience the addition of a new set of parents-in-laws-when they marry, and perceived satisfaction with in-law relationships can be related to the quality of the relationships and exchanges of support. Serovich and Price (1994), based on data from the National Survey of Families and Households find that generally, husbands perceive a better relationship with in-laws than do wives, and relationships with fathers-in-law are more satisfactory than with mothers-in-law. Overall, though, most couples report high satisfaction with the relationship and low amounts of open disagreements with their in-laws, indicating that in-law relationships may not be as problematic as once believed.

Research has also begun to examine how ethnicity and race have an impact on intergenerational relations when a couple marries. In particular, there is a burgeoning area of research on interracial marriage. Notably, Majete (1999) studied how interracial (black and white) couples perceive their families' adjustment to their marriage, and significant differences by race and gender are found. Overall, black females reported the highest levels of support, and white females the lowest. Whites were more than twice as likely as backs to experience a negative response from their families. Black males were most likely to report a negative response by a mate's family, while white males were opposite. Although several respondents reported extremely hostile/negative reactions, the majority did not; in fact, most respondents stated that their parents and in-laws accepted their interracial relationships.

Similarly, in Europe there appear to be variations in intergenerational exchanges of support once a couple marries based upon factors such as the timing of the marriage, distance, contact patterns, and the quality of the relationships. For instance, a distinctive aspect of Italy is its comparatively low level of internal mobility and it is very common for young married couples to live very close to at least one set of parents (Tomassini, Wolf, and Rosina, 2003). Dalla Zuanna (2001) argues that this is partly due to Italian housing policy, which encourages home ownership and familism, such that prospective homeowners are actively encouraged to live near their family. As a result, many Italian couples receive housing and other related assistance from their parents relative to many other countries, and there are high economic and non-economic flows between parents and children. Indeed, many Italian couples report very close relationships with their parents and in-laws: 91 percent and 86 percent of couples have at least one weekly visit to the wife's and husband's parents, respectively (Tomassini, Wolf, and Rosina, 2003).

## Having Children

Similar to marriage and other family-related transitions to adulthood, having a child is a key marker event and is age-graded in that most people become parents during their young adulthood years. Moreover, dramatic changes have occurred in the timing and nature of this transition since our primary historical benchmark of the 1950s. Although the pressure on couples to have children is almost as strong as ever, the average age of motherhood has steadily climbed over the past several decades, while family size has been shrinking. Also, more children are being born outside of traditional, legal marital unions, although rates of teenage pregnancy have been declining and are at their lowest level in over fifty years (U.S. National Center for Health Statistics, 2000).

It is beyond the scope of this book to examine all aspects of parenthood during the transition to adulthood and all types of parents. Obviously, biology alone does not determine parenthood—one can become a parent yet never give birth to a child, for example, by "inheriting" stepchildren or through adoption. It is also possible that a young adult remains childless, either for life or until they enter their adult years. In this section we will provide an overview on contemporary trends in parenthood. This will include a focus on variation in the timing of motherhood and family size between North America and our selected European countries of interest, as well as within these societies. Similar to marital timing, we will also review the factors associated with "early" versus "later" childbearing, and consider the effects of parenthood for aging parent-child relations.

### Variations in Maternal Age at First Birth

Figure 5.3 displays the mean maternal age at first birth for selected countries in 2001. The mean age of mothers in the United States was 25.0, an increase of almost four years since 1970. Interestingly, the birth rate for U.S. teenagers declined steadily throughout the 1990s, falling from 62.1 births per 1,000 teenagers fifteen to nineteen years in 1991 to 48.5 in 2000, a decrease of 22 percent (Ventura, Mathews and Hamilton, 2002). In Canada, the average age of mothers was 29.5 years in 2001, up almost five years from 1970 (also see table 3.3 in chapter 3). Remarkably, only 47.9 percent of births were to Canadian mothers aged twenty to twenty-nine in 2002, and 44.8 percent of births were to mothers aged thirty to thirty-nine.

In Europe, the postponement of first parenthood up to age thirty is also strong. Specifically, the average age of first birth for mothers in these countries in 2001 is: Britain (28.6), France (29.4), Germany (28.8), Italy (30.3), the Netherlands (30.3) and Sweden (30.0). It is also important to acknowledge that birth rates and average family size have been rapidly declining since the 1960s in most industrialized countries.

Why are so many young adults postponing marriage and parenthood and having fewer children? Based on previous discussions, it is clear that numerous individual, socio-cultural, economic, and political factors are at play. In particular, economic conditions, education, and career factors are reported as important in women's decisions to delay marriage and parenthood. From 1970 to 2000, for

**Figure 5.3**
**Mean Maternal Age at First Birth for Selected Countries, 2001**

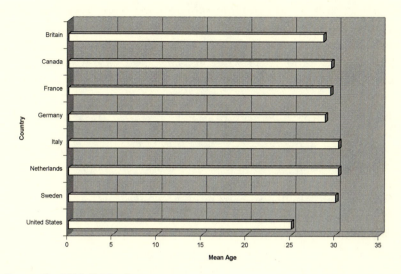

Source: See Table 3.3 for data sources.

example, the percent of women having completed four or more years of college nearly tripled while the female labor force participation rate increased 39 percent. Contraceptive use at first intercourse, particularly condom use, rose dramatically, and the effects of economic cycles (e.g., cost of marriage and children), the marriage squeeze, and marital disruption are all factors considered to be important in understanding these trends (Mathews and Hamilton, 2002). Further, with lengthening life spans and new reproductive technologies, the age at which biological parenting occurs is increasing.

## Parenthood and Marital Status

As previously noted, more babies are now born outside marriage in most industrialized countries, along with the rise in cohabitation and decline of legal marriage. For example, the U.S. and Canada's extramarital birth rate is calculated at approximately 30 percent of all live births (Baker, 2005; Bianchi and Casper, 2000). This is moderate compared to Sweden's rate at 55 percent and Italy's at 9 percent (Lewis, 2003). Overall, countries with higher rates of cohabitation generally have higher rates of extramarital births and extramarital childbirth is on the rise in North American and across Europe

(Baker, 2005; Liefbroer, 2003). Furthermore, there are also racial and cultural differences with respect to childbearing in cohabiting unions. In the U.S., for example, children are more often present in minority cohabiting households than in white families. Also, Hispanic women are found to be 77 percent more likely to conceive a child in cohabitation than white women and black women are 69 percent more likely than white women to do so (Manning, 2001).

Another striking trend is the dramatic increase in one-parent families in most Western industrialized countries over the past half-century. In 1950, only about 6 percent of U.S. family households with children under the age of eighteen were single-mother families. This rose to 22 percent in 1998 as the percentage of families with two parents present in the household declined (Casper and Bianchi, 2002). Overall, single-mother families increased from 3 million in 1970 to 10 million in 2000 in the U.S., while the number of single-father families grew from 393,000 to 2 million (Fields and Casper, 2001). A dramatic trend in the formation of single-parent households over time is that pathways to this family structure have changed. In the late 1970s, the vast majority of single mothers were either divorced or separated, with only one in five single mothers having never married. By 1998, 42 percent of single mothers had not married, representing an increase of almost 20 percent. Differences by ethnicity/race are also evident. For example, by 1978, the most common marital status for black single mothers was "never married" at 43 percent, and this increased to 64 percent in 1998. More and more white and Hispanic single mothers were also never married during this time period, although the proportion of single mothers who had never married was higher among Hispanics than among whites (Casper and Bianchi, 2002).

### Factors Associated with "Early" versus "Late" Childbearing

Similar to the factors associated with early and late marital timing, studies document a number of factors related to those prone to have children early versus later in the transition to adulthood. Generally, women with lower educational attainment have their first birth earlier. For example, the average age at first birth for women with a high school diploma was 23.7, while it was 31.9 for women with a master's degree. Overall, older parents are more likely to be married, highly educated, and working in professional careers with higher incomes (Seccombe and Warner, 2004). With regard to social class, young adults from wealthier families generally have their children later in life, and rarely outside of marriage. In sharp contrast to those from privileged or more middle-class families, children from poorer families often have unplanned children and these children are often born into unstable families (Furstenberg, 2003).

Recent U.S. data also show that the mean age of mother varies by race and Hispanic origin. In general, black, Hispanic and American Indian women have lower mean ages at first birth than non-Hispanic white and Asian or Pacific Islander women (Mathews and Hamilton, 2002). In 2002, for example, Japanese women had the highest mean age at first birth at thirty-one years, whereas American Indian women had the lowest at 21.8 years. Also, from 1990 to 2002, the mean age at first birth increased (on average one year) for nearly all race and Hispanic origin groups (Martin et al., 2003). The mean age of mother at first live birth also varies considerably by geographical region. Notably, in 2000, Mississippi had the lowest mean age at 22.5, while Massachusetts had the highest at 27.8 (Mathews and Hamilton, 2002).

While variations in mean of age of mother by ethnic group have not been recently documented in Canada, in British Columbia and Ontario first-time mothers were the oldest on average among the provinces at 28.5, whereas Yukon mothers were the oldest on average among the territories at 29.0 years of age. Conversely, Saskatchewan mothers were the youngest on average among the provinces at 27.5 years of age, and the youngest first-time mothers were those in Nanavut, with an average of 21.5 in 2002 (Statistics Canada, 2004a).

European research also documents that individual, family, and geographical factors can affect the timing of parenthood. Generally, parenthood is delayed for those with higher education and for those from more advantaged socio-economic backgrounds. Being more religious also appears to accelerate first parenthood in countries such as France, Italy, and the Netherlands (Corijn, 2001; Ongaro, 2001; Jansen and Liefbroer, 2001). Also, women whose parents had divorced tend to have children earlier (Corijn, 2001) and mothers who delayed marriage into their late twenties are less likely to have been a parent in their teens (Berrington, 2001). There are also regional variations in the timing of parenthood. For example, Italian men and women who spent their adolescence in the South become parents sooner than those who lived in the center or north of the country (Ongaro, 2001).

## Implications of Parenthood for Intergenerational Relations

The entry into parenthood has a significant effect on inter-generational relationships because it creates the countertransition of grandparenthood. Thus, grandparenthood is a "contingent" transition because having grandchildren is typically in the hands of one's children (Troll, 1985). In fact, about 80 percent of North American older persons are grandparents, although the transition to grandparenthood remains a phenomenon of middle, not old age, since more than half of all grandparents are under the age of sixty (Aldous, 1995; Connidis, 2001, Szinovacz, 1998). However, regardless of the age of grandparents, it is generally assumed that since the status of parenthood and grandparenthood is central to many persons, it influences the quantity and quality of intergenerational contacts (Brubaker, 1990).

Studies show that generally, the birth of a grandchild is a milestone event and a joyous occasion for both generations, although the arrival of grandchildren does not typically alter the closeness of parent-child relationships (Kaufman and Uhlenberg, 1998). However, the closeness of the relationship and the exchange of supportive behaviors after the birth of a child can be affected by a number of characteristics such as: age, proximity, race/ethnicity, gender, retirement plans of grandparents, personality attributes, quality of relationships, and the health or marital status of either generation (e.g., see Hodgson, 1995; Uhlenberg and Hammill, 1998). For example, those who become grandparents at younger ages are less likely to be able to provide assistance to the middle generation since they are more likely to be engaged in other activities, such as paid work. Conversely, those who are relatively old for the transition tend not to engage in more demanding forms of support to their children, such as babysitting and childcare (Aldous, 1995). Also, mothers of young children tend to feel far greater affinity with their mothers than their mothers-in-law, in that the advice and involvement of their own mothers is usually welcomed, whereas that of their mothers-in-law are often resented (Fischer, 1986).

The concept of "social timetables" also has relevance for understanding how parenthood impacts the relationship between young adults and their parents. Generally, it is presumed that non-normative transitions can threaten parent-child solidarity (Logan and Spitze, 1996; Rossi and Rossi, 1990). Therefore, individuals who enter par-

enthood and grandparenthood unexpectedly or at an "inappropri-
ate" time are more likely to experience intergenerational stress and
conflict. Conversely, studies have shown that individuals who enter
grandparenthood at the expected time are more ready to be actively
involved in the role than are persons who are "off time." For example, Burton (1985) documents that when grandchildren arrive too
early, grandmothers often reject their new role, since it is "out of
synch" with the roles and relationships of mid-adulthood, such as
parenting, working, and building friendships (Hagestad and Burton,
1986).

Generational conflict, resentment and ambivalence can also be produced if grandparents unexpectedly become surrogate parents or become the primary caregivers of grandchildren (Burnette, 1999; Jendrek,
1994). Some grandparents become second-time-around parents because of factors that include alcohol and drug abuse, mental illness,
teenage pregnancy, divorce, incarceration, and AIDS (Minkler and
Roe, 1996; Minkler and Robinson-Beckley, 1994). As a result, many
grandchildren are currently living with their grandchildren in North
America and some European countries, although this trend appears
most prevalent in the U.S. For example, it is estimated that approximately 4.7 million American grandchildren coreside with their grandparents (Casper and Bianchi, 2002). In these households, neither parent is present in over a third of these families, which are commonly
dubbed "skip generation" households. Indeed, skipped generation
households are one of the most rapidly growing coresidence living
arrangements in the U.S. and Canada (Bryson and Casper, 1999).

Moreover, many cultures immigrating to North America place high
value on custodial grandparenting and the use of extended families
and multigenerational households for parenting grandchildren. For
example, relying on grandparents as the primary source of child
care while at work is most common among black mothers, followed
by Hispanic and then White mothers (Ries and Stone, 1992). Also,
in both the U.S. and Canada, multi-generational households, although
relatively rare (5 percent of Americans and only about 4 percent of
Canadians reside in a household with three or more generations),
are on the rise (Kemp, 2003). In Canada, many recent immigrants
are from Asian societies, and many form multi-generational households for economic and cultural reasons. In these families, grandparents often spend considerable amounts of time in the rearing and
socialization of their grandchildren in exchange for other support-

ive behaviors. This day-to-day contact and mutual assistance typically enhances intergenerational solidarity among all generations who report mainly positive consequences when they live "under one roof" (Gee and Mitchell, 2003).

Finally, although research is lacking on the effects of grandchildren on intergenerational relations in Europe, it appears that grandparent roles and intergenerational relations can vary across countries because of divergent norms, customs, traditions, expectations, and family obligations. Smith (1991), for instance investigated grandparental roles across Europe (such as the intergenerational transmission of parenting among grandmother-mother dyads in the Netherlands), and found unique processes related to cultural origin.

## Divorce and Union Break-Up

Despite the continuing popularity of marriage, divorce remains common in many Western countries. Divorce rates have been declining slightly in the U.S. and Canada since 1982, however, rates are still at historically high levels. In Table 5.4, we observe that in 2001, the U.S. exhibited the highest crude divorce rate among all countries of interest at 4.00, whereas it is calculated at 2.30 in Canada.

**Figure 5.4**
**Crude Divorce Rate for Selected Countries, 2001**

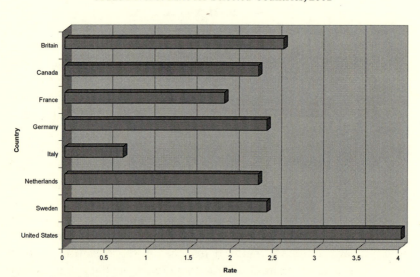

Source: See Table 3.4 for data sources.

Thus, the likelihood of divorce remains extremely high, particularly in the U.S. Indeed, it is estimated that nearly 50 percent of first marriages in the U.S. and approximately 33 percent of first marriages in Canada will end in divorce (Cherlin, 1999; McDaniel and Tepperman, 2004). With regard to European countries, crude divorce rates, in ascending order of prevalence are: Britain (2.60), Germany (2.40), Sweden (2.40), Netherlands (2.30), France (1.90), and Italy (.70).

The overall trend toward increased divorce is commonly explained by fundamental social, cultural and legal shifts. For example, some researchers argue that the higher divorce rates are the result of a change in the ties that bind family embers to one another. Whereas family bonds once rested on strong economic interdependence, today they rest more often on emotional ties. Others point to economic development and how this stimulates individualism and secularization by changing the values, norms, and preferences in the larger society. Women's economic independence, for instance, makes them less dependent on a male breadwinner. Finally, some writers focus on how laws governing divorce have also liberalized over time, making divorce relatively simple to obtain. Yet, many researchers are quick to point out that laws only reflect ideological change. In this vein, liberal divorce laws have been described as "merely tools" for the ready user" (McDaniel and Tepperman, 2004).

## The Divorcing Kind: Who is Likely to Divorce?

At the individual level, age at marriage is consistently found to be the strongest predictor of divorce in the first five years of marriage. People who enter marriage at the youngest ages, particularly during their teenage years, do so with the greatest risk for marital dissolution (Ambert, 2002). Also, those who cohabit prior to marriage are more likely to divorce, possibly due to adverse selectivity. That is, cohabitation may attract some who are less keen on commitment and stability, although as cohabitation becomes more normative this effect may be diminishing. Moreover, the relationship between premarital childbearing and the likelihood of divorce is overwhelming (McDaniel and Tepperman, 2004) and couples who divorce tend to have no children, or fewer on average than those with more children (Ambert, 2002). Interestingly, sons appear to reduce the risk of marital disruption, possibly due to greater parental involvement by fathers (South, Trent, and Shen, 2001).

With regard to family background factors, numerous researchers have found that children who experience the disruption of their parent's marriage are more likely to see their own marriages dissolve (Amato, 1996; Wolfjinger, 1999; 2000). In particular, the children of divorce are more likely to see their own marriages end in divorce than are children who grew up with both parents. It is postulated that parental divorce affects the risk of offspring divorce through three mediating mechanisms: life course and socioeconomic variables (i.e., early marriage, lower socioeconomic origins), commitment and attitudes toward divorce, and patterns of interpersonal behavior that are detrimental to marital stability (Amato, 1996). Interestingly, however, children born out of wedlock (and who did not experience parental divorce or death) are as likely, if not more likely, to have their own marriages dissolve (Teachman, 2002).

Race/ethnicity is also found to affect divorce rates. African-American women are 1.8 times as likely to divorce as white American women (Kposowa, 1995), and this pattern holds after controlling for such factors as socioeconomic status and background factors such as fertility, sex ratios, and age at marriage. Asians, however, have the lowest incidence of divorce (Kreider and Simmons, 2003). Similarly, in Canada, divorce is very low among persons from Asian backgrounds (e.g., Chinese, Indo), as well as for those from traditional ethnic groups in which divorce is still largely taboo (Mitchell, Wisteri and Gee, 2004).

Geographical locale and regional factors are also related to the risk of divorce in both the United States and Canada, although the relationship is not clear cut. Generally, urban living is positively related with divorce, while rural living is negatively correlated and. divorce rates typically increase as one moves from east to west. Part of this may be due to the frontier tradition that includes migration for work that seems to characterize the West. Also, the age distribution of the population differs, with the younger and more divorce-prone people being found in the West and some of these migrants may have lost the stabilizing influences of extended family and family traditions (McDaniel and Tepperman, 2004). Yet, it is interesting to note that some states, such as Oklahoma, Arkansas, and Wyoming have highly conservative social and political cultures, yet have some of the highest divorce rates in the country (U.S. Bureau

of the Census Bureau, 2000). These finding suggest that more conservative gender ideologies and greater religious activity do not create an immunity to divorce (Hawkins et al., 2002).

In Europe, many similar predictors of those prone to divorce are
also evident. In addition, researchers have found that young adults
who score high on "planful competence" (a concept introduced in
chapter 2) have lower rates of divorce. Planful competence is defined as the ability to think through choices in many domains, and is
associated with making "wise" transitions to adulthood (e.g., attending college or university) and at later ages. Thus, both men and women
who exhibit this trait experience life crises less often and are easily
able to adapt to marital difficulties (Goossens, 2001).

## Cohabitation and Union Dissolution

Finally, although technically one cannot speak of divorce among
unmarried cohabitors (homosexual or heterosexual) one can speak
of relationship dissolution. Obviously, there are fewer barriers to
dissolving these relationships, since there are generally neither legal
nor religious supports for these relationships (Connidis, 2001). As
previously noted, cohabiting unions are more likely to dissolve than
marital relationships, and this appears to be evident in all countries
(Kiernan, 2002). For example, more than 50 percent of cohabiting
unions in the United States end by separation within five years compared to only 20 percent of marriages (Bumpass and Lu, 2000).
Similar differentials exist in Canada, although absolute levels differ
somewhat. In particular, cohabiting unions that do not convert to
legal marriage are the most fragile, although the role of premarital
cohabitation in union dissolution may be more variable across nations (Kiernan, 2002).

With regard to same-sex unions, cohabitors also have less family pressure to remain together, since there is generally less support for same-sex than an opposite-sex union (Kurdek, 1998).
Despite this, the probability of breaking up over an eighteen-month
period among longer-term (ten years or more) is very similar for
straight, gay, and lesbian couples (Peplau et al., 1996). In shorter-
term unions (under two years), dissolution rates are lower for married couples but similar for cohabiting couples, regardless of sexual
unions. Unfortunately, the long-term effects of dissolving same-
sex partnerships and the implications of the break-up for
intergenerational relations have received scant attention. However,

research on the effects of marital dissolution among heterosexual couples on intergenerational relations has received some attention, and these studies will be briefly reviewed in the following section.

## Impact of Divorce on Intergenerational Relations

It is not surprising to learn that divorce can be a very distressing experience for both the divorcing couple and their parents, evoking feelings of sadness, loss, powerlessness, disappointment, confusion, guilt, and for some, bitterness (Connidis, 2001; Pearson, 1993). Studies show that many parents are quite shocked to learn about their child's divorce, having been unaware of the inner workings of their child's marriage (Hamon and Cobb, 1993; Matthews and Sprey, 1984). This lack of foreknowledge of a child's marital problems can make parents' adjustments to the divorce more difficult (Hamon and Cobb, 1993). Moreover, as observed by Connidis (2001), this lack of awareness "reflects a cultural preference to maintain intimacy at a distance once children are adults, with both parents and children seeking to respect mutual independence" (p. 190). She further notes that a key challenge presented by a child's divorce is the need to renegotiate the parent-child relationship based on changed circumstances.

Despite mixed results regarding the immediate effect of a child's divorce on intergenerational ties, aging parents and their children usually adopt transitional strategies for renegotiating relationships following divorce. Some young adults may rely heavily on their parents for support and parents can be particularly helpful in making this transition. If grandchildren are involved, grandparents can play an important role as caretakers. Yet, greater involvement in their children's lives also means more scrutiny of the previously private domain of the child's intimate partnership, which can create ambivalence in the parent-child tie (Johnson, 1988). Indeed, divorce clearly introduces ambiguity in family boundaries, leaving some parents confused about how to interact appropriately with their child and former child-in law (Hamon, 1995; Hamon and Cobb, 1993).

Overall, in-depth reports of parents concerning the help they give their children following a divorce suggest extensive emotional and instrumental support in the aftermath of divorce (Hamon, 1995). However, inconsistent findings are found with regard to the impact of a child's divorce on the help offered to parents. Some research (e.g., Cicirelli, 1984) finds that divorced children provide less support than their married peers, possibly because the challenges of divorce may make children less sensitive to the needs of their parents. Other studies (e.g., Logan and Spitze, 1996) show no change in parental support when children divorce. Furthermore, divorce is also found to affect individuals' relationships with their former in-laws. The quantity and quality of post-divorce interaction, however, depends on the history of the relationship prior to the dissolution of the marriage. Notably, those with a good quality relationship during the marriage, experienced continuing support from former in-laws (Duran-Aydintug, 1993).

## Summary and Conclusions

From a life course perspective, this chapter has presented an overview of contemporary trends in partnership formation and parenthood, with a focus on unmarried cohabitation (heterosexual and homosexual), marital timing, maternal age at first birth, and divorce. Primary emphasis was placed on North American family-related transitions to adulthood, although variations across a number of European countries (Britain, France, Germany, Italy, the Netherlands, and Sweden) were also highlighted. These modern trends are especially important because they are part of a broader pattern of social transformation affecting the family and converge to produce the "boomerang age." The institution of marriage has remained the dominant form of family living in most Western, industrialized countries, yet divorce rates are high from a historical perspective and young adults are increasingly experimenting with cohabitation. And as more young adults divorce and cohabit, they become active agents in destigmatizing behaviors that were once considered unacceptable and as such, are directly contributing to social change.

However, it should be recalled from chapter 2 that in a broader sweep of history, marriage has been dominant for a relatively short period and that the "1950s family," characterized by universal and low ages of marriage and parenthood was a relatively anomalous period. Therefore, family institutions express the needs and values of society at a particular time and place. From this perspective, marriage is not necessarily a permanent institution, nor is it necessarily the best form of family organization. Moreover, if the decline in marriage rates and increase in cohabitation rates tell us one thing, it is that the family is a flexible and adaptable institution (Wu, 2000).

In addition to considering broad economic and cultural changes that have fuelled transformations in these family-related transitions to adulthood, we also considered diversity in family-related transitional events across societies. While many Western industrialized countries exhibit remarkable similarity in the timing of many family-related behaviors, some countries, such as Sweden and Italy, display very different behaviors (e.g., cohabitation and divorce trends). It was also recognized that there is diversity within countries, and that the timing of family-related transitional events is shaped (and reshaped) at an intermediate group level. For example, research on the role of primary groups, such as the family of origin, illuminate important linkages between macro-level societal processes (e.g., economic and cultural change) and individual, history and biography. As such, the primary group is "a sutured zone where there is a reciprocal articulation and mutual merging of the public and the private, of social structures and the self, of the social and the psychological, of the universal and the singular" (Ferrarotti, 1981: 24).

In this vein, we have sought to highlight interdependencies among linked lives by focusing on how the timing and negotiation of transitional behaviors occur within unique social and historical locations and are dialectically connected through intergenerational ties. For example, the timing of transitional behaviors is often subjected to normative societal age norms and mutually reinforced via parental expectations, and individual-level resources linked to generational position. Time-disordered roles arise when "an individual's various social spheres and role sets are not temporally synchronized" (Seltzer, 1976:111-112). Thus, the timing and nature of transitional behaviors have the potential to affect the quality of intergenerational relations (e.g., create ambivalence), alter parental roles and exchanges of support over the life course.

We also considered how family-related transitional behaviors affect intergenerational relations through expanded kin networks, by producing in-laws, children, and grandparents. For example, the transition to parenthood produces the countertransition of grandparent, and grandparents are an important part of the "latent matrix" of kin connections (Riley and Riley, 1993). As a result, grandparents often sustain the younger generations in times of need and help weave the network that supports family member over the life course. Similarly, when adult children divorce, parents often provide much needed support. This network of contact and exchange highlights the characterization of contemporary family life as "modified extended" (Shanas, 1979). In other words, family ties beyond the nuclear family operate on a principle of revocable detachment wherein "dormant emotional ties can be mobilized when they are needed or desired" (George, 1981:79).

This chapter also alluded to how the timing of transitional behaviors can affect the life course of young adults, and how young adults can play an important role as innovators of the life course, themes that will be developed in more detail in the next chapter (chapter 6— "Through a Policy Lens: Social Policy and Social Action in the Boomerang Age"). Marriage and parenthood at a young age increases the probability of transition reversals such as divorce, and early family transitions can adversely affect educational and long-term occupational trajectories. Thus, the past has the potential to affect the present and future, which can viewed as a "ripple effect." This long-term view, with its recognition of cumulative advantage or disadvantage is particularly valuable for understanding social inequality later in life and for creating effective social policy and programs (O'Rand, 1996).

## Questions for Discussion and Debate

1. It has been argued that most societies are essentially pronatalist and that the North American cultural commitment to parenthood stems from a Judeo-Christian tradition that depicts children as "blessings" and childlessness as a curse or punishment (Miall, 1989). Do you agree or disagree that we live in this type of pronatalist society? What about in various European countries?

2. Discuss why there has there been a narrowing of the gender gap in median age of first marriage over the last century. Moreover, if you consider age to be an indicator of social power, with older people typically having more power than younger ones, how might the changing gender gap in age at marriage affect contemporary and future power relations between husbands and wives?

3. What is the evidence for the claim that a pervasive ideological opposition is set up between gay and lesbian partnerships and "the family"?

4.    As cohabitation continues to rise, how will this effect social institutions such as: government, religion and the media. What kinds of reciprocal effects will occur?

5.    Provide an argument for and against the following statement: "Grandparenthood is a roleless role" in relation to intergenerational relations and exchanges and support.

6.    Outline some possible similarities and differences between legal union dissolution and non-legal union dissolution with regard to its short term and long-term impact on other family related transitions to adulthood.

# 6

# Through a Policy Lens: Social Policy and Social Action in the Boomerang Age

Despite the fact that many people maintain that the state has no place in the bedrooms of the nation and that people should be able to develop intimate relationships as they choose, there will always be a need for governments to support and regulate certain aspects of family life (Baker, 2001). Indeed, for over a century, the state has regulated many domains of family life in Western, industrialized societies by enforcing government legislation and regulations. Moreover, the welfare state has been a defining feature of advanced capitalist society, especially since the end of World War II. The welfare state refers to government-sponsored programs designed to improve the social and economic well-being of families and individuals. It is comprised of an intricate web of supports to individuals and families. This includes aspects such as: income and security payments, social insurance, universal and targeted cash transfers, a wide range of social services (including housing, education, and health care), as well as several related laws and regulatory measures (Coles, 1995; Olsen, 2002).

However, as social programs became more costly, most of which were developed from the 1950s to the 1970s, governments began to question their ability to improve them or even to maintain them (Baker, 1995). Also during this time, we witnessed generally slower levels of economic growth in the late 1970s, 1980s, and 1990s. Spurred by factors such as global trade and production, this was a period punctuated by severe worldwide recessions and rapidly escalating rates of unemployment (Baker, 1995; Olsen, 2002). As a result of these and other tumultuous economic, social, and political transformations, the welfare state has been dramatically restructured and reshaped. A notable outcome of this retrenchment has been massive cutbacks in state supports and a heavier reliance on family and community resources. High levels of inequality and disparities both across and within countries have also deepened. Taken together, these trends have introduced a number of new challenges for young people and their families as they navigate their lives en route to "full" adulthood. Notably, young adulthood has become extended and midlife parents commonly shoulder the economic responsibility for the care and survival of its "grown" children.

There is little question that changing socio-demographic and other macro-level conditions, such as educational inflation, in conjunction with existent social policy and government programs dramatically influence the transition into adulthood. These factors shape opportunity structures and the developmental experiences of young people and their middle-generation parents. Homeleaving, for instance, entails moving into an independent accommodation apart from the family-of-origin, and this decision can be influenced by the job and housing market, including availability, and the cost and provision of accommodation for students. Therefore, if housing choices are scarce or limited, some young adults will be deterred from leaving home in the first place.

Concurrently, it is recognized that the decision to leave home (or family-related transitions more generally) also entails some degree of human agency. From a life course perspective, human agency is conceptualized as goal-oriented behaviour aimed at strategies of adaptation and which becomes especially salient during social change (e.g., see Elder, 1998; Marshall et al. 2001). For example, young adults may view extended coresidence as a positive life style strategy in order to maximize a wide variety of social and economic benefits, such as being able to save money while enjoying the comforts of home (Mitchell, 2004). In fact, research on a broad array of transitions to adulthood positioned within a life course theoretical lens, suggests the need to examine from both the volitional, choice patterns of young adults, as well as how the economy and social policies help to mold opportunity structures. The interplay of each side of this equation produces the "social structuration" of young adulthood, a concept developed by Giddens (1979; 1991a, 1991b). This term implies that we must take account of social and economic institutions and change that determine structures of opportunity, as well as the agency of young people in choosing a particular trajectory and in affecting their own lives through social change.

Yet is well documented that some young people have fewer opportunities and resources than others, and this can place them in a vulnerable position. Inequality of opportunity means that some young adults have lower likelihoods than others of creating economically viable family units. In short, with inequality of opportunity, "success" is not guaranteed for all (Hill and Yeung, 1999). Most people would agree that vulnerable young people need to be protected, and that families require sufficient health and social services to ensure healthy and safe childbirth and development. However, as the availability of safety support networks shrinks, new debates and challenges surface in the social policy arena.

In light of these trends and issues, this chapter presents a summary of key social and family policy issues relevant to the lives of today's young adults and their families in Western, industrialized societies. We begin by considering the unique socio-historical environment in which the current generation has grown up. This backdrop is needed to contextualize the life course of individuals within a particular historical time and place (e.g., see Elder, 2003). It is also necessary so that we can tailor policies to reflect current diversities and realities.

Also, in recognition of the role that human agency plays in transitional behaviors and the development of social policy, we will also consider how members of today's generation can instigate social change. Social and family policy development and the factors that affect it will be highlighted, including cross-national differences. We will also provide an overview of how young adults in the past have played a pivotal role in fostering social change, using the example of youth movements of the 1960s. Additionally, we will explore ways that young people can potentially influence social policy by serving as active innovators. In particular, it will be seen that young people can further develop and refine their knowledge base and critical analysis skills in order to forge alternative solutions to problems facing individuals, families, as well as advocates, and policy researchers. Finally, the chapter will conclude with some general recommendations for family policy reform and community programs.

## Changing Boundaries of Youth and Young Adulthood

There is little disagreement among social scientists that the advent of industrial society has heralded a significant change in the process by which young adults "come of age." Unlike pre-industrial times, youth has become associated with a period of dependency and relative leisure due to changes in such realms as child labor laws and compulsory education. Recent transformations in social policies and programs, as well as the occupational and educational structure of advanced industrial societies have further contributed to an extended period of youth. Côté and Allahar (1994) observe that this trend has been particularly pronounced since the 1950s because new technologies have reduced the work force and have altered the social fabric. Young adults are now conditioned to stay younger longer and are dependent upon parents until later ages. And, despite having fewer jobs, young adults are now being targeted as consumers rather than producers.

As a result of these demographic and socio-economic shifts, many social scientists (e.g., Arnett, 2000) have focused on young adulthood as a period of "emerging adulthood," since it is theoretically and empirically distinct from both childhood and adulthood. Consistent with our boomerang age metaphor, these years are characterized by a high degree of demographic diversity and instability, reflecting change and exploration. In fact, Rindfuss (1991) characterized the age range of eighteen through thirty as "demographically dense" because of the many demographic transitions that take place during that time, especially in the late twenties, such as leaving home, marriage and parenthood. Yet many of these transitional behaviors are subject to reversibility, such that linear models of family development do not realistically capture contemporary transitions to adulthood.

Despite the existence of age inflation and the potential reversibility of family-related transitional behaviors, there is controversy with respect to whether or not this has resulted in more difficulties for young adults during this phase of the life course. Some theorists (e.g., Côté and Allahar, 1994; Miles, 2000) express grave concern over current trends faced by youth, while others (e.g., Aquilino) view the extension of youth and adolescence in a more positive light. Pessimists, for example, argue that young people have lost an important "franchise," since they participate less in the labor force. And when they do participate, it is in a more subservient manner.

As a result, it is argued that many young adults do not have the full rights and privileges of citizenship and they must wait longer before they are fully recognized as adults. In addition to not being able to contribute to the economy in a meaningful fashion, they are viewed as being forced to stay in school and at home longer under the watchful eyes of educational bureaucracies and their parents. Moreover, young adults are increasingly targeted as consumers of "leisure industries" (e.g., media and music) and "identity industries" (e.g., fashion and education), in part because of the globalizing influences directed at the disenfranchised young to "manufacture their consent" (Herman and Chomsky, 1988). Consequently, it is asserted that we have created a culture in which the development of a viable adult identity has become increasingly tenuous (Côté and Allahar, 1994: xvi-xvi).

Conversely, those in the "optimistic" camp, view a number of positive outcomes for young adults as the result of the lengthening of youth and adolescence in advanced capitalist societies. Aquilino (1996), for instance, argues that the trend toward longer periods of dependency on parents and of training and preparation for the labor market are advantageous. Notably, youth may benefit from more years of experimenting with intimate relationships and a variety of living arrangements before marriage. Delayed marriage has been found to lengthen the number of years young people have to develop emotional maturity and the capacity for intimacy and caring (Erikson, 1963; Kahn et al., 1985). Delayed transitions can also be optimal for later role performances. For instance, living at home with parents or in other semiautonomous living arrangements can facilitate preparation for other work and family roles through continued family support. It can also contribute to increased intergenerational solidarity in later life since parents and children can reciprocate support and develop more peer-like relationships (Veevers and Mitchell, 1998).

Accelerated transitions, on the other hand, are argued to create disadvantage because young people may move into adult roles before they have acquired the resources, abilities, or experiences necessary to succeed in them (Aquilino, 1999:170). Thus, from this perspective, prolonged dependency and delayed transitions to adulthood are viewed as "developmentally appropriate" and represent an emerging strategy for developmental success, given current social and economic realities.

Regardless of whether there are positive and/or negative implications associated with the prolongation of youth, it has been well documented throughout this book that an extended transition to adulthood has become available for many, but not for all. This is because not all young adults have the opportunity (or desire) to delay adult transitions. And with ongoing cutbacks to social policies and programs, these young adults face even greater challenges relative to those with more individual and family resources. For example, young adults facing crisis situations (e.g., teenage pregnancy, poverty, mental health issues) with poor or unsupportive family relations may not have the choice to live at home to save money and receive family support. This can set up a chain reaction of disadvantage over the life course. Therefore, it is critical that we consider how changes to family policy can promote more equitable opportunities for disadvantaged members of our society.

## Defining Social and Family Policy and Factors Affecting Family Policy

On a general level, social policies and programs are those social arrangements aimed at the distribution of social resources and the promotion of the welfare of the individual and society, and are formed out of competing values (Gee and McDaniel, 1994). Family policy, therefore, is a sub-field of social policy concerned with the problems of families in relation to society and advancement of family well-being as its goal. It can be defined as "a coherent set of principles about the state's role in family life which is implemented through legislation or a plan of action" (Baker, 1995: 5), although numerous definitions have been advanced and are characterized by differences in scope, content, target, and source. For example, Kamerman and Kahn (1978: 3) defined the scope of family policy as "everything that government does to and for the family," while others have defined it broadly enough to include defense policy or economic arenas (e.g., see Bogenschneider, 2000). Moreover, Baker states that family policy can be divided into three categories: (1) laws relating to family issues (e.g., marriage, adoption, divorce, child support); (2) policies to help family income (e.g., tax concessions, maternity leave); and (3) the provision of direct services (e.g., child care, home care health services, subsidized housing). Thus, the range of programs and policies affecting families is very broad—some support a nurturance or social function while others support economic ones.

It is also important to recognize that some governments have developed an explicit written family policy, in which the state's role is very clear (e.g., marriage laws), whereas most governments create implicit family policies. Many people assert that implicit family policies establish general legislation and social programs that contain a particular ideological view of the role of the state in family life. These policies can be found within laws, social policies, and regulations, rather than within one specific document. For example, an implicit assumption in U.S. social policy, such as tax policy and poverty classification, is that married nuclear families behave as an economic unit who pool income in order to share a common standard of living (Kenney, 2004).

Many of these implicit policies have been developed over the years and have been influenced by the ideology of the party in power, the concerns of the day, and the pressure of powerful advocacy groups. They are especially prevalent within labor market and social welfare programs, and relate to notions of how families are defined with respect to their responsibilities; family values; and under what circumstances the state will assist or intervene in family life. Thus, it may be necessary to review a wide variety of laws or to "read between the lines of these laws" (Baker, 1995).

Furthermore, the term *family policy*, although not a common household phrase, is probably more familiar to people today than in the past. For example, Al Gore used the term on *The Oprah Winfrey Show* during the 2000 presidential campaign (Zimmerman, 2001). Zimmerman (2001, p. 3) also notes that the discourse on family policy at the beginning of the 21$^{st}$ century is very different from the discourse of the 1960s, when the term family policy was first introduced into American policy vocabulary. At that time, discourse was premised on the belief that government had a responsibility to help individuals and families meet their needs and could play a positive role. As a result, attention became focused on problems that many families were experiencing, such as poverty, health care affordability, and related issues of social sharing of its costs.

It should also be recognized that the expansion of the government's role in matters pertaining to families from the mid-1960s to the mid-1970s was influenced by Swedish sociologist Alva Myrdal. She introduced the idea of family policy in her book *Nation and the Family* (1941, 1968), which described Sweden's experience in the development of a democratic welfare state, having replaced a strongly centralized monarchy (Zimmerman, 1999). Sweden's welfare state was founded on a highly developed bureaucratic model of centralized administration and control made possible by the homogeneity and size of its population and circumscribed geography

(Dempsey, 1981). Concern over demographic changes such as falling birth rates led to systematic efforts to make connections between population policy and family policy and their demographic and social implications. As a result, Sweden set goals to initiate ways to better understand the consequences of policies in many areas, maintaining that family policy was nothing less than social policy (Zimmerman, 1999).

The reaction to Myrdal's book in the United States was largely skepticism, although many social scientists and family professionals followed the "Swedish experiment" with interest. That experience led to the value of having something called family policy, since it appealed to a society that almost uniformly valued family. It also brought to the forefront the fact that an explicit comprehensive national family policy had not been a conscious part of the American tradition, largely because family life was viewed as a private matter. Also, a number of European innovations, such as child care and maternity leave, during a period of economic expansion and a favorable political climate made it an opportune time for the country to initiate some family policy initiatives (Zimmerman, 1999).

It was also during that period that Daniel Patrick Moynihan (1965), who later became a senator for New York, wrote one of the first American papers on family policies. In this article, he issued a dire warning of the negative consequences that emanated from the enactment of laws that ignored their family implications. Fortunately, since that time, family dimensions have received more attention, such that the words family policy no longer sound as out of sync with policy discourse as when Moynihan first used them. Thus, the field of family policy was conceived in the United States in the 1970s, and it "came of age" in the 1990s, although it has not achieved a status commensurate with that of economic or environmental policy (see Bogenschneider, 2000 for a full discussion). Yet, as previously noted, the increasing dominance of the markets in American society has partly eroded the belief that the government is responsible for addressing the problems of individuals and families.

In Canada, early settlers brought their European marriage customs and legal traditions. Similar to the U.S., social and family policy has always been influenced by the development of social programs in other countries, including the U.S. but especially Britain. For example, *The Married Women's Property Act,* which was first passed in England in 1870, was gradually introduced to the Canadian provinces after 1872 (Dranoff, 1977: 48). Also, when Britain developed its unemployment insurance program in 1911, there was considerable discussion in Canada's Parliament about the need for such a program, although the Canadian unemployment insurance program was delayed until 1940 (Cuneo, 1940). More recently, Canadian policy discussions concerning the enforcement of child support have been based on an examination of policies in the United States, Australia and Sweden (Baker, 1995). Overall, the Canadian system of family policy is characterized as "liberal welfare state," similar to the United States, since both of these countries rely mainly on means-tested benefits to those who have exhausted their family resources (Baker, 2001).

Turning to Europe, although the development of family policy in Europe is more complex than in North America, many trace the origins of North American family policy to Europe. This is because these countries industrialized much earlier and this process is usually related to increasing labor force participation by women, declining birth rates, and an aging population (Baker, 1995). The earlier development of more generous family benefits in countries such as France and Sweden, relative to the U.S. and Canada, for example, have been explained by differences in demographic and social trends. Also, many European nations take an approach to social protection that differs from both the social insurance and means-tested programs in the United States. Notably, in Sweden, the government offers benefits on the basis of citizenship, rather than on the basis of need or contribution (Esping-Andersen, 1990).

However, European family policy is generally characterized by a great deal of diversity with regard to the generosity and implementation of its social programs. Epsing-Andersen (1990, 1998), for example, identifies three clusters or regimes of welfare capitalism: liberal, continental or Christian-democratic, and social democratic. Nations such as Sweden (and Denmark) fall into the category of "social democratic" because they have established relatively generous universal benefits, funded through general taxation. Germany and the Netherlands are "continental or Christian democratic," according to Epsing-Anderson, although other policy researchers such as Baker consider Germany (as well as Italy) "conservative" or "corporatists," since these citizens rely largely on social insurance for employees (and their dependents), financed through contributions from employees, employers and government (Baker, 2001). Britain, on the other hand, is classified as "liberal," similar to Canada and the United States (Epsing-Anderson, 1990). Moreover, countries such as France and Sweden continue to be interventionist and to devote a significant portion of state spending to family policy while countries such as Italy lag behind (e.g., see Bonke and Koch-Weser, 2004; Letablier, 2004).

Similar to North America, European social and family policy has also been affected by the politics of cutbacks, downsizing and retrenchment which have become endemic as spending on social programs has been targeted as problematic (Jenson and Sineau, 2001). European Union (EU) concerns over the impending "crunch" due to falling birth rates and an aging population has generated some common cross-national patterns. Although absolute spending on family policy rose, it lost ground relative to other social polices. Different responses to impending issues are also emerging. For example, in France, there has also been an effort to coordinate across many policy dimensions, while in Sweden, a private market in services is being proposed as a way to reduce the burden of expensive public services in a high-end welfare state (Jensen and Sineau, 2003).

## The Intergenerational Equity Debate

It is also important to note that family policy discussions in Westernized countries have been affected by "the intergenerational equity debate." Although this "debate" appears to be particularly pronounced in the United States (Marshall et al., 1993), generational concerns, especially as they pertain to family relationships and the provision of social support, are a worldwide issue (Antonucci and Jackson, 2003). As articulated by Connidis (2001), the intergenerational equity debate has strong roots in the United States where, in 1984, Americans for Generational Equity (AGE) was created. Its objective was to apply Thomas Jefferson's opinion that each generation should ensure that the succeeding one experience similar or greater levels of prosperity (Bengtson, 1993). The debate centers on the view that each generation must receive its fair share of government spending (public transfers).

One side of the intergenerational debate argument focuses on the idea that the old are receiving too much at the expense of the younger generation. On the other side of the argument are those who disagree and contend that discussions of equity must include more than current government expenditures. For example, some argue that the so-called Generation X, born during the 1960s, have already experienced the growth of poverty and rising divorce as children; limited economic opportunities while young adults; and high taxes while working as adults. As a result, some members of this generation blame older generations for leaving them a bleak economic future (Pampel, 1998).

Yet many oppose the claims of generational inequity and argue and that generations contain more diversity within them than between them, and furthermore, that all generations are vulnerable to poverty and the loss of public support. Interdependence rather than conflict also characterizes generations. Viewed from the long-range perspective that current age is "a brief point in the life course," it may make little sense to favor one's own age group at the expense of others, since each age group has a stake in the well-being of all groups (Kingson et al. 1986, Pampel, 1998). And finally, critics dispute arguments that suggest problems of generational fairness based upon the experiences of European nations. Many of these countries, despite having already reached levels of old-age dependency that the United States will not reach for decades, have not experienced disastrous problems (Myles, 1995 and see Pampel, 1998 for full discussion of exaggerated claims).

We will now turn our attention to how young adults have engaged in political movements and social change in the past. This will be followed by a discussion on how young people can affect social and family policy in the present, as well as the future.

### Young Adults as Social Innovators in the Past

It should be recognized that young people have always played a role as active agents of social change throughout history. Toward the end of the nineteenth century, for instance, many American students embraced the new theories of socialism and communism being advanced in Europe, forming the Intercollegiate Socialist Society (1905) to advance their Marxist ideas (e.g., see Johnston, 1998). Yet, their force as a collective counter culture in the sixties has assumed almost mythical proportions. This era was created after the calm of the 1950s and the "cult of domesticity" and it had a revolutionary impact on society compared with adjacent generations. Of course not everyone was "radical" and large proportions of 1960s youths were not true "hippies"—in fact most remained apolitical or opposed to the radicalism that is associated with this time period.

However, this was the age of the "generation gap," student protest, the Beatles, rock and folk music, flower power, free love, drugs, and militancy in which political activism and the influence of radical ideas were highly pronounced. This period was inseparable from that of the baby boom (individuals born between 1946-1965) and this was a moment in history that forever defined the baby boom as a distinct generation (Owram 1998).

Soares (2000) observes that in the 1960s and 1970s, youth action was often focused on the student movement, which was inseparable from its historical moment. This included a number of favorable conditions, events and social tensions, including: affluence and optimism, civil rights, the Cold War, Vietnam, Kennedy, Johnson, Nixon, the assassinations of Kennedy, Malcolm X, King and worldwide upheavals seeming to promise "the founding of a new age in the ashes of the old" (Gitlin, 1989: 5). From this period emerged a tumult of movements aiming to remake virtually every social arrangement America had settled into after World War II.

However, to a large extent, the student movement of the 1960s and early 1970s faced structural tensions, lacked autonomy, and often acted in line with the needs of political movements and parties. In particular, the tendencies of revolutionary politics played a major role in the shaping of ideology and the activities of the student movement. Large-scale plans for transforming society were therefore predominant, and this often amounted to a certain rejection of "the system," in which authority figures were often viewed as the enemy (Soares, 2000). There was also a growing fear that, in the words of C. Wright Mills, that "increased rationality may not make for increased freedom" (cited in Owram, 1998: 205). Thus, many young people searched for alternative experiences, which were afforded by the prosperity of the decade and changing labor market requirements. Also, many young people enrolled in higher education, had higher disposable incomes than previous generations and were free from immediate worries about the future. Moreover, advances in technology (e.g., cheaper air fares) made travel cheaper, such that thousands backpacked around Europe and other countries to escape the domesticity of suburbia (Owram, 1998).

During the 1960s, many student-led events sparked widespread attention, which further fuelled youth protest, activism and social change. One notable event occurred in Greensboro, North Carolina on February 1, 1960, when four black (then known as Negro) students wearing jackets and ties, sat down at a Woolworth's whites' only lunch counter. They claimed their right to be served and refused to leave. These four—Ezell Blari, Jr., Franklin McCain, Joseph McNeil, and David Richmond—belonged to the Youth Council of the National Association for the Advancement of Colored People (NAACP). Familiar with earlier sit-ins across the country, these young people had been socialized in a tradition of liberation transmitted to them by many individuals such as their parents, ministers, teachers, and the leader of the Southern Christian Leadership Conference (SCLC), Martin Luther King. The four returned on February 2 with twenty-five other young people, and by the fifth day there were more than three hundred. This event triggered a wave of sit-ins at lunch counters across the urban south, and within two months, sit-ins had been organized in fifty-four cities in nine states (Gitlin, 1989).

Overall, group action was not just a means but a core of the student movement's identity. It also represented a significant break from the fifties, which dictated adjustment, acceptance, and middle-class mores, as well as predictable paths of career, propriety and family. Many young women, for example, were active participants in both the civil rights and anti-war movements, and they also formed the basis of emerging feminism. Sharing the idea of liberation from male authority, many began to challenge the rigid gender roles that they had learned growing up in the 1950s and the presumption that they should be spending their young adult years waiting for a husband who would continue to protect them from the real world. As Tischler (1998: 189) observes, "Marches not marriage, teach-ins not PTA meetings, and getting arrested for civil disobedience not disciplining children, all became subjects of discussion and action for women who sought an identity beyond husband, home, and children."

Many of these social movements, particularly The New Left and the SDS (Students for a Democratic Society, est. 1959), were heavily influenced by the idea of participatory democracy, in which, as the landmark political manifesto for SDS the *Port Huron Statement* reads, "the individual [should] share in those social decisions determining the quality and direction of his life." This document was primarily written by Tom Hayden, a twenty-two year old former editor of the student newspaper at the University of Michigan, and criticized the American government for failing to address a myriad of social ills such as poverty, racism and materialism. Overall, the SDS was part of a more general youth movement aimed at correcting social injustice in the U.S. and it became famous for its many slogans such as: "Make love—not war!" "The issues are interrelated and need to be addressed together," "War on Poverty—Not People," and "Negotiation" (Blue, 2002, Gitlin, 1989).

In Canada, young people were also involved in social movements, although most commentators assert that they were not quite as radical or as large as their southern neighbors. By the early 1960s, a minority of Canadians were beginning to question the nature of the Cold War alliance that had developed since 1945. Moreover, many events in the U.S. provided a major impetus to Canadian movements and protests. For example, the Political Science, Sociology and Anthropology Department (or PSA) at Simon Fraser University, British Columbia, was one of the most radical departments in a generally radical university and much of this activism was inspired by American political culture (Owram, 1996). This is hardly surprising, given that many professors were educated in the U.S. and the baby boom generation had grown up in the era of the American "superpower" under the heavy influence of American politics, television and music. Some Canadians youth also wanted Canada to emulate Sweden and wanted to exist outside the framework of the Western alliance. It is also striking to note that none of the major Canadian domestic themes of the 1960s—Quebec separatism, Native's rights and women's liberation, racism, the poor—were viewed as politically important in the 1950s (Owram, 1998).

There were also a number of youth protest movements during the 1960s in Europe, which were mobilized earlier and more massively in Germany than in other European countries, such as Britain, France, Italy, the Netherlands, and Sweden (e.g., see Ellis, 1998). Notably, West Berlin was the undisputed centre of student protest in Europe both in terms of numbers participating and in the radicalism of thought and action. Perhaps this is not surprising, given that the divided city had been at the centre of the Cold War for two decades and there were conflicting ideologies of communism and the "free world." Also, with its cheap housing and the exemption of its residents from military service, there was an unusually large student population and student subculture (Minnerup, 1998).

In the latter half of the 1960s, a radical form of idealism developed across Europe based on the idea that traditional political parties had failed to provide a vision which extended beyond post-war materialism and wealth creation. Many of these ideas were inspired by American civil rights movements, revolutionaries in South America, and student protesters at Berkeley. Similar to many Americans, European young people were searching for new values and new ways of living together in solidarity (Cornils, 1998). For example, British students demanded increased participation in university policymaking, especially from 1967 onwards, although they were politicized over a whole range of local, national and international issues.

Today's youth movements, on the other hand, are often characterized as less radical and as going through a period of disorganization. This is due to the general fragmentation of social movements, the disappearance of points of reference, and the current neo-liberal model which promotes individual solutions with an 'everyone for him or herself' attitude (Soares, 2000). That being stated, there have been some notable youth movements in recent years, such as the demonstrations and protests against globalization (e.g., the World Trade Organization (WTO) meeting in North America in 1999, and the marches against the war in Iraq following the terrorist attacks to the World Trade Buildings in New York and in Washington, September 11, 2001. For example, the WTO meeting was a watershed event that demonstrated that the new youth movement had sophistication in both its tactics and its analysis of the international situation. It was also the beginning of a series of similar mass protests that have occurred when leaders from different countries or international organizations meet to promote "freer trade" and neo-liberal policies (Shragge, 2003).

Moreover, identity politics and social movements have reshaped the community sector, creating a new kind of pluralism in which many "new" concerns and divergent interest groups have surfaced. For example, following the lead of the women's movement in the 1960s and 1970s, groups such as gays and lesbians, the physically and mentally challenged, and immigrants have influenced the way that these groups have been treated. The emphasis is now on their respective social rights and the building of new opportunities. And, although service provision and mobilization are not necessarily in contradiction, integrating other activities becomes more difficult. This is partly because an organization becomes enmeshed in the demands of provision and also because governments support only the service aspects of their programs, Also, since the community sector is not well-financed (with no long-term guarantees), a relationship of dependency is thus established, leading to less risk-taking and political engagement (Shragge, 2003).

Despite huge gains, many authors purport that there is a "global crisis," with no blueprint for change, a defining element of previous periods. Although some argue that this is a pessimistic view, there are ways in which the young people of today can continue to play a role in effecting their lives and the world around them during the "boomerang age." These recommendations are offered in the next section.

### Empowerment and Social Action Strategies for Young Adults

There are a number of tactics that today's young people can employ in order to serve as agents or innovators of social change. This includes the need for young people to have a vision of a more humanistic and caring society, a strong knowledge base, and the need to take individual and civic responsibility. Young adults can also become directly involved in policy change by developing careers as policy researchers and practitioners. Each of these strategies will be discussed below and some key barriers to change will also be highlighted.

It is sometimes argued that many of the decisions affecting young people have been made by those that have interests not shared by young people, such as capitalists, legislators, advertisers, educators and religious groups. Moreover, it is also observed that there does not appear to be a political revolution on the horizon that would eradicate the problems facing young people today (Côté and Allahar, 1994; Soares, 2000). As a result, it is commonly asserted that young people need to focus on the "real" cause of family problems by adopting the premise that personal troubles, which many ascribe to an individual's shortcomings, can often be explained by larger problems within society. This insight was developed by C. Wright Mills (1959) and forms the basis of what he calls the "sociological imagination."

An important starting point to bring about positive change is for young people to have a clear vision of what a more compassionate and caring society would be like, with the assumption that all youth share the same basic needs, albeit some groups may have unique needs and interests. Therefore, policies need to be created that are informed by humanistic values and that take into account the experiences and perspectives of those they are supposed to benefit. On an individual level, young people can gain strength by learning about the history of the world in which they live, the roots and reproduction of social inequality (e.g., racism, sexism, poverty) and by becoming aware of the limitations of the institutions governing their lives. With this knowledge, young people can play a role in navigating their own development instead of relying on others to act in their best interest.

Young people can also learn important insights by having a broader knowledge based about life in other countries. Sweden, for example, is commonly offered as a model of social democracy with a reputation of a relatively egalitarian family policy with a strong emphasis on gender equality (e.g., see Duane-Richard and Mahon, 2003). It is also characterized by effective and rational service delivery with generous parental leave insurance and a publicly funded childcare system. Also, large numbers of young people belong to "party political youth organizations" funded by state grants (Côté and Allahar, 1994). In fact, the Swedish government has taken many steps to involve young people in many aspects of decision-making and actively encourages all nations to include Youth Delegates of both genders at the United Nations General Assembly (Klang, 2003).

Moreover, although many people believe that government is not working as it should, many writers (e.g., Roe, 1998; Putnam, 2000, Zimmerman, 2001) contend that our current problems do not lie with government but rather with individual citizens who have neglected their citizenship responsibilities. Therefore, it is argued that we need to have new relationships with governments and each other and new ways of making decisions and acting together. Government, according to Roe (1998) is about the collaborative efforts of all citizens and elected and appointed officials to meet common needs. This could entail improvements in civic education for all generations. It also means that young people have a responsibility to vote since it is a seminal act of citizenship in a democracy and a sign of the level of commitment to the democratic process. Indeed, Putnam (2000) observed that voter turnout has dropped by nearly 25 percent since 1960 in the United States. In fact, young people notoriously have low rates of voting in North America as well as in many European countries. However, beyond voting, citizens must be actively engaged in election campaigns, deliberative forums, and a range of other activities that are related to family policy.

Furthermore, according to Putman, there is a need for improved civic engagement. This refers to people's connections with others in their communities, like those facilitated by small-scale face-to-face associations. It also increases social capital, which he defines as certain features of social life—namely social networks, norms and basic trust—that enable people to act together to pursue shared objectives more effectively, such as family policies that enhance family well-being. Thus, when citizens become actively engaged in public life, it rejuvenates their communities, culturally and economically (Roe, 1998). In short, it increases the social capital that makes solutions possible (Zimmerman, 1999).

Young adults can also affect family policy as advocates, community organizers and as researchers. Generally, the advocate endorses and actively works for a course of action that improves family life and improves family life and the well-being of its members, and this typically requires some type of leadership and group mobilization. Community organizing can be defined as "a search for social power and an effort to combat perceived helplessness through learning that what appears personal is often political" and creates a capacity for democracy and for sustained social change (Shragge, 2003: 41). It is therefore not surprising to learn that advocacy can be a daunting task, since it requires many skills, perseverance, and pragmatism.

As researchers, there are a variety of ways to establish family policy (see Eshelman, 1994, for full discussion). "Think tanks" such as the Urban Institute and the Heritage Foundation are actively involved in both family policy research and advocacy. Members of these institutes and foundations publish books, special reports and position papers, testify before congressional committees and hold seminars and conferences to disseminate their information. With regard to the policy research process, it typically begins with a general statement that some kind of social action may be desirable. Researchers seek to examine whether or not recommendations need to be made with respect to changing laws, the development of programs, or action taken to fulfill specific needs.

A second type of policy research conducted is to evaluate existing policy. This is done at a programmatic level to determine the extent to which social programs have achieved or are achieving their stated goals. The need for family-evaluation research is evident on many issues, not the least of which is parental leave. For example, in 1992, President Bush vetoed a family-leave bill, largely based on the justification that it would be an added financial cost to businesses. Others asserted that such a bill is unnecessary because many firms already offer parental leave and that what parents really need is child care, not parental leave.

A third type of policy research is family-impact analysis, with the attempt to assess intended and unintended consequences. For example, what is the impact of a program such as Head Start on mothers as well as children? What is the consequence of not allowing dependent coresident young adults to be eligible for welfare benefits? Unlike evaluation research, family impact analysis examines how families are affected beyond the explicit intentions or goals of the policy or program. Evaluation research may demonstrate that intended goals are being met, but impact analysis may show that the goals are counterproductive, producing unintended or undesirable consequences for families.

Finally, the adoption of a long-term temporal perspective can promote a more fundamental reappraisal of assumptions that inform policy analysis and advocacy. This framework has been well articulated by Dey (1999), in which he criticizes current social policy initiatives and welfare debates. Although he focuses on policy and research on parental support for young adults, many underlying assumptions of this approach complement our previous discussion as well as a life course theoretical conceptualization of family transitions to adulthood. In particular, this framework can be used to highlight and link aspects of time, social structure and human agency in the context of social change.

Specifically, Dey's temporal or "morphogenetic" approach as similarly proposed by Archer (1995), stresses the temporal interplay of structure and agency. Structural conditions (e.g., the state of the economy) are viewed as "generative mechanisms," and are independent factors preceding social interaction, with effects mediated by the latter. However, although young adults cannot alter the conditions they inherit, they can alter their effects through interaction over time.

Notably, Dey argues that time is a much neglected dimension of social policy. Instead, most welfare debates are preoccupied with the distribution of material goods and social services to satisfy immediate needs rather than such aspects as past actions or the prospects of future benefit through investment. Thus, from a social policy perspective, "time" is often conceived in terms of the "instant" or the "eternal" and related empirical concerns tend to identify current deficits in the fulfillment of needs. This results in a "universalist moralism" which tends to generalize such needs across time and place at one point. Instead, he asserts that we need to recognize the diversity of time frames through which transitional events occur. For example, policies that shift the burden of welfare spending from the state to families assumes that all parents are able to meet the needs of their adult children at all times. Thus, the related issue of "who cares?" cannot be examined without reference to the related question of who has time to care, and the changing structures and needs of families over the life cycle.

Overall, recognition that social needs are constructed within (or through) varying temporal frames of reference encourages a more sensitive analysis of the diverse and changing needs of young adults and their families. Moreover, a temporal perspective also reminds us of that young adults are not just passive recipients of social structure. Instead, young adults have the potential to play an important role in questioning social policy assumptions. In this way, young adults can serve as pioneering "innovators" in questioning and altering existing social structures and in the creation of more equitable social policies and programs. It can also contribute to meeting the diverse needs of young adults and their families in a rapidly changing world.

It is also important to acknowledge the barriers that impede the progress of the field of family policy, such as a lack of research that can inform decisions about how policies actually affect families, coordination among many interrelated sectors delivering policies and programs, piecemeal "funding," and inconsistency with regard to implementation.

Conflicting values and the ideological clashes that undercut the consensus for political action (Bogenschneider, 2000) are also a major barrier. Big policy agenda items, according to McKenzie (1991) are addressed only when there is sufficient consensus to do so.

These factors stand in the way of developing an interested, attentive public that is informed and engaged in policy issues related to families (Zimmerman, 1995). McKenzie (1991), for example, argues that a key challenge stems from our Western cultural penchant for individualism, material success, social status, instant gratification, and luxury goods. According to McKenzie, there is a widespread cultural assumption that an "invisible hand" produces individual, family and societal well-being from the sum of our individual, not collective pursuits. Yet, this assumption runs counter to engagement in public and family policy issues. It is also argued that consumerism has invaded our culture, such that many families have little leisure time because they work long hours not out of necessity, but to purchase materials goods. In fact, Americans own and consume twice as much as their 1948 counterparts. Bellah (1990) warns that one of the greatest threats to strong families and a good society is an economy that creates a culture of consumerism, a culture that has become so potent that it transforms "today's luxuries" into "tomorrow's necessities" (Schor, 1991:122).

Another threat to creating an interested public is institutional competition, whereby family policy practice/education competes with a number of other institutions, such as religious institutions, voluntary associations, media, and community in transmitting civic and social values (Zimmerman, 1995). Moreover, Putnam (2000) highlights various social and technological challenges that contribute to civic disengagement by identifying the media (especially television) as a major culprit. He maintains that older people have consistently been more engaged and trusting than younger people, although people do not become more engaged and trusting as they age. Also, generational effects reveal themselves in disparities among age groups at a single point in time. This produces real social change as successive generations, enduringly imprinted with divergent views, enter and leave the population. With generational effects, individuals do not change, but rather, society does.

According to Putnam, the visible effects of generational disengagement began in the U.S. in the 1940s and 1950s. However, they were delayed in part because of the postwar boom in college enrollments. This raised levels of civic engagement and offset generational trends. Television watching per household, for instance, was more than 50 percent higher in 1995 than in the 1950s, resulting in a significant change in the way that Americans spend their time. He further observed that newspaper circulation per household in 1996 dropped by more than half from its peak in 1947. Television viewing, Putnam asserted, privatizes leisure time and comes at the expense of nearly every social activity outside the home. In particular, people are less likely to participate in social gatherings, community meetings, and informal conversations—the very venues of family policy discourse and family policy practice (Putnam, cited in Zimmerman, 1995).

## Recommendations for Policy Reform and Community Programs

Based upon the research presented in this book, several suggestions for policy reform and community programs can be identified. This will include focus on the following five areas: (a) education and income; (b) housing and dependency issues; (c) cohabitation, marriage and divorce; (d) parenthood and childcare; and (e) gender and racial equity. It is recognized that many of these areas intersect, but they do allow for a focus on the key family-related transitional events focused upon in this book (homeleaving and intergenerational coresidence; partnership formation and dissolution; and parenthood). Linkages to intergenerational issues will also be made, whenever appropriate, throughout this discussion. It should be emphasized that these recommendations are only meant to highlight some general issues rather than to provide a comprehensive critique of existing social policy in North America and our selected international comparisons.

It is also recognized that there is considerable variation across nations with regard to the generosity of social policies and in the state of their respective economies. Therefore, this overview primarily focuses on the United States and Canada, but could be extended to other countries that need to improve the social conditions of vulnerable young people and their families. This emphasis is warranted given the fact that current trends appear to be widening social inequality in many of the countries examined in this book. Therefore, it is critical to equalize opportunities for youth based on the belief that that these formative periods are crucial determinants of the subsequent adult life one leads (Becker, 1991, as cited in Marshall and Mueller, 2003; Heinz, 1996). In other words, the timing and nature of earlier life course experiences significantly impact the long-term transitional behaviors and trajectories of young adults. By the end of their lives, initially disadvantaged cohort members are doing worse relative to their advantaged counterpart, a view that has been extensively explored in North American life-course research (Marshall and Mueller, 2003; O'Rand and Henretta, 1999).

### Education and Income

Research presented in this book and elsewhere establishes a myriad of benefits associated with higher education and income, both from the family of origin, as well as based on the personal characteristics of the individual. Notably, young adults from higher socio-economic families are less likely to experience poverty, tend to marry and have children later, and are at less risk of becoming teenage parents, to divorce and to become high school dropouts. Overall, educational qualifications are a key determinant of life chances in industrial societies and generally and are a strong correlate of making a higher income. Higher income enables young people to have more choices. For example, they may have more housing options, since relatively low income makes it difficult to live alone or in a small household, as the latter is relatively more expensive than a large one (Burch and Matthews, 1987).

It is also well documented that less educated workers have been disadvantaged in the labor market during the past two decades and that income inequality has also grown in many countries. For example, in 1970, the bottom 20 percent (the lowest quintile) of households controlled only 4.1 percent of all household incomes in the United States, whereas the top 20 percent of households (the highest quintile) controlled 43.3 percent of income. By 1998, the gap had widened as the share of the bottom 20 percent plummeted to 3.6 percent and the share of the top 20 percent increased to 49.2 percent (Casper and Bianchi, 2002). Additional evidence shows that if wealth were measured rather than income, the inequality in economic well-being would be even greater (Oliver and Shapiro, 1995).

Moreover, the level of income in minority families is significantly lower in the United States, although minority two-parent, dual-earner families are advantaged relative to other types of minority families. However, they are disadvantaged relative to comparable white families. Black two-parent families have per capital income levels that are only 79 percent of those of white families, and poverty rates are 44 percent higher. Hispanic families, in particular, face disadvantage, with per capita income levels only 60 percent of those in comparable white families and poverty rates are five times greater (Casper and Bianchi, 2002).

Although poverty rates in the United States have declined since 1980, a large number of families live in poverty, a trend that seems an anomaly in an otherwise strong economy with low unemployment rates and rising consumer confidence. In particular, single-mother families experience extraordinarily high rates of poverty when compared to that to two-parent families (Casper and Bianchi, 2002).

Also, children and young adults remain at a higher risk of living in poverty than most other age groups. Nearly one in five up to the age of twenty-four live below the poverty line, and 10.5 percent aged twenty-five to thirty-four live below the poverty line. This compares to only 6.7 percent of those aged forty-five to fifty-four (Dalaker and Proctor, 2000). Poverty is most pronounced among minority children: 32.7 percent of black children and 29.9 percent of Hispanic children live in poverty, compared to 12.9 percent of whites (Newman and Grauerholz, 2002).

Furthermore, the United States has very high rates of child poverty in the industrialized world, with Canada also near the highest poverty rates. Notably, the after-tax poverty rate for children in the United States is 22 percent, while in Canada it is lower at 14 percent. These rates are much higher than all of our selected international comparisons. These rates are: Sweden (3 percent), the Netherlands (6 percent), France (7 percent), Germany (7 percent) and Britain at 10 percent (Canadian Institute of Child Health, 2002). Although comparable data are unavailable for Italy, evidence shows that child poverty rates are the highest in this country, and fall slightly above Britain (BBC News, 2002).

Therefore, aims to eradicate poverty (particularly in North America, Italy, and Britain) and to improve the educational opportunities for all young people should be paramount. A number of policies have been implemented to address family poverty (e.g., see Bogenschneider, 2000 for overview), although many argue that family scholars and advocates typically exclude education from their policy agendas. Moreover, it is also recognized that not all students are willing or able to attend college or university. Thus, it might be useful to devise incentives to increase the proportion of at-risk adolescents from high school. For example, it might be beneficial to have an expanded system of apprenticeship and vocational education as other options to formal college attendance (also see Galston, 1996 for a discussion of these issues). Also, greater attention should be given to the likely impact of government policies on the economic well-being of families and children, especially those living at or near the poverty line.

## Housing, Homelessness and Dependency Issues

As noted throughout this book, the parental home is increasingly being used as a type of social safety net or as a secure home base (denoting a "normal base of operations) for many young adults (e.g.,

Goldscheider and Goldscheider, 1999). They are remaining at home until later ages, and are increasingly likely to refill the parental nest as boomerang kids in North America and many European countries. Moreover, research establishes that extended coresidence can provide young people with many important benefits, such as receiving day-to-day parental support, the use of household resources, the ability to save money and a chance to complete an education.

Yet, research also documents that intergenerational coresidence, as the result of either delayed homeleaving or home returning, is not an option for some young adults. For example, Looker (1993) highlights how the transition to adulthood in rural areas is quite different in urban areas. Youth living in rural areas may not have the option of residing at home after high school, either to work or while attending post-secondary institutions. Also, those young adults with a lack of "social capital" usually do not have the option to remain or return home due to strained or unsupportive relations. Not being able to return to the security and comforts of home could have a devastating effect on the lives of young adults who are not psychologically prepared to be launched as adults An inability to co-reside in the parental home while attending college or to save money can also widen the gap between groups of young adults, perpetuating social inequality (Mitchell and Gee, 1996b). Therefore, with regard to policy reform, young adults require adequate housing options and other related supports.

Housing policies and favorable economic conditions are found to influence the timing of homeleaving in many countries. For example, in the Netherlands, the housing needs of young people are recognized, which probably explains the relatively low proportions of young people living at home. In countries such as Italy, on the other hand, the housing situation deters many young people from leaving home, since there is an absence of a substantial market for houses to rent and the financial charges incurred when buying or selling property inhibit the attainment of residential autonomy at a young age (Ongaro, 2001). Therefore, social security measures in the form of public assistance, student grants, child benefits and rent subsidies can have an important impact on household formation and dissolution. The choice between leaving home and studying, for example, partly depends on the availability of student grants and rent subsidies which provide a greater degree of independence to those who are not able to obtain a mortgage (Alders and Manting, 1998).

Reform is also needed with regard to tax credits and the housing of dependent children. Many policies are dated on the premise that once a child is eighteen they are no longer financially dependent on parental support. However, with changing times young adults are often staying at home well into their twenties (see chapter 4). Therefore, the government needs to acknowledge the present diversity of caring or supportive relationships by considering tax provisions or benefits for those housing financially dependent adult children, at least for low-income families. Students also need sufficient financial support so that they are not forced to overly rely on parents and/or employment. For example, in many countries such as Britain, there has been a reduction in support (for example, the withdrawal of maintenance grants, introduction of student loans and £1,000 annual fees). This has contributed to the necessity of youth to live with their parents and/or work long hours while attending higher education (Berrington, 2001).

At both a societal and a community level, many people are also concerned about the tendency of some young adults to leave home at an early age, especially before the completion of high school. The majority of these young people are escaping conflict ridden or abusive households. In short, many of these youths lack "social capital" in the form of supportive home environments. A small number of these youths are homeless and live on the streets of major metropolitan cities. These "street kids" often sleep in stairwells and abandoned buildings or cram together in tiny hotel rooms. As one would expect, these young people also experience numerous health problems because of poor hygiene and inadequate nutrition. Drug use, prostitution and crime present other risks (Kines, 1993). Many of these young adults are not eligible for income assistance or most kinds of housing, including social housing and landlords typically will not rent to them.

Preventive strategies could be highly effective. Identification of those youths most at risk of leaving home could be made by high-school teachers, counselors, and social workers. The targeting of such youths may facilitate additional intervention strategies, such as the provision of special programs that may be of great value both to young adults and their families. The education of family members about the repercussions of early homeleaving and of sexual exploitation and physical abuse is also important.

Therefore, there should also be crisis services for youths on both an emergency and a regular basis, for such items as food, clothing and shelter, safe houses or environments in which to obtain information and counseling, life skills training, and medical and financial services. As a first step, greater community awareness and involvement in what is seen as a growing social problem is necessary. Money spent on social services, in the long run, will reduce the necessity to spend money on policing, courts, probation, parole, and incarceration.

## Cohabitation, Marriage, and Divorce

As previously noted, cohabitation has increased dramatically in the United States, Canada, and in many Western European countries. However, with the exception of some countries (i.e., Sweden), family policy has been inattentive to the implications of this highly popular family type. For example, some American researchers argue that social policy is inconsistent in its treatment of cohabiting households compared to their married counterparts. In the case of cohabiting-parent households, welfare policy typically assumes that marital status should not affect the extent to which children benefit from each adult's income. Yet, tax policy and the poverty classification system assume income pooling among married but not cohabiting parents, which is contrary to research findings such that the income of both parents should be considered in setting family policy (Kenney, 2004).

Ooms (1998) argues that marriage should be on the public agenda for a number of reasons. Married men and women are healthier, live longer, and have fewer emotional problems (Eastman, 1996). In fact, a recent study confirmed that the relationship between marriage and personal happiness in sixteen of seventeen industrialized countries, with marriage contributing to happiness significantly more than cohabitation (Stack and Eshelman, 1998). Married fathers tend to be more involved with their children, and there is little question that children fare better socially, psychologically and financially (assuming a conflict-free marriage) in families with both biological parents compared to those in single parent or stepfamily environments (Glenn, 1996, McLanahan and Sandefur, 1994). However, policy efforts to strengthen marriage have been met with considerable controversy and have been sporadic, uncoordinated and unsupported by think tanks, foundations and government commissions. This has been partly due to ideological concerns that marriage is a code word for an agenda to de-liberate women, stigmatize single parents or force women to remain in an abusive patriarchal relationship (Bogenschneider, 2000).

With regard to relationship dissolution, as previously demonstrated, young adults who experience parental divorce growing up are at a higher risk of a number of adverse effects, many of which affect their own transitional behaviours. For example, young adults exposed to stepfamilies tend to leave home earlier and experience higher divorce. Many individuals are also concerned over the high rates of divorce, particularly in the United States relative to many other industrialized countries. As a result, many states are considering legislation that would place restrictions on no-fault divorce. Proponents of this change assert that when laws are more restrictive, such as in Italy, divorce rates are lower (Alders and Manting, 1998). Therefore, making divorce more difficult to obtain or to increase the number of children living with both parents is assumed to have a positive effect on children and their families (Amato and Booth, 2000).

Many researchers argue that this view is too simplistic because divorce may be advantageous for children under certain conditions, such as when parents are in highly conflicted marriages. Therefore, laws making it harder to divorce can actually create more problems, such as keeping children and parents trapped in conflict-laden environments. Similarly, requiring deeply aggrieved spouses to battle each other in court over who is at fault for terminating the marriage will further burden children. Therefore, new legislation to restrict access to divorce is unlikely to make couples want to stay together and does not seem to be the most effective way of dealing with the high rates of divorce and their generally negative implications (see Amato and Booth, 2000).

Instead, it may make more sense to think about policies that support coupled partnerships more generally and try to prevent many of the problems that contribute to breakdown. Common "micro-sociological" marital problems for example, include alcoholism or drug abuse, infidelity, domestic abuse and violence, a lack of commitment, and poor conflict-resolution and communication skills (McDaniel and Tepperman, 2004). Policies related to social services, income, education and the workplace could therefore have positive effects on relationships and alleviate financial strain. In particular, supports and services need to be tailored to meet the specific needs of couples, regardless of marital status. Thus, providing greater awareness, support, and access to workshops, seminars, and family counseling could be very helpful, and is described in greater detail below.

Another issue that legislators must confront is the "same-sex marriage debate." Same sex couples want to be able to marry, or at least, have civil unions available to provide legally guaranteed coupler and family rights currently not available to them. Many argue that they have ignored the continuing cultural and legal shift from viewing marriage as a patriarchically based system to an egalitarian one, and the parallel societal trend that legal rights and protections should be available to everyone (Kitson, 2004). However, while some countries and states have made strides in this area, the issue remains highly controversial. Over the past years, U.S. national polls remain fairly stable with 53 percent of the public opposed to same sex marriage with 46 percent in favor. The option of civil unions giving homosexual couples "some of the same legal rights of married couples" has gained some ground, with 34 percent favoring it; 41 percent opposing and 25 percent expressing no opinion (http://www.gallup.com, 3/26/04). Not surprisingly, opposition is greater among Republicans, social conservatives and in more conservative religious groups. For example, President Bush recently tried to amend the U.S. constitution to ban gay marriage although it was recently struck down in a Senate vote on July 13, 2004.

Overall, there appears to be growing consensus that we need policy reform and community programs to support healthy families and intimate relationships more generally, with a focus that extends beyond legal, heterosexual marital relationships. This can strengthen the intimate ties of young adults and their families, as well as to prevent young adults from other risky behaviors such as leaving home at an early age and teenage parenthood. Family and marital counseling can be an effective means to support families, since it appropriately focuses attention on specific problems such as intergenerational conflict or the marital relationship. Also, although some marriages cannot be salvaged, future generations would be well served if some of the divorcing parents remained together.

Moreover, community resources are needed to support the diverse relationships of young people. In chapter 5, it was noted that gay/lesbians experience more resistance to partnership choices and their decision to cohabit or marry. Generally, gay and lesbian young adults receive more support from non-family member than their families-of-origin. This suggests that this group of individuals and their families requires community supports of a specific nature (e.g., education and counseling to overcome homophobic ideologies).

## Parenthood and Child Care

As mentioned throughout this book, although overall rates of teenage pregnancy have declined in industrialized societies, becoming a parent at a young age can set up a chain reaction of disadvantage over the life course. Therefore, continuing efforts to reduce teenage pregnancy are required. For example, home visiting programs from nurses offering education and resources that target disadvantaged young women have been found to significantly reduce teenage pregnancy (Olds et al., 1998). Similarly, "second chance homes," aimed at preventing subsequent pregnancies among young unmarried mothers have also been highly effective. Currently, 132 of these programs are in operation in the United States with Massachusetts having a particularly well-established network (Social Policy Action Network, 2001).

Moreover, young parents and single parents are particularly prone to poverty and many parents face enormous problems in accessing good quality and affordable day care. As a result, many parents and women's groups are demanding that governments acknowledge the need for improved day care and pre-school programs, both as an equity issue and as an investment in children as a future national resource (e.g., Baker, 2001; Jenson, 2004).

Furthermore, the concern voiced most often by parents is conflict between work and family, and this may transcend class, race, ethnicity, and family structure (Bogenschneider, 2000; Moen and Jull, 1995). For example, access to affordable day care is an enormous problem for parents who work untraditional hours, such as night shifts, weekends, or part-time. Also, many young adults trying to accommodate family life while fulfilling career ambitions face the dilemma of either "subcontracting" care responsibilities to other family members or a paid worker or a "specialization strategy." This specialization strategy entails one parent (usually the mother) to specialize in childcare, but this can lead to negative consequences in the paid labour realm, such as less career advancement and more economic vulnerability (Folbre, 2002).

Not surprisingly, researchers characterize family and work conflict as the "double squeeze," since there is often pressure on economic resources and a simultaneous squeeze on the time and energy needed for family and community commitments (Skocpol, 1997). And although many policies have emerged that provide more flexibility for employees with family responsibilities, in comparison with Europeans, many argue that North Americans have "policy deficits" in relation to work-family and other policy supports (Raabe, 2003). Many of the policies emerging in Northwest European countries, for example, can be described in terms of "new norms for organizing market work and unpaid care work" (Appelbaum et al., 2002). In fact, some advocates have argued for a more fundamental restructuring that moves beyond a "family-friendly" corporation to a "family-friendly" society (Goggins, 1997). The family-friendly society is one in which family life is more broadly supported by friends, schools, service agencies, and civic organization (Bogenschneider, 2000).

## Gender and Racial/Ethnic Equity

Finally, as we have noted throughout this book, the family-related transitions of young adults are experienced differently by young men and women and across racial/cultural groups. In chapter 3, for instance, we noted that males are more likely to remain at home than females, either as the result of delayed coresidence or home returning. One implication of this is that males may have more advantages than females in being able to draw upon household resources and to save money during the transition to adulthood. Moreover, women tend to marry at younger ages than men (described as the marriage gradient in chapter 4), and this can significantly affect the life course of women. With regard to parenthood, women are more likely to be single parents and to spend time balancing work and family obligations. They are also more likely to suffer economic hardship after a union dissolution, since they tend to earn less money than men in the paid labour market.

Moreover, the wage differential between certain racial groups and the sexes continues to be large. For example, although women have made substantial progress in narrowing the gap in both occupational attainment and average wages after 1970, job segregation is still evident, and women are estimated to earn 79 percent of men's wages (Bianchi and Casper, 2002). This narrowing of the gender wage gap has led to considerable debate between those who attribute it to gains made by women in education, work experience, and resulting wage gains, and those who argue that it is more a result of stagnation or decline in male wages (Bernhardt, Morris, and Hancock, 1995). Nonetheless, there is little doubt that wage inequity and discrimination persist and that policies should seek to redress this problem.

There is also a need to promote men's greater involvement with their children and in housework, since women still bear the brunt of childcare and domestic chores in most industrialized nations. Bianchi and Mattingly (2004) find that men have increased their participation in housework and that there has been a sizeable increase in time with children among fathers who live with their children. According to this study, the gap has improved over time and the allocation to these activities was more equal in 1998 than in 1965. However, women still do more child care and domestic labor than do fathers, even when both are working full-time in the paid labor force.

With regard to paid parental leave, Sweden was the first nation to provide this support to all employed fathers, while in the U.S., unpaid parental leave has only recently become available from larger employers (Seward, Yeatts, and Zottarelli, 2002). And while many industrialized nations have mandated employment leave benefits for fathers, only a minority of fathers is found to take paternity leave. This suggests that a number of institutionalized barriers still exist to the creation of shared parenting and a more equitable division of domestic labor.

At a community level, services and outreach programs are needed to help disadvantaged young men and women. For example, young people need access to organizations that can assist them with pregnancy planning, crisis situations and day care. Also, given that many countries are comprised of a diverse range of ethno-cultural groups, communities need to eliminate racism and to offer culturally sensitive program and services, which target such issues as language barriers and intergenerational conflict when young people do not share their parent's values.

## Summary and Conclusions

This chapter provides an overview of social and family policy issues pertinent to the "boomerang age" and considers how young people in the past, and well as in the present and future, can play a role in affecting social change. We began by considering how the retrenchment of the welfare state and the movement toward neo-liberal agendas in Western industrialized nations has affected the transition to adulthood. Indeed, some researchers characterize today's generation of young people as "on hold" since the full passage to adulthood has become delayed, relative to earlier generations (Côté and Allahr, 1994). The trend toward privatization in welfare states has also affected intergenerational family ties and the formation of close relationships more generally. This is because policy inattention to young adults and their families contains an implicit assumption that their families will and should look after them. Rhetoric and assumptions are that the family is a private institution that should be shielded from state intervention. The reality, of course, is that the state has a substantial investment in the way that families operate (Mitchell and Gee, 1996b).

Attention was also paid to defining social and family policy, as well as its development in the United States, Canada, and Europe. Notions of intergenerational equity and how these have entered into political rhetoric and discussion were also explored. We also considered how young adults in previous generations have played a role in social change, focusing on their role as leaders and participants of youth movements, especially during the 1960s. Several strategies for social action in the boomerang age were also presented. A number of social policy recommendations were also offered, with the recognition that nations differ with regard to generosity and implementation. Despite these variations, issues pertinent to the needs of vulnerable young adults and their families were highlighted, with the recognition that not all young adults have adequate family resources and support.

Therefore, as we begin the twenty-first century, policy makers should try to devise progressive family policies that reflect the fact that contemporary society has experienced what has been termed "age inflation" (Vobejda, 1991) for many family-related transitions. We also need to carefully consider policies that highlight ties across the generations (Pampel, 1998) and the caring work that occurs within these contexts. Policies also must reflect a non-linear model of family development over the life course. Notably, the family-related transitions of young adults are less predictable and orderly than they were compared to the 1950s, and are subject to high rates of reversibility. This has presented even more challenges for aging, middle-generation parents who are increasingly responsible for the economic well-being of their young adult children, who may be well into their twenties and thirties.

Therefore, legislation and programs should be adjusted to more equitably meet the needs of young adults and their families. Approaches include alleviating youth poverty and unemployment; widespread creation of work programs, including job counseling, training and placement; a fair distribution of national income to ensure that employed young adults receive a sufficient wage, job security, and benefits; providing government-sponsored student incomes, loans and grants for students to live independently of parents; and the creation of affordable housing. Community-based organizations are also needed to provide information, resources, and socio-cultural activities to young adults.

And of course, young people (and their families) need to take personal responsibility in creating social change and more equitable opportunities, in addition to more collective responsibility from government. For example, young adults can learn more about family and social issues and the sources of inequality, question current policies and participate in the creation of new ones as researchers and practitioners, engage in collaborative efforts, and make themselves heard by government. Implementation of these measures could have a large-scale positive impact on the lives of today's young adults in ways that would benefit them, the local community, and society as a whole. This also represents an exciting opportunity to serve as role models for younger children and to help future generations by creating a social legacy of profound importance.

It is crucial to emphasize that investment by individuals, communities and governments have massive potential to significantly improve the lives of the next generation of young adults, a topic which we turn to in chapter 7. For example, given the high long-term payoff of public investments in education, a current policy challenge is to search for methods to maintain the quality of institutions and to guarantee educational opportunities to students from all income backgrounds.

In closing, rather that viewing "government" and social policy in adversarial terms, governments can be viewed as important mechanisms for connecting micro- and macro-level concerns. They are also a potential relational network for fostering political and social integration and the development of a humanistically oriented collective conscious. In this way, the concerns of individuals, families and communities, can be linked with the concerns of the larger society via family policies as outputs of the political system (MacRae, 1985; Zimmerman, 1992). Thus, young people can wisely see government as a potential form of valuable social capital that family policy practice requires for constructing policy solutions to family problems. This will ultimately lead to the enhancement of individual, family and societal well-being in both the short- and long-term.

## Questions for Discussion and Debate

1.  How do definitions of "family" influence government public policy? Provide specific examples and consider cross-cultural variations.
2.  Why do governments need to intervene in private matters such as partnering and sexuality?
3.  Provide an argument for and against the following statement: "Family policy should be value free."
4.  Compare and contrast the ideological positions toward family life taken between conservative and progressive governments. How do these stances translate into directives on issues such as abortion, same-sex marriage, day-care, the employment of young children? Are there any points of convergence?
5.  What arguments can be made for and against establishing family policy at a federal level as opposed to a state or local level?
6.  Should family policy be directed at all intimate relationships or only those with problems? What are some of the effects of labeling certain life styles or structural inequities as "problems"?
7.  Suggest some additional recommendations for how members of the boomerang age generation can become more involved in creating more caring and healthier relationships, families and communities.

# 7

# Back to the Future: Is the Boomerang Age Here to Stay?

Throughout history, family scholars and writers have tried to predict what the transition to adulthood and family life would be like in the future. In many of these discussions, one finds a number of common themes—a sense of uncertainty about the future, a tendency to romanticize past family life, and calls for reform to end a multitude of social problems. At the turn of the nineteenth century, for example, many academics, community and religious leaders, as well as politicians speculated and worried about the fate of the family in industrial societies. They also were concerned about other signs of impending family crisis, such as poverty, divorce, and falling birth rates, which led many to profess the breakdown of "the" family (Skolnick, 1996).

Not surprisingly, concerns about the future of the family that reappear with regularity in the history of the United States, Canada and Western Europe seemed to become more optimistic after World War II. By way of illustration, in the early 1960s, experts and leaders from a wide array of fields were asked by a national magazine to envision what American society would look like twenty-five years in the future (Mandel, 1987). According to Skolnick (1996), similar to other futurists, virtually all of these thinkers predicted that the United States would be a streamlined, high tech, orderly place in which robots took care of domestic drudgery and family life was stable and predictable. Poverty and other social problems had been erased, and the family car was replaced by 500-mile-an-hour car planes. Automated kitchens that cleaned up after themselves would predominant in family homes, and the "traditional" nuclear family icons of the 1950s—such as Ozzie and Harriet and the Cleavers— remained the ideal model of families for the future. In general, growing technological advances in science and technology, coupled with a strong economy at the time, were thought to solve most of our problems and create stability in family behaviors.

Looking twenty-five years after the fact, it is obvious that most of these predictions did not come to fruition, although they did reflect what many people thought at the time. Ironically, many of these writers had no idea that they were living in the decade that was going to be part of the most turbulent time in American history since the Civil War (Gitlin, 1989). In particular, they could not imagine that the supposedly unchanging institutions of marriage and family were going to be so strongly affected by such changes as divorce, the sexual revolution, the women's movement, and the other social upheavals of the 1960s and 1970s. Moreover, the impact of major socio-demographic changes such as population aging, changing patterns of immigration, and the impact of globalization on family life and generational relations were not fully realized at this time. The field of social gerontology, for example, only emerged in the 1940s and it was not widely recognized as a "legitimate area of inquiry" until at least 1975 (McPherson, 1983:19).

Despite our long-standing penchant for trying to predict the future of family life, there is little disagreement that speculation can be a futile endeavor. According to Gerson (2000: 180): "The looking glass remains opaque not simply because our analytic tools are imprecise. The human capacity for growth and creativity, for responding in unintended ways to new contingencies, renders prediction a risky business." Hence, assuming that current patterns will continue is often reasonable, but it can be speculatively incorrect, particularly since there are so many unknowns. Also, events such as widespread economic recessions, terrorist attacks, wars, or natural disasters (including epidemics such as AIDS) are essentially unpredictable, yet can produce profound changes. For example, the recent tsunami (December 26, 2004) in Southeast Asia resulted in the deaths of over 150,000 persons and massive regional and economic devastation. This catastrophic event forever changed the lives of countless numbers of young people due to the deaths of family and friends, illness, injury, loss of homes, schools, work, and displacement. In this sense, family patterns may be subject to change due a particular historical event (Elder, 1978). In addition, some family trends are short term (e.g., the early ages of marriage in the 1950s and 1960s) and are tied to the economic climate of prosperity while others are non-linear and fluctuate over time (e.g., home leaving patterns).

Government actions can also affect family-related socio-demographic and economic realms, such as immigration policies. These policies influence the age, family composition, origin, and occupation of various segments of the population. Other state policies and programs can dramatically shape the decision-making of young people and their families through taxation, income distribution and service provision (Ward, 2002). It is also widely recognized that the complexity of numerous determinants influencing behavior makes it difficult to predict future behaviours, and that it is not easy to predict whether or not differences between countries will become smaller or larger.

That being stated, there remain a number of reasons to attempt projections of family trends. First, as family life course scholars, we are interested in the influence of the past in shaping the present and future so that we can identify and assess current developments, and project their anticipated and unanticipated consequences. These projected changes raise important questions about the future for young people and of their families more generally. Social forecasts can also make it possible to prepare for future demands of public and private services and for outlining policies in areas such as youth housing, education, welfare, health, and care giving across the generations (Alders and Manting, 1998). Overall, knowledgeable projections about how young people experience family-related transitions to adulthood and how they are likely to be transformed in the future are vital. These projections can shape agendas for research, alert educators, policymakers, and practitioners to new realities and can facilitate the formulation of thoughtful responses to emerging dilemmas (Mortimer and Larson, 2002).

So, is there a way to develop sensible forecasts about the future for young adults and their families, since projections are generally fraught with problems of accuracy, given the complexity of social change? Kain (1990) presents a number of guidelines, which we will consider in this chapter. Notably, projections should be probabilistic rather than deterministic. In other words, we should not necessarily assume that what appears likely to happen will actually occur. Moreover, it is often argued that speculating trends in areas such as the economy, politics, and religious ideology is more tenuous than in other realms, such as socio-demographic change. For example, few social analysts before the 1980s expected the rebirth of the kind of religious fundamentalism that had not been experienced in the United States since the 1920s. The emergence of the New Religious Right in the 1980s and 1990s was provoked by a growing perception that the women's movement had created enormous social upheaval and challenged the institution of family (Newman and Grauerholz, 2002). As one New Religious Right minister stated, "We're not here to get into politics. We're here to turn the clock back to 1954" (quoted in Faludi, 1991: 230). Therefore, it is not enough to examine "trend lines on a graph" to make predictions. Rather, we need to understand what lies behind the patterns in order to understand the social, economic and political factors that facilitate and perpetuate patterns of family life.

In recognition of the pitfalls associated with social projection, including the associated ideological problems in conceptualizing families, this chapter will present two possible future scenarios based on "educated guesses." This exercise is primarily undertaken in order to summarize the major themes of this book and to identify the trends and issues that young people and their families are likely to encounter over the next twenty-five years. However, it should also be emphasized that we will only be providing some broad "brush stroke" generalizations of reasonable changes. The aim is to highlight important family trends, rather than attempting to undergo the type of demographic forecast analysis that is commonly conducted by national statistical agencies (e.g., see Alders and Manning, 1998).

Specifically, in this chapter we will present and evaluate the possibility of two "ideal type" scenarios: (1) the Increased Individualization Scenario; and (2) the Increased Familism Scenario. First, each of these scenarios and their theoretical rationales will be offered in relation to the primary family-related transitions to adulthood considered in this volume. These include: homeleaving and intergenerational coresidence, non-marital cohabitation, marriage, and partnership dissolution patterns (i.e., divorce). We will also consider major patterns of intergenerational relations under each of these two scenarios. Once this stage has been set, a review of empirical evidence in the family literature will be conducted. This will be done in order to ascertain whether or not there is support for either of these models by focusing on themes of change and continuity. In addition, these themes will be explored in relation to current economic, political and technological landscapes (e.g., educational and labor market requirements, technological developments), and cultural and socio-demographic shifts (e.g., secularization, attitudinal change and family values, role of women in society, population aging, immigration patterns).

## The Increased Individualization Scenario

As described in chapter 2, until the end of the nineteenth century, the major transitions of young people—leaving home, securing employment, completing school, getting married, and setting up an independent household—all occurred at more variable ages and in more random order than they have during most of the twentieth century. During our primary historical benchmark of the 1950s, however, transitions became more predictable in their sequence, as well as more prevalent throughout the population. Since that time, family-related transitions have been characterized by growing impermanence, diversity, fluidity, and reversibility. A significant difference between historical patterns and contemporary ones is that the latter exhibit a higher degree of voluntary "choice" with regard to the timing, sequencing, duration, and nature of family-related events and transitions (e.g., single parenthood, divorce).

Theorists argue that the recent "destandardization" has occurred because of two of the most salient features of most Western cultures —a movement towards secularization and individuation. As outlined in chapter 5, secularization reduces formalized religious commitment and diminishes the strength of religious theology and moral values supporting much "traditional" behaviour (Lesthaeghe and Surkyn, 1988). A shift toward more individualistic goals and self-fulfillment is also made possible by the growth of the global capitalist system, increased affluence, and the emancipation of women. These processes erode "traditional" social norms because they are incompatible with values such as individual choice, companionship and self-gratification (Burch and Matthews, 1987). Thus, behaviours that have become more commonplace since our historical benchmark of the 1950s (e.g., non-marital cohabitation and divorce) would be compatible with an individualistic cultural value system.

An Increased Individualization Scenario assumes a growing emphasis on individual pursuits, choice, autonomy, and self-determination in the timing and nature of family-related transitions to adulthood and the unfolding of the life course. This is not to say that structure and position no longer play a significant role in these decisions, but that the individual increasingly gains the freedom to choose and create his or her own lifestyles during transitional events

(Johansson and Miegel, 1992). As a result of broad social change, such as secularization, urbanization and gender role flexibility, young people's collectivities are seen as becoming increasingly informal in nature, such that their loyalty to a particular territorial focal point becomes undermined (Miles, 2000). As a result, family-related transitions to adulthood (and family-ties more generally) have become less traditional, formalized and rigid. Young adults are also less dependent upon rituals, such as formal marriage and the wedding ceremony. Overall, this scenario assumes that young people are becoming less bound to do what a particular informal or formal group is doing and can legitimately choose their own pathways en route to adulthood.

Gidden's (1992) theorization of the emergence of "plastic sexuality" and "pure relationships" also helps us to conceptualize a global convergence toward individuation and informal, weak traditional family structures. Although the origins of plastic sexuality are traced by Gidden's to ideas favoring fertility control, he maintains that the major impetus for this phenomenon originates from the proliferation of sophisticated contraceptive and reproductive technologies since the 1960s. In essence, Giddens argues that the increasing separation of sexuality from the exigencies of reproduction – a process that started with the demographic transition in Europe – has produced what he coins "plastic sexuality." This term refers to sexuality that serves as medium or means for self-expression and self-actualization that is largely freed from reproduction. It has also surfaced in response to a reduction in institutional, normative, and patriarchal control. Unlike traditional sexuality, which is defined and regulated by a constellation of norms, laws, religious proscriptions, and institutions such as marriage, plastic sexuality is malleable and can be molded and defined by the individual as a personality trait (Giddens, 1992: 1-17).

According to Giddens, the emergence of plastic sexuality is important because it is purported to be a major cause of the recent dramatic changes in marriage and family in Western societies. It is also a potent catalyst for a profound transformation of human intimacy and the timing and nature of family-related transitions to adulthood (Hall, 1996). In particular, Giddens asserts that plastic sexuality is changing family relationship forms into what he calls "pure relationships." This term denotes the idea that intimate relationships are organized and sustained primarily from within the relationship itself. Rather than being supported or anchored in external social criteria such as norms, traditions, or formal institutions, pure relationships are voluntarity constituted and maintained by individuals on the basis of the relationship's value as a "site" for their self-actualization.

A significant implication of the rise in pure relationships is that "traditional" behaviors such as formal marriage and childbearing (particularly at a young age) are not perceived intrinsic to the pure relationship. This is because they can be seen as an "externality" or potential threat to the pure relationship, unless these behaviors directly contribute to self-actualization of the individual. Thus, in the case of the formation of intimate partnerships, although plastic sexuality may become fully realized, the stability and durability of pure relationships cannot be taken for granted by the partners. This is because it is possible for them to be terminated by either partner at any time (Giddens, 1991a: 185-188; 1992: 157).

Within the Increased Individualization Scenario, the following changes are expected to occur in family-related transitions to adulthood and intergenerational relations. Although the average age of (first) homeleaving may not significantly change, young adults will increasingly leave home to live in non-traditional family settings (e.g., as "primary individuals" or singles) or to cohabit in non-marital partnerships to achieve individual goals. Returning to the parental home will also become increasingly common because of the economic and convenience benefits that it affords young people during transitional periods. Unmarried cohabitation will predominate as a preferred partnered living arrangement (both heterosexual and homosexual) prior to marriage as young adults experiment with a wide range of relationships and living arrangements. Also, young people with divorced parents will show a continued reluctance to enter into legal marriage without some previous experience of what it is like to live with a partner.

Moreover, as opposition to traditional gendered martial roles and traditional expectations continue to grow, and the legal distinction between marriage and cohabitation declines, the latter will become an alternative to legal marriage for more people. Marriage rates will continue to decline as more young people question the social importance of legal marriage as a rite of passage to adult status.

The Increasing Individualistic Scenario also predicts that the average age of marriage and (first) parenthood will continue to be delayed and that more children will be born outside of legal marriage. Fertility will continue to be low as children become increasingly regarded as threats to "pure relationships" and as "consumers" rather than "producers." Greater proportions of individuals will become childless by choice (Veevers, 1979), although rates of involuntary childlessness may rise as young women delay the timing of parenthood. Many will become accustomed to a childfree lifestyle and decide to continue with it permanently. In fact, more childfree marriages could lead to higher divorce rates, as relationship dissolution are much simpler without having to deal with concerns over child custody, care and support (Baker, 2005). However, a general delay in marriage should offset this trend since the risk of divorce is lower when couples are older in age.

Intergenerational relations will continue to be characterized by mutual cooperation and reciprocity, and flows of financial assistance will generally flow down the intergenerational ladder. Young people will still highly value their relationships with their parents and many midlife and older-aged parents will continue to be economically responsible for their children well into their twenties (and even their thirties). Yet intergenerational relations will be primarily characterized as independent and autonomous, with family members continuing to place a high value on privacy and independence. "Intimacy at a distance" (Rosenmayr and Kockeis, 1963) will predominant as the preferred living arrangement. This refers to the notion that family members desire to interact with their relatives, but generally do not want to live with them in the same household. Yet, there will be an expanded range of living arrangements and relational styles as some young adults remain at home longer or return for temporary periods of time (and often more than once). For example, extended coresidence provides opportunities for parents to extend the socialization process and develop less hierarchically based and more individual or peer-like orientations with their adult children.

Furthermore, some relationships will become increasingly characterized by "intergenerational ambivalence" (as discussed in chapter 5), as family life becomes more individualized and complex and there is rise in a multiplicity of structures and forms, due to factors such as unmarried cohabitation, divorce, remarriage, and blended families. A rising emphasis on the achievement of individual goals and pursuits over the wider kinship structure will also create greater geographical mobility. This will contribute to reduced physical and emotional interaction between the generations, although new forms of communication will continue to develop to meet the diverse needs of individuals in response to these changing patterns.

## Increased Familism Scenario

While the Increased Individualization perspective on youth transitions in post-industrial societies theorizes a general decline in the centrality of "traditional" formal family bonds in young people's lives, the Increased Familism Scenario assumes the opposite. The term "familism" generally implies that family roles and relationship are at the core of people's lives (Goldscheider and Goldschedier, 1993). For the purpose of this discussion, the familism scenario builds upon this concept and assumes that future family-related life course transitions to adulthood will be characterized by a higher degree of "traditional" familistic behaviours than is currently witnessed. By "traditional" we are referring to family-related behaviours mainly evident during our historical benchmark of the 1950s. This was a time period of early and near universal marriage and parenthood, and relatively low rates of unmarried cohabitation and divorce. Intergenerational coresidence, however, which was more characteristic of family life prior to the 1950, was relatively uncommon during this time period.

Specifically, the idea of familism denotes the centrality of family relationships. It is associated with the idea of family solidarity, which refers to familial social relations that include exchange, affective closeness, interaction, normative obligations and value consensus (White and Rogers, 1997). This matrix of social interaction, normative expectations, and preferences influence "family values," which in turn, affect the timing and nature of family-related transitions to adulthood and intergenerational relations. Therefore, a strengthening of familistic patterns should theoretically re-emphasize traditional family values and loyalties and ignite the importance of relationships with extended and family-of-origin family members (Goldscheider and Goldscheider, 1993).

What factors are found to contribute to familism which might lead to this scenario? The first sets of factors emphasize religion and racial/ethnic components. As noted by Boyd (1998), religion typically stresses the centrality of family life by reinforcing family obligations, and family centered values such as intergenerational coresidence and legal marriage. Familism is also associated with traditional gender roles, such that gender role differentiation is generally strong and women are expected to value motherhood over education and paid work roles for women; and legal, marriage rather than unmarried cohabitation.

Moreover, it is well documented that throughout history, family members have a stronger need to rely on each other when economic times are tough and state supports are lacking. Hareven and Adams (1996), for instance, document that in regimes of economic insecurity, which was characteristic of family life prior to World War II, kin assistance was the only constant source of support for family members. Young adults were expected to subordinate their own careers and needs for those of the family as a collective and did so out of a sense of responsibility, affection and familial obligation, rather than with the expectation of eventual gain. Moreover, this sense of obligation toward kin was a manifestation of "family culture"—supported by a commitment to the well-being and self-reliance or survival of the family. This took precedence over individual needs and personal happiness.

The Increased Familism Scenario would manifest several trends. We will expect to see fewer young people leaving home to live in non-family households and for "independence," with greater proportions remaining at home until later ages and leaving home for marriage. Cohabitation will decline (especially homosexual cohabitation), and this will propel young adults to marry at younger ages. Legal marriage will be regarded as preferable, partly because of the known health benefits and stability that it affords. Age at parenthood will be more closely tied to age at marriage, and family sizes will either remain stable or increase, with no significant increases in childlessness. Divorce rates will stabilize, or possibly decline because there will be an emphasis on "intact" nuclear families.

Intergenerational relations will become characterized by a more intense exchange of support and resources. This will be due to a strong emphasis on "family values" and familial obligation, and perhaps due to economic necessity. Immigration patterns may also perpetuate normative expectations that family members take care of one another. For example, the norm of "filial piety," common to Asian familistic cultures, is rooted in the idea that the core of moral behavior lies in deference and several obligations that offspring owe to parents (Ishii-Kuntz, 1997; Lin and Liu, 1999). As a result, adult children, through a heavier religious upbringing and socialization, internalize and express a strong moral and ethical obligation to obey and assist their aging parents. This may encourage staying at home until marriage and extended coresidence. Moreover, as the population ages, government supports shrink (e.g., pensions, home care), and there is widening social inequality, more and more young people will find themselves in multigenerational households. This preponderance of multiple generations has the potential to intensify supportive behaviors across the generations, but could also create new challenges for young adults and their families. Grandparents will also play a much more significant role in the day-to-day lives of their grandchildren because they will be more likely to share households and pool resources.

### Is the Boomerang Age Here to Stay? Evidence For and Against Each Scenario

Now that we have presented two possible scenarios for the next generation of young adults with respect to the timing and nature of their family-related transitions to adulthood, the question arises as to whether they can be reasonably supported. Specifically, we will review economic, technological, cultural and socio-demographic trends widely accepted as instrumental in shaping the life course of young adults and their families. We will also consider their broader implications for the future of intergenerational relations in aging families. The chapter will conclude with a summary of predominant themes and issues woven throughout the book.

### (1) The Economy and State, Schooling and Technological Advances

Economic and political factors play a critical role in the timing and nature of family-related transitions to adulthood. Favorable economic conditions (e.g., good paying jobs and affordable housing) and supportive government policies (e.g., student grants and loans to live independently), for example, are generally associated with more choice in young adults' living arrangements. In short, economic fortunes and family relationships remain intertwined (Casper and Bianchi, 2002). Historical patterns covered in chapter 2, for example, reveal that during tough economic times (e.g., the Great Depression), young adults are more likely to remain at home and are less likely to marry. The current trend toward neo-liberal agendas and the restructuring of the welfare state amidst globalization in many Western societies is also associated with a heavier reliance on family households. This contributes to a delayed transition to adulthood, as well as growing social and income inequality.

However, predicting future economic and political trends, such as the state of the economy and knowing which governments will be in power is very difficult, if not impossible. This is because the economy is not impervious to corrections, downturns, and stagnations, which are natural events in any business cycle (Alch, 2000). Local job markets in the West can also disappear in a year or two, as entire industries are suddenly exported to developing countries (Mortimer and Larson, 2002). Governments, laws and policies also change, and these factors can determine the propensity or legality of particular "non-traditional" family forms. By way of example, conservative activists in California (a highly liberal jurisdiction) were recently successful in securing support for a constitutional amendment to ban gay marriage. As a result, the California Supreme Court voted 5-2 in favor of annulling close to 4,000 marriage licenses signed in the early part of 2004 (Gordon, 2004). In light of these unknowns, it may be more fruitful to speculate how general changes in the interrelated realms of the labor market and in the institutions of post-secondary education, as well as in technological, cultural and socio-demographic realms will likely affect future family-transitions to adulthood.

## The Interface of Family/School/Work Transitions

Most scholars would agree that one trend that shows little sign of changing in the near future is the need for higher levels of education. "Credentialism" or rising skill requirements account for the increasing educational inflation that we have witnessed, particularly since the 1990s, as many professions now require more education. High-growth fields, such as health care, education, technology and other professional services usually require a college degree, while low-growth and highly cyclical blue-collar industries (e.g., manufacturing, transportation, construction) on the other hand, rarely require an education beyond high school. College graduates also earn more money than those with only a high school diploma. The mean wages of twenty-one-year-old men and women, according to the U.S. Census Bureau surveys, is $17,000 and $13,000, respectively, for high school graduates and $26,000 and $24,000, respectively for college graduates (Francese, 2003).

It is also well established that educational attainment affects the timing of transitional events and intergenerational relationships. For example, young adults often delay the formation of family roles and responsibilities until they have completed their education. College students may also live at home or in semi-autonomous dwellings (e.g., dorms) to save money while attending school. If they leave home to attend college, they often return to live with their parents (Goldscheider and Goldscheider, 1999).

It is observed that the structure of the labor market is changing in Western societies and that as global influences on everyday life grow stronger, the dynamics of family lives will be affected. In particular, the competitive pressures of the international capitalist marketplace have forced many employers to make greater use of so-called "disposable workers" (Kilborn, 1993). Increasingly, companies are cutting costs by relocating their manufacturing facilities to other countries, where they can pay lower wages. Thousands of U.S.-owned manufacturing plants, such as plants run by Ford, General Motors, RCA, and Zenith, are now located in northern Mexico alone (Baca Zinn and Eitzen, 1996). However, while these companies benefit financially, displaced workers and their families do not (Newman and Grauerholz, 2002).

These labor market trends have led to a widespread consensus that more employed people will experience increasing uncertainty in the labour market, and change jobs or careers several times throughout their lives. Others will be employed in temporary or contractual jobs with little job protection, low pay and few benefits (Giele, 2004; Kilborn, 1993; Torjman and Battle, 1999). Indeed, the last decades of the twentieth century have been characterized by a general shift toward freer markets and fewer worker protections (Levy, 1998). Youth who do not obtain college credentials are particularly vulnerable to finding themselves in a "revolving door" of low paying and unstable jobs, which are usually insufficient to support a family (Kerckhoff, 2002). In fact, recent studies in the U.S. and Europe reveal that many young people have low expectations that they will be able to attain career jobs, despite the need for a post-secondary education. Many young adults also anticipate that their employers will provide them with flexible working hours and opportunities for developing skills and employability, but without lifelong commitment (e.g., see Brannen, Nilsen and Smithson, 2001).

Young adults are also often characterized as well-informed, media-savvy and as very comfortable with the new digital economy. Having grown up with technology in school and at home, a revolution in telecommunications has made instant global interaction possible. Thus, this "net generation" is purported to represent a potentially more powerful and influential cohort who will create a new culture of work. In particular, they will be characterized by more independence in the work force, since many of these future workers will become entrepreneurs (Alch, 2000). Yet many argue that this independence in the work force is also potentially unstable and volatile, since these kinds of jobs are subject to the effects of economic cycles.

Within this context, there is likely to be an economic component relevant to future transitions to adulthood and living arrangements, as work lives become less permanent and more unstable. The average earnings of employed young adults are also usually insufficient to pay for a place to live. As a result, this lack of job security and stable income may encourage many young adults to rely upon their parents and remain at home until later ages. Interestingly, a primary reason for many young married couples living apart is so that one partner can live in the parental home in order to save money (Statistics Canada, 2003b). Others may find it necessary to share accommodation, cohabit, marry, or repartner in order to afford a home or to support their children. For example, many college grads have large student loan payments; and the median rent, plus utilities of an urban apartment can exceed $10,000 a year. Young adult households often spend slightly more than half of their food budget outside their home, compared with 42 percent of other households (Francese, 2003). It is also observed that young adults are increasingly re-enrolling in school after entering into full-time work (Mortimer and Larson, 2002). Therefore, living with parents or a partner may become an economic necessity for the next generation of young adults.

In addition, many young adults are finding that living at home until later ages represents a positive strategy in order to save for the future. According to Alch (2000), if history is our guide, young adults will probably follow the spending habits of the baby boomers and Gen Xers, rather than their grandparents, whom he labels, the "conservative traditionalists." And unless there is a significant tumultuous event such as the Great Depression of 1920-1940, this new generation will likely follow the spending tendencies established after World War II. Thus, young people are expected to save for the future, invest and play the market as the economy becomes more expansive and as baby boomers continue to work well into their retirement years. Indeed, a recent survey of college students found that 31 percent had money invested in the stock market. The survey also found that the younger generation often voices concern that Social Security might not be able to provide for them when they reach retirement age. It is also speculated that this new generation of consumers will create a new economic boom of increased productivity, real-wage gains, rising savings, and falling debt (Alch, 2000).

Another significant and probably irreversible shift in the contours of family life is the revolution in medical, contraceptive and reproductive technology. Improvements in these areas reduce the portion of a woman's life spent in bearing and rearing children (Giele and Holst, 2004). This transformation allows the prevention of pregnancy and an almost complete disassociation of the sex act from the act of procreation. For example, new methods of in vitro fertilization, sperm banks and ovum transfers increasingly permit childbirth to occur with very little relation to actual intercourse or biological rhythms. These advances suggest that alternatives to traditional biological constraints are likely to become more widespread, not less (Coontz, 1992). In 1997, for example, there was a great deal of media attention on a sixty-three-year-old Los Angeles woman who gave birth to a normal baby girl created from her husband's sperm and an anonymous donor's egg (Kalb, 1997). Therefore, it is reasonable to assume that age at parenthood will continue to rise as the boundaries of biological parenthood continue to become expanded through new technological advances.

A more widespread phenomenon of delayed parenthood also has the potential to create important changes in intergenerational relations in both the family-of-origin and the family-of-procreation. For example, later ages of motherhood can delay the postparental stage of family life and the age of grandparenthood. Some critics argue that older parents may face unique strains and challenges, such as having to provide care giving to elderly parents while raising their own children. They also contend that these older parents will be unable to "keep up" with their children, while children may worry that their parents may die at any moment. Yet others observe that becoming a parent at older ages has always been a biological option for men, especially well-to-do men. The Hollywood actor Tony Randall (aged seventy-seven at the time) and his wife (aged twenty-six at the time), for example, had their first baby in 1996. In fact, these so-called "start-over-dads" have always existed (although not commonplace), and their later age of parenthood has rarely raised the sorts of ethical questions raised by older women bearing children (Newman and Grauerholz, 2002).

Other technological advances, such as those related to digital and electronic communication, are also expected to continue to transform future intergenerational relations in profound ways. Of course, there is some controversy with regard to whether these advances will facilitate or hinder the formation of strong intergenerational relations and exchanges of support. On one hand, communication technology (e.g., cell phones, web cams) can help physically distant family members keep in touch and have a bonding effect. On the other hand, these technologies can produce "virtual families" and have a privatizing effect on individuals and their families, even when they live in the same household. As a result, family relationships may suffer and fade through a lack of face-to-face contact and meaningful social interaction (Ward, 2002).

Taken together, these projected changes in labor market, educational attainment and technological spheres most strongly support a movement toward an increased individualization scenario, with a strong emphasis on flexibility and possible reversibility in the timing and nature of transitional events. Over the next twenty-five years, it is reasonable to expect that young people will continue to delay their "complete" transition to adulthood in order to pursue individualistic goals. This will occur in response to technical and occupational change (e.g., continuing shift to service-based economy) that demands higher levels of education and greater flexibility. In Western Europe and North American, achieving flexibility has also meant an expansion of the variety of acceptable work schedules and adaptive mechanisms for the use of time, a trend that will continue to provide individuals with more role options (Giele and Holts, 2004, Plantenga, 2004). Increasing enrolment in education and a more unstable job market also means that many young adults will change jobs and living arrangements several times during the transition to adulthood. These changes may lead to a greater reliance on parental households and on non-traditional partnerships for temporary or transitional periods.

Moreover, the majority of young adults will eventually marry and have children, which although characteristic of familistic behaviors, will increasingly occur at later ages and in response to individual need. This is because marriage will often be preceded by cohabitation and other less traditionally based "alternative" relationships. Overall marriage rates will likely decline slightly and divorce rates should stabilize since many will wait to marry, and later age of marriage is related to a lower propensity to divorce.

Also, differences among nations may become less pronounced, depending upon their public policies. For example, Alders and Manting (1998) project that despite the tendency to leave home at later ages, the number of European young adults who live at home will decline over the next twenty-five years (with the exception of Italy). This is based on the premise that the proportions of young persons living alone has increased substantially since the 1980s. It is argued that young adults are increasingly becoming individualistic in their family-related behaviours, but at the same time are also adopting a flexible life course strategy in which they try to keep their futures "open." They accomplish this by avoiding long-term commitments in the household and in their housing careers and by prolonging formal partnership formation and parenthood. Made possible by the availability of supportive government policies (e.g., subsidized housing for young people), young adults individualize their life paths by living in one-person households. The Netherlands, for example, has special housing units for those who opt to live alone.

It is also evident that we are experiencing a widening of social inequality in an era of globalization and the decline of social reform (Teeple, 2000). This means that not all young adults will have the opportunity to attain higher levels of education and suggests an increasing diversification in the life course, which further supports the increased individualization scenario. For example, a growing number of young adults may face even greater uncertainty and more decisions to make during the transition to adulthood, while others will have a number of advantages and options that positively affect their lives, such as strong, supportive intergenerational bonds (social capital). Countries with strong social safety nets (e.g., Sweden and the Netherlands), however, may be partly immune to the effects of widening social inequality.

An overview of these trends in relation to the future of intergenerational relations lends further support to an increased individualization model. For example, rapid developments in technological spheres provide individuals with a multitude of methods to communicate. Many of these advances have the potential to bring the generations closer together, particularly if family members are geographically dispersed. At the same time, these advances can also be perceived as threats to the formation of familistic behaviors, especially when viewed within the context of individualization, social isolation, and patterns of physical and social contact (e.g., see Hellenga, 2002).

## (2)  Cultural and Attitudinal Changes and Socio-Demographic Shifts

In addition to economic, political and technological transformation, we can also consider how cultural and attitudinal shifts have the potential to affect the future life course of young adults. As noted throughout this volume, we have observed a long-term trend of secularization throughout most Western countries. This has led to a declining commitment of people to normative guidelines espoused by formal religion (Lesthaeghe, 1983). As a result, non-traditional social bonds such as one-parent families (due to choice or divorce) and unmarried cohabitation, as well as living along, have been increasingly accepted. Together with a quest for individual freedom, non-traditional relationships and sex before marriage have become increasingly common.

Will this pattern of secularization continue in the future? Recent surveys reveal that religious attendance and participation in youth groups is declining in virtually all Western industrialized nations. In Canada, for example, relatively few teenagers place much value on religious involvement, although many expect to use the services of the country's religious institutions for ceremonial purposes, such as marriages, births and deaths (Bibby and Posterski, 1992). Moreover, it is acknowledged that young people are usually the recipients of family-transmitted religion, which is passed on via intergenerational socialization. Thus, unless there is another revival of religious fundamentalism, the trend toward secularization is likely to persist.

Furthermore, we have witnessed many cultural changes with respect to the role of women in families and society, which may affect future life course behaviors of young adults. Many researchers predict that in the face of increased opportunities for women outside the home, their financial incentives to marry lessen. There is also less need for women to remain in marriages if they become unsatisfactory, which may contribute to more divorces. However, it is expected that most individuals will eventually marry and have children, although average ages will continue to be delayed and fertility will remain low. Moreover, as more women attain professional degrees and careers, it is reasonable to assume that we will continue to see a small and growing number of "commuter" marriages and dual residences of orientation.

There is also ample evidence to suggest that societal-level norms are shifting toward greater acceptance of many "non traditional" family values and behaviors. Normative change means that young adults today are more likely to believe that behaviors such as extended coresidence (e.g., home returning), cohabitation and divorce are acceptable, and are less likely to believe that marriage is a lifelong commitment than was true in the past. The overwhelming evidence is that values have changed from those favoring family commitment and self-sacrifice to those favoring self-fulfillment, individual growth, and personal freedom (Lasch, 1979; McLanahan and Casper, 1995). Yet, as previously noted, some researchers argue that the increasing acceptability of extended coresidence (which includes home returning) among young adults represents an emergent "pro-family" strategy at odds with many other individualistic behaviors (Alwin, 1996). However, as previously noted, this living arrangement has been largely adopted in response to economic circumstances and in order to accommodate personal goals (e.g., to save money).

As a result, most observers argue that we will become increasingly tolerant and accepting of a diverse set of family structures and associated meanings of family in the future. For example, there is rising social acceptance of gay and lesbian partnerships and in having children outside of legal marriage, as well as returning to live in the parental home. And as these family structures become "institutionally complete" (Cherlin, 1978) and clear normative standards emerge, these behaviors may become more widespread. As lives change, new norms develop and become widely accepted and institutionalized in structural transformations (Riley, 1996). Indeed, Riley and Riley's (1994) analysis of "structural lag" supports the view that changing lives far outpace social institutions. However, over time, as normative change in life course patterns occurs, new behaviors become widespread and reproduced through the socialization process and cultural expectations. The widespread practice and acceptance of unmarried cohabitation in Sweden is a good example of how certain behaviors can become "institutionally complete" over long periods of time. Swedish family law, for instance, has come to be applied to married and cohabiting couples in the same way (Bradley, 1996).

Despite the convergence toward individualization and a growing acceptance of a wide range of relationship options, living arrangements, and more flexible definitions of family in North American and European societies, it is important to emphasize diversity both within and between countries. Although transitions to adulthood have become generally extended in all countries under study in this book, there is some diversity with regard to specific life course transitions. For example, in Italy, similar to other countries, delayed coresidence is extremely common (especially among young men) and the family of origin continues to play a very significant role in the care and development of young adults. However, home returning is relatively uncommon, and while Italy has one of the lowest fertility levels in the world, unmarried cohabitation and divorce remain rare and have not reached the levels of other European countries. Catholic moral values are still widely present, and family and housework continue to be a women's responsibility. In fact, women have relatively low levels of paid employment activity relative to men. Thus, although there has been a tendency toward greater individualization (e.g., with dramatic increases in cohabitation and divorce), the individualization and de-standardization as seen in other European populations have not taken root to the same degree in Italy (Bonke and Koch-Wester, 2004; Ongaro, 2001).

Turning to socio-demographic changes and their potential to influence the future lives of young people, one of the most significant changes in human history has been the recent explosion in population aging. This has been the result of dramatic increases in longevity and decreases in fertility, which have caused age pyramids to become rectangularized in most industrialized societies. Indeed, population aging is a global issue and there is concern about long-term the effects of population aging and its consequences for family life (e.g., see Bengtson, Lowenstein, Putney and Gans, 2003). According to the U.S. Bureau of the Census (2002), the current growth of the elderly population (aged sixty-five and older) in the developed countries is expected to rise above 3.5 percent annually from 2015 through 2030 before declining in subsequent decades. At present, the United States and Canada have approximately 13 percent of elderly, and these rates are expected to rise to between 21 and 23 percent by 2030. Projected proportions are even higher for many Western European nations at between 24 to 26 percent (U.S Bureau of the Census, 2002).

What are the implications of population aging for the timing of future family-related transitions to adulthood and intergenerational relations more generally? Most would agree that population aging per se is not a major determinant of the timing of family-related transitions to adulthood (unlike economic and political and technological factors). It is possible that more young adults will return home to assist aging parents, although care from children usually occurs when both generations are older in age. Yet, there is little doubt that increased life expectancy translates into extended length of family relationships. Since this will continue to increase the duration of intimate relationships (e.g., marriages), it may become more challenging to sustain only one lifetime "till death do we part" relationship. Indeed, some social scientists (e.g., see Casper and Bianchi, 2002) assert that increased longevity may be partly responsible for a rise in the divorce rate. It can also provide young people with more opportunities for individualized sexual expression through a series of relationships with different partners before marriage and over the life course.

Lengthening life spans also provide a number of implications with regard to the impact of population aging on future intergenerational relations. In fact, Bengtson (2001) has recently hypothesized that as life expectancy rises and families undergo change, relationships across the generations are becoming increasingly important, perhaps even more so than nuclear family ties. Notably, it is observed that we now have more years of "co-survivorship between generations." This means that more and more aging parents and grandparents are now available for family continuity and stability across time (Silverstein, Girarrusso, and Bengtson, 1998).

Population aging will likely have positive and negative consequences for young people and their families. On the positive side, increased longevity represents a resource of kin available for help and support that can be activated in time of need, since older kin will be in better health than in the past. On the negative side, there will be protracted years of care giving for dependent elders, although this may not affect many young adults until they become older themselves. However, it may affect them indirectly, as their middle-generation parents (commonly refereed to as the "sandwich generation) may be increasingly responsible for the simultaneous care of the younger and older generations.

Some commentators also express concern that there will be fewer resources for young people, as more societal-level resources are channeled to older people (e.g., Mortimer and Larson, 2002). These concerns raise issues of intergenerational equity, conflict, and a variety of other challenges in the future (e.g., see Bengtson, Lowenstein, Putney, and Gans, 2003; Kingsmill and Schlesinger, 1998).

As the composition of the family broadens, it is also speculated that interactions and living arrangements among the generations will be transformed. Population aging may also further strengthen family relationships and family bonds and create the possibility for more contact, interaction and a wider array of household structures among the generations. For example, it is expected that there will be more multigenerational households, which will provide greater opportunities for daily contact and socialization (e.g., see Gee and Mitchell, 2003). Changes to leisure activities involving multiple generations are also expected. Fueled by an aging population, technological advances, and increased mobility, we are already beginning to witness a rise in the number of multiple generations traveling together, including "grandtravel" (grandparents traveling with their grandchildren). Young people are also increasingly likely to travel with other extended kin, and it is expected that as baby boomers head for grandparenthood and retirement, there will be even greater opportunities for intergenerational contact through travel (Gardyn, 2001).

Finally, it is important to recognize future changes in immigration and the ethnic composition of a population, since many studies document key differences in family processes for certain racial and ethnic groups. Most "traditional" ethnic groups retain certain aspects of their culture (e.g., food, clothing, language, rituals), although the tendency is for some degree of integration and acculturation over time. Therefore, life course patterns are expected to further diversify in the future. This is because high levels of immigration from countries in which familistic behaviors are normative may result in an increasingly pluralized array of trends and family structures. However, the presence of immigrants in industrialized nations is likely to become more prominent in North American than in European countries. While there is variation among European countries, their immigrant policies are not as pro-immigrant compared to more migration-based countries such as Canada and the United States (Fussell, 2002).

Indeed, data from the U.S. Bureau of the Census and Statistics Canada indicate that the racial and ethnic backgrounds of the populations are becoming more diverse. Future population projections show that the population of whites will shrink, while the percentages of other racial groups will expand. In particular, the largest increases are expected among Asian Americans and Hispanics, both typically regarded as "familistic family cultures." For example, by the year 2025, it is anticipated that the white population will decrease from 70 percent to 62 percent, while the percentage of Hispanics will grow from 12 percent to 18 percent. Longer-term projections to the year 2050 show that the proportion of Hispanics will rise to 25 percent, and the Asians population will double from 5 percent to 10 percent (U.S. Bureau of the Census, 2001, cited in Seccombe and Warner, 2004). Moreover, ethnic diversity may be further enhanced since some North American social policy analysts are advising the government to actively recruit more immigrant young people and their families into the population to meet the needs of an aging workforce. An important implication of policies supporting ethnic pluralism is that some young people will retain their traditional ethnic practices (e.g., remaining at home until marriage, disapproval of unmarried cohabitation), while others will adopt "mainstream" or broad ideological values which are less traditionally based.

Moreover, researchers project that a rise in multigenerational households in the future will be partly because of immigration patterns. High levels of immigration to North America will also contribute to more flexible and expanded meanings and definitions of family, since many recent immigrants (e.g., Hispanics and Asians) arrive from countries in which familism is operant. In these families, fictive kin (e.g., godparents and other nonrelatives) often assume real obligations, and will become increasingly significant with the rising numbers of minorities in the U.S. population (Riley and Riley, 1996). However, there may be differences across nations, since high rates of immigration are not forecasted for many European countries.

In light of these trends and issues, the strongest support is found again for a modified Increased Individualization Scenario, which emphasizes greater flexibility and diversity. A cultural shift toward secularization, the emancipation of women, and a greater occurrence and tolerance of a wide diversity of intimate relationships and living arrangements suggests a proclivity towards a wider range of family behaviours. Exposure to these diverse family paths will contribute to increased individualization because young adults will perceive a number of "acceptable" alternatives to traditional practices. Moreover, as non-traditional behaviours rise, such as non-marital cohabitation, it is reasonable to forecast greater impermanence (at least in the near future) because these behaviours are often not permanent and can become reversed.

However, familism in the traditional sense will remain strong in some families, although not the majority experience. This will be due to an adherence to cultural tradition (e.g., among recent immigrants) and/or because of religious membership (e.g., among Evangelical Christians, Islamics). Finally, while relatively uncommon during our historical benchmark of the 1950s, multigenerational households will become more common (but still relatively rare) due to population aging and immigration patterns. And while this can be considered a familistic living arrangement, it can also meet the needs of individual family members at specific points in the life course in response to changing economic and health needs (e.g., see Gee and Mitchell, 2003).

## Summary and Conclusions

In summary, while it is virtually impossible to forecast family life in the future, there is little doubt that the family paths that young adults of the future will follow from childhood to adulthood will continue to become more individualized, flexible and diverse. Throughout this book, we have seen how the life course of young adults is embedded in, and transformed by, conditions and events that occur during the historical and geographical locations in which they live. Within this context, we have also seen how family-related transitions to adulthood are shaped by economic, political, cultural and technological forces. Revolutions in these realms have provided today's young people with tremendous opportunities to delay adult transitions and decide among a variety of life options and to experiment and explore different lifestyles, residences and types of work.

The changing timing and nature of family-related transitions are also found to have important implications for "linked lives," since societal and individual experiences are linked through the family and its network of shared relationships (Elder, 1998). As such, we have paid considerable attention throughout this volume to how the life trajectories and transitional behaviors of young adults affect, and are affected by, intergenerational relationships during midlife and aging family development.

Moreover, from a wider historical lens, the transition to adulthood during the 1950s—characterized by early homeleaving (and low rates of returning), nearly universal and early marriage and parenthood, and low rates of unmarried cohabitation and relationship dissolution—was somewhat of a "fluke" and not completely characteristic of previous family life. Thus, family life courses are clearly subject to fluctuations and cycles. Changes in family life and in family development are not necessarily linear (nor universal) and the pendulum of family change can swing back and forth. Transitional behaviours can also become "reversed," from both the perspective of long-term historical change, but also especially in modern times. For example, as outlined in chapter 3, the tendency to delay marriage among young adults today was also commonplace at the turn of the twentieth century. Additionally, intergenerational coresidence and union dissolution were prevalent in earlier parts of the twentieth century (but not during the 1950s), although the circumstances fuelling these family states have changed considerably over time.

Taken together, a review of empirical trends supports a modified Increased Individualization Scenario which incorporates greater flexibility and more choice in family-related transitional behaviors and kinship bonds. Yet, many family-related behaviors do persist across time and place, although not technically "traditional" in their timing and formation. This includes the widespread popularity of marriage and parenthood, the need for people to live in family settings and to form intimate relationships more generally. Marriage, for instance, is the modal type of living arrangement for American young adults aged twenty-five to thirty-four (50 percent of men and 57 percent of women) and the vast majority (74 percent) of men and women marry by the age of thirty-five (U.S. Bureau of the Census, 2000). Also, parenthood continues to be embraced by most European and North American couples (e.g., see Therborn, 2004), and similar to other time periods, many couples prefer to postpone their age of (first) parenthood although average ages are at a historical high point.

Not surprisingly, a review of past and current trends has led to commentary that young people are increasingly experiencing a new period of unprecedented opportunity for identity and human capital development prior to the adoption of full adult responsibilities (Aquilino, 1996). These provide unique opportunities for experimentation and experiences in a number of relationships and living arrangements, as well as for continued or renewed intergenerational contact. This is partly because the key markers of the transition to adulthood have been postponed and are subject to more individual choice. Also, the ordering of the transition markers has become more variable, particularly since our historical benchmark of the 1950s (Shanahan, 2000). For example, leaving home at later ages (either due to extended coresidence or home returning) has become a popular adaptive strategy and life style choice for many young people, and this behavior has the potential to bring the generations closer together and to strengthen their stock of "social capital." Thus, many argue that social change bodes well for the future of generational relations. From this perspective, emergent kin connections hold promise of modulating, rather than exacerbating, whatever intergenerational strains and conflicts the future may bring (Riley and Riley, 1996).

Other commentary is less optimistic, however, asserting that these changes produce greater complexity, instability, and uncertainly in the experience of family-related transitions to adulthood and more challenges for intergenerational relationships and aging families. Thus, age-based tensions could escalate because of growing generational equity concerns and issues. Unprecedented inflation in longevity over the past century and the decline of welfare states could also force some aging families to rely on each other as important sources of financial, instrumental and social support. Given these competing views, there is little doubt that generational issues will persist and grow as important areas of discussion in scholarly and family policy arenas. As such, topics such as financial compensation for caregivers, the value of unpaid work, parent-child socialization, and the role of women in families and households will gain added significance.

Furthermore, in reviewing the key themes of this book, it has become apparent that there is no "one" family life course that provides a workable model for all young people, either within or and across societies. Although there is a proclivity toward delayed transitions, enhanced individualization and free choice, diversity in the life course predominates, and this variability is socially structured and constructed by factors such as gender, race/ethnicity, socio-economic status and geographical region. Some young adults have greater access to family, institutional and societal resources than others, and this can affect the kinds of decisions they make, their living arrangements and day-to-day intergenerational interactions, and their opportunities over their life course. For example, home returning is relatively uncommon in some countries (e.g., Sweden, Italy) because young adults have less need to rely on parental households after an initial "launch." Also, in countries such as Italy, there is less public and familial support for young people to practice premarital residence independence (particularly among young men), as well as for unmarried cohabitation and divorce. Even within countries, we have observed considerable heterogeneity in the timing and nature of family-related transitions to adulthood. For example, the location of educational institutions, local job markets and the availability of affordable housing have been found to mould youth transitions to adulthood.

It has also been established that the past has the potential to shape the present and future, which can be viewed as a "ripple" or "domino effect." Becoming a teenaged parent or leaving home at a young age, for instance, has been demonstrated to set up a chain reaction of disadvantage for young people and their families. These early transitional behaviors also have significant implications for intergenerational relations and the exchange of support across generations. This long-term view, with its recognition of cumulative advantage or disadvantage is valuable for understanding social inequality later if life and for creating effective social policy and programs (O'Rand, 1996). Moreover, in an era of globalization and the retrenchment of welfare states, issues of inequality are sure to become intensified, particularly in countries such as the United States, Canada, Britain, and Italy, countries in which rates of child poverty remain very high. In fact, family income is a principal factor in differentiating the life paths youth take through their transitional years (Mortimer and Larson, 2002).

What does an analysis of the past and present suggest for strategies of change for the future? As Luxton (1987) points out, it illustrates the problems inherent in familial ideology and the social practices that accompany it. Conformity to a single model of family life in an attempt to recapture family traditions that either never existed or occurred in a different socio-historical location does not allow us to create responsible social policy. Instead, as discussed in chapter 6, young people need multiple options and flexible policies which allow them to make realistic choices about how they will live their lives, and which meet their diverse needs at different points in their life course. These options need to be based on public policies that recognize the importance of reducing inequities and discrimination, investing in the future, recognizing that we live in an era of "age inflation," and the growing salience of generational concerns amidst rapid population aging.

Thus, social policy needs to take precedence over economic policy and its current ideological bent toward cost containment or cost reduction. There is also a need to forge more equitable methods of resource allocation and the creation of sustainable collectivities or communities in which networks of people can live and work together. We also need to discover better ways to build and support the formation of healthy family relationships that can accommodate a wide variety of family forms and intimate relationships. Vulnerable young people, in particular, require protection and need to be provided with personal and community resources that allow them opportunities in both the short and long-term. As previously noted, a long-term view is especially critical since it is well documented that the timing of earlier transitional behaviors reverberate into old age and this can have significant repercussions for societal costs on many levels.

In closing, a prominent theme of this book is the importance of looking beyond macro forces in order to recognize that young people are agents in the course of their own and society's destiny. Macrostructures depend on the existence of social reproductive processes that are perpetuated through the everyday intentions and interactions of individuals. From heroic acts of revolution and protest to everyday strategies such as staying in school or delaying marriage and parenthood, young people can re-shape the entire course of their own lives and alter the structure of young adulthood for future generations (Youniss and Ruth, 2002). In short, human agency, or the actions of individuals organizing together, can play a significant role in shaping these choices, and in turn, how social change occurs.

This is because social change involves the complex interaction of many forces, but it can also be affected by deliberate intervention such as youth social movements and changes to social policy legislation.

As previously outlined, young adults have always played a pivotal role in fostering social change which is probably best illustrated by their noteworthy political activism during the 1960s. However, today's young adult members of the "boomerang age" have and can continue to forge alternative and innovative solutions to problems facing individuals and their families. This can be fostered by learning more about family and social issues and the sources of inequality, by critical evaluation of current policy practices, and by working as activists, researchers, policy analysts, educators, and practitioners. And yet, resourcefulness and commitment to building a brighter future for all families must come from the actions and efforts of all generations. In this way, we all participate in the making of a new family history, a new generation of young people and their families, and a new society.

## Questions for Discussion and Debate

1.  Do you agree or disagree with statement that: "Although future families will face some issues that are very different from those faced today, they will struggle with the same question and dilemmas that families have always struggled with throughout history"? Provide examples to illustrate.

2.  Some futurists maintain that advancements in medical and reproductive technology will fuel greater social inequality by creating a genetic underclass. This is because wealthier families have the resources to ensure that their offspring will be genetically "superior" (e.g., by being able to purchase the latest genetic testing or in vitro therapy in an attempt to "order a baby engineered to their specifications"). Is this a reasonable forecast? What are some implications of improved reproductive technologies for future family-related transitions to adulthood and intergenerational relations?

3.  It is argued that advances in digital technology (e.g., email, text and photo messaging) will continue to transform family and intergenerational relations in significant ways. Discuss this idea in relation to both: (1) the potential for privatizing family relationships and; (2) with respect to creating more

opportunities for interaction and support among family mem
bers and the generations.

4.    Written in West Berlin and Alabama, Canadian-born
      Margaret Atwood's (1986) classic best-selling novel entitled,
      *The Handmaid's Tale,* forecasts a cataclysmic fascist revolu-
      tion, in which a group of religious extremists create Gilead,
      a society founded on "a return to traditional values" and
      gender roles, and on the subjugation of women by men.
      Consider how this work reflected both the place and time in
      which it was written (e.g., during a historical period of in-
      creasing political influence of female voters, fears of declin-
      ing birthrates and infertility and the dangers of nuclear power).
      Also try to envision how a future major political upheaval or
      a revival of religious fundamentalism could alter family re-
      lated transitions to adulthood and intergenerational relations.

5.    Despite the broader trend toward individualization, some
      futurists maintain that the long-term effects of globalization
      will have a homogenizing influence on Western societies.
      This will result in the construction of a common global cul-
      ture and a widespread convergence in family transitions, con-
      sumption-based lifestyles. It will also produce large popula-
      tions of "Stepford Kids" on college campuses. Discuss this
      idea in relation to past and current trends and life course
      theorists' notions of social structure and human agency.

# References

Ainley, P. 1991. *Young people leaving home*. Cassell Educational Ltd.: London: England.

Alch, M.L. 2000. The echo-boom: a growing generation force in American society. *The Futurist* September-October: 42-46.

Alders, M. and Manting, D. 1998. Household scenarios for the European Union: Methodology and main result. Netherlands: Netherlands Official Statistics.

Aldous, J. 1996. *Family careers: Rethinking the developmental perspective*. Thousand Oaks, CA: Sage.

Aldous, J. 1995. New views of grandparents in intergenerational conflict. *Journal of Family Issues* 16:104-122.

Alwin, D.F. 1996. Coresidence beliefs in American society – 1973-1991. *Journal of Marriage and the Family* 58:393-403.

Ambert, A.M. 1994. An international perspective on parenting: Social change and social constructs. *Journal of Marriage and the Family* 56:529-44.

Amato, P.R. 1996. Explaining the intergenerational transmission of divorce. *Journal of Marriage and the Family* 58:628-640.

Amato, P.R. and Booth, A. 2000. *A generation at risk: Growing up in an era of family upheaval*. Cambridge, MA: Harvard University Press.

Ambert, A.M. 2002. *Divorce: Facts, causes and consequences*. Ottawa: The Vanier Institute of the Family.

Anderson, K.L. 1987. Historical perspectives on the family. In K. L. Anderson et al. (eds.), *Family matters: Sociology and contemporary Canadian families* (pp. 21-39). Toronto: Methuen.

Anderson, M. 1971. *Family structure in nineteenth century Lancashire*. Cambridge: Cambridge University Press.

Andersson, G. and Philipov, D. 2002. Life-table representations of family dynamics in Sweden, Hungary, and 14 other FFS countries: A project of descriptions of demographic behaviour. Demographic Research 7, article 4, published by the Max Planck Institute for Demographic Research, Germany, August 2, 2002 at www.demographic-research.org.

Anisef, P. and Axelrod, P. (eds.). 1993. *Transitions: Schooling and employment in Canada*. Toronto: Thompson Educational Publishing.

Antonucci, T.C. and Jackson, J.S. 2003. Ethnic and cultural differences in intergenerational social support. In V. L. Bengtson and A. Lowenstein (eds.), *Global aging and challenges to families* (pp. 355-370). New York: Aldine de Gruyter.

Applelbaum, E., T. Bailey, P. Berg and Kalleberg, A.L. 2002. Shared work, valued care. New norms for organizing market work and unpaid care work. Washington, DC: Economic Policy Institute.

Aquilino, W.S. 1999. Rethinking the young adult life stage: Prolonged dependency as an adaptive strategy. In A. Booth et al. (eds.), *Transitions to adulthood in a changing economy: No work, no family, no future?* (pp. 168-175). Westport, CT: Praeger.

Aquilino, W.S. 1997. From adolescent to young adult: A prospective study of parent-child relations during the transition to adulthood. *Journal of Marriage and the Family* 59:670-686.

Aquilino, W.S. 1996. The returning child and parental experience at midlife. In C.D. Ryff and M.M. Seltzer (eds.), *The Parental experience in midlife* (pp. 423-458). Chicago: University of Chicago Press.

Aquilino, W.S. 1991. Family structure and home-leaving: A further specification of the relationship. *Journal of Marriage and the Family* 53:999-1010.

Aquilino, W.S. 1990. The likelihood of parent-child coresidence: Effects of family structure and parental characteristics. *Journal of Marriage and the Family* 52:405-419.

Archer, M.S. 1995. *Realist social theory: The morphogenetic approach.* Cambridge: Cambridge University Press.

Arnett, J.J. 2002. The psychology of globalization. *American Psychologist* 57:774-783.

Arnett, J.J. 2000. Emerging adulthood: A theory of development from the late teens through the twenties. *American Psychologist* 55:469-480.

Arnett, J.J. and Arnett, J.L. 2002. A congregation of one: individualized religious beliefs among emerging adults. *Journal of Adolescent Research* 17:451-467.

Atwood, M. 1986. *The handmaid's tale.* Toronto: McClelland and Stewart.

Avery, R., F. Goldscheider and Speare, A. 1992. Feathered nest/gilded cage: The effects of parental resources on young adults' leaving home. *Demography* 29:375-388.

Axinn, W.G. and Thornton, A.T. 1993. Mothers, children, and cohabitation: The intergenerational effects of attitudes and behaviour. *American Sociological Review* 58:233-246.

Axinn, W.G., Barber, J.S., Thornton, A. 1999. Values and beliefs as determinants of outcomes in children's lives. In A. Booth et al. (eds.), *Transitions to adulthood in a changing economy: No work, no family, no future?* (pp. 118-127). Westport, CT: Praeger.

BBC News, U.K. Edition. 2002. Young cannot afford to leave home. Retrieved March 12, 2004 at www.http://news.bbc.co.uk/1/hi/business/2844295.stm.

BBC News. 2001. Child poverty high in the UK. Retrieved July 15, 2004 at www. http://news.bbc.co.uk/1/hi/health/1184856.stm.

Baca Zinn, M. and Eitzen, D.S. 1996. *Diversity in families.* New York: HarperCollins.

Bachrach, C., Hindin, M.J. and Thomson, E. 2000. The changing shape of ties that bind: An overview and synthesis. In L.J. Waite (ed.), *The ties that bind: Perspectives on marriage and cohabitation* (pp. 3-16). New York: Aldine de Gruyter.

Baker, M. 2001. *Families, labour and love: Family diversity in a changing world.* Sydney: Allen and Unwin and Vancouver: UBC Press.

Baker, M. 2000. *Families, labour and love: Family diversity in a changing world.* Vancouver: UBC Press.

Baker, M. (ed.). 1995a. *Families in Canadian society,* 5th ed. Toronto: McGraw-Hill Ryerson

Baker, M. 1995b. *Canadian family policies: Cross-national comparisons.* Toronto: University of Toronto Press.

Baker, M. (ed.). 1993. *Families in Canadian society,* 2nd ed. Toronto: McGraw-Hill Ryerson.

Banner, L.W. 1984. *Women in modern America: A brief history,* 2nd ed. New York: Harcourt Brace Jovanovich.

Beaupré, P., M. Declos, A. Milan and Turcotte, P. 2003. Junior is still at home: Trends and determinants in parental home leaving in Canada." Paper presented at the annual Canadian Population Society Congress meeting, Dalhousie University, Halifax, 2-5 June.

Beck, U. 1992. *Risk society. Towards a new modernity.* Thousand Oaks, CA: Sage Publications.

Becker, H. (ed.). 1991. *Life histories and generations.* Utrecht: Isor.

Becker, G. 1981. *A treatise on the family.* Cambridge, MA: Harvard University Press.

Belanger, A. and Ouellet, G. 2002. A comparative study of recent trends in Canadian and American fertility, 1980-1999. In A. Belanger (ed.), *Report on the demographic situation in Canada, 2001*. Ottawa: Statistics Canada.

Bellah, R.N. 1990. The invasion of the money world. In D. Blankenhorn, S. Bayme and J.B. Elshtain, (eds.), *Rebuilding the nest: A new commitment to the American family* (pp. 227-236). Milwaukee, WI: Family Service America.

Bengtson, V.L. 2001. Beyond the nuclear family: The increasing importance of multigenerational relationships in American society. The 1998 Burgess Award Lecture. *Journal of Marriage and the Family* 63:1-16.

Bengtson, V.L. 1996. Continuities and discontinuities in intergenerational relationships over time. In Bengston, V.L. (ed.), *Adulthood and aging: Research on continuities and discontinuities* (pp. 271-303). New York: Springer.

Bengtson, V.L. 1993. Is the "contract across generations" changing? Effects of population aging on obligations and expectations across age groups. In V.L. Bengtson and W.A. Achenbaum (eds.), *The changing contract across generations* (pp. 3-23). New York: Aldine de Gruyter.

Bengtson, V.L. and Allen, K.R. 1993. The life course perspective applied to families over time. In W. Boss, R. Doherty, W. LaRossa, W. Schumm and S. Steinmetz (eds.), *Sourcebook of family theories and methods: A contextual approach* (pp.469-499). New York: Plenum Press.

Bengtson, V.L., R. Giarrusso, J.B. Mabry and Silverstein, M. 2002. Solidarity, conflict, and ambivalence: Complimentary or competing perspectives on intergenerational relations. *Journal of Marriage and the Family* 64:568-576.

Bengtson, V.L., A. Lowenstein, N.M. Putney and Gans, D. 2003. Global aging and the challenges to families. In In V. L. Bengtson and A. Lowenstein (eds.), *Global aging and challenges to families* (pp. 1-24). New York: Aldine de Gruyter.

Bengtson, V.L., C. Rosenthal, and Burton, L. 1995. Paradoxes of families and aging. In R.H. Binstock and L.K. George (eds.), *Handbook of aging and the social sciences*, 4th ed. (pp. 253-282). San Diego, CA: Academic Press.

Benokraitis, N.V. 1993. *Marriages and families: Changes, choices, and constraints*. Englewood Cliffs, NJ: Prentice-Hall.

Berman, H.J. 1987. Adult children and their parents: Irredeemable obligations and irreplaceable loss. *Journal of Gerontological Social Work* 10:21-34.

Bernstein, R.A. 1995. *Straight parents, gay children: Keeping families together*. New York: Thunder's Mouth Press.

Berrington, A. 2001. Transition to adulthood in Britain. In M. Corijin and E. Klijzing (eds.), *Transitions to adulthood in Europe* (pp. 67-102). Dordrecht: Kluwer Academic Publishers.

Bernhardt, A., M. Morris and Handcock, M.S. 1995. Women's gains or men's losses? A closer look at the shrinking gender gap in earnings. *American Journal of Sociology* 101:302-28.

Berrington, A. 2001. Transitions to adulthood in Britain. In M. Corijin and E. Klijzing (eds.), *Transitions to adulthood in Europe* (pp. 67-102), Dordrecht: Kluwer Academic Publishers.

Bianchi, S.M. and Casper, L.M. 2000. American families. *Population Bulletin* 55:1-42.

Bianchi, S.M. and Mattingly, M.J. 2004. Time, work, and family in the United States. In J.Z. Giele and E. Holst (eds.), *Changing life patterns in Western industrial societies* (pp. 95-118). New York: Elsevier Jai.

Bibby, R.W. and Posterski, DC 1992. *Teen trends: A nation in motion*. Toronto: Stoddart.

Black, D., G.Gates, S. Sanders and Taylor, L. 2000. Demographics of the gay and lesbian population in the United States: Evidence from available systematic data sources. *Demography* 37:139-154.

Blank S. and Torrecilha, R.S. 1998. Understanding the living arrangements of Latino immigrants: A life course approach. *International Migration Review* 32:3-19.

Bliezner, R., J.A. Mancini and Marek, L.I. 1996. Looking back and looking ahead: Life course unfolding of parenthood. In C.D. Ryff and M.M. Seltzer (eds.) *The parental experience in midlife* (pp. 607-637). Chicago: University of Chicago Press.

Blossfeld, H.P. and Mills, M. 2001. A causal approach to interrelated family events: A cross-national comparison of cohabitation, non-marital conception, and marriage. *Canadian Studies in Population* 28:409-437.

Blue, T. 2004. SDS: Students for democratic society. Retrieved July 7, 2004 at http://ma.essortment.com/sdsstudentsfo/rmsx.htm.

Bogenschneider, K. 2000. Has family policy come of age? A decade review of the state of U.S. family policy in the 1990s. *Journal of Marriage and the Family* 62:1136-60.

Bonifazi, C., A. Menniti, M. Misiti, and Palomba, R. 1999. Giovani che non lasciano il nido. Atteggiamenti, speranze, condizioni all'uscita di casa. Technical Report, Consiglio Nazionale delle Ricerche sulla Popolazione. Retrieved June 25, 2004 from http://www.irp.rm.cnr.it/pubblica.htm.

Bonke, J. and Koch-Weser, E. 2004. The welfare state and time allocations in Sweden, Denmark, France, and Italy. In J.Z. Giele and E. Holst (eds.), *Changing life patterns in Western industrial societies* (pp. 231253). New York: Elsevier Jai.

Booth, A., A.C. Crouter, and Shanahan, M.J. (eds.). 1999. *Transitions to adulthood in a changing economy: No work, no family, no future?* Westport, CT: Praeger.

Boyd, M. 2000. Ethnic variations in young adults living at home. *Canadian Studies in Population* 27:135-158.

Boyd, M. 1998. Birds of a feather…ethnic variations in young adults living at home. Paper presented at the annual Population of America meeting, April 2-4, Chicago, Illinois.

Boyd, M. and Norris, D. 1999. The crowded nest: Young adults at home. *Canadian Social Trends*, Spring, Statistics Canada, Catalogue No. 11-008.

Boyd, M. and Pryor, E. 1989. The cluttered nest: The living arrangements of young Canadian adults. *Canadian Journal of Sociology* 15:462-479.

Bourdieu, P. 1986. The forms of capital. In J.G. Richardson (ed.), *Handbook of theory and research for the sociology of education* (pp. 241-258). New York: Greenwood Press.

Bozon, M. and Villeneuve-Gokalp, C. 1994. Les enjeux des relations entre génération à la fin de l'adolescence. *Population* 6:1527-1556.

Bradley, D. 1996. *Family law and political culture: Scandinavian laws in comparative perspective*. London: Sweet and Maxwell.

Bramlett, M.D. and Mosher, W.D. 2002. *Cohabitation, marriage, divorce and remarriage in the United States*. National Center for Health Statistics, Vital Health Statistics.

Brannen, J., Lewis, S., Nilsen, A. and Smithson, J. (eds.). 2001. *Young Europeans, work and family: Futures in transition*. London: Routledge.

Brines, J. and Joyner, K. 1999. The ties that bind: Principles of cohesion in cohabitation and marriage. *American Sociological Review* 64:652-688.

Brubaker, T.H. 1990. An overview of family relationships in later life. In T.H. Brubaker (ed.), *Family relationships in later life*, 2nd ed. (pp. 13-26). Newbury Park, CA: Sage.

Bryson, K. and Casper, L.M. 1999. Co-resident grandparents and their grandchildren. Current Population Reports, Series P-23, No. 198. Washington, DC: Government Printing Office.

Btopenworld. 2002. Boomerang kids keep bouncing back to the family nest, 21 March.

Buck, N. and Scott, J. 1993. She's leaving home: But why? An analysis of young people leaving the parental home. *Journal of Marriage and the Family* 55:863-874.

Bumpass, L.L., T. Castro Martin and Sweet, J.A. 1991. The impact of family background and early martial factors on marital disruption. *Journal of Family Issues* 12:22-42.

Bumpass, L.L. and Lu, H.H. 2000. Trends in cohabitation and implications for children's family contexts in the United States. *Population Studies* 54:29-41.

Bumpass, L.L., T.C. Martin and Sweet, J. 1991. The impact of family background and early marital factors on marital disruption. *Journal of Family Issues* 12:22-42.

Bumpass, L.L., R.K. Raley and Sweet, J. 1995. The changing character of stepfamilies: Implications of cohabitation and nonmarital childbearing. *Demography* 32:425-36.

Burch, T.K. and Mathews, B.J. 1987. Household formation in developed countries. *Population and Development Review* 13:495-511.

Burnette, D. 1999. Social relationships of Latino grandparent caregivers: A role theory perspective. *The Gerontologist* 39:49-58.

Burton, L.M. 1985. Early and on-time grandparenthood in multigenerational Black families. Unpublished PhD dissertation, University of Southern California.

Callan, S. 2005. A brief history of marriage: The implications of civil divorce. Retrieved July 29, 2005 from http://www.2-in2-1.cou.uk/articles/brhistory/index5.html.

Canadian Institute of Child Health. 2002. *The health of Canada's children: A CICH profile*, 3rd ed. Ottawa: CICH.

Card, D. and Lemieux, T. 2000. Adapting to circumstances: The evolution of work, school, and living arrangements among North American youth." In D.G. Blanchflower and R.B. Freeman (eds.), *Youth employment and joblessness in advanced countries* (pp. 171-213). Chicago: University of Chicago Press.

Casper, LM. And Bianchi, S.M. 2002.*Continuity and change in the American family*. Thousand Oaks, CA: Sage Publications.

Castleton, A. and Goldscheider, F. 1989. Are Mormon families different? Household structure and family patterns. In F. Goldscheider and C. Goldscheider (eds.), *Ethnicity and the new family economy: Living arrangements and intergenerational financial flows* (pp.93-109). Boulder, CO: Westview.

Chafe, W.H. 1972. *The American woman: Her changing social, economic, and political roles, 1920-1970.* New York: Oxford University Press.

Chappell, N., E.M. Gee, L. McDonald and Stones, M. 2003. *Aging in contemporary Canada.* Toronto: Prentice-Hall.

Cherlin, A. 1999. *Public and private families: An introduction*, 2nd ed. Boston: McGraw-Hill.

Cherlin, A. 1992. *Marriage, divorce, remarriage*. Cambridge, MA. Harvard University Press.

Cherlin, A. 1978. Remarriage as an incomplete institution. *American Journal of Sociology* 84:634-650

Cherlin, A., E. Scabini and Rossi, G. 1997. Delayed homeleaving in Europe and the U.S. *Journal of Family Issues* 18:572-575.

Chudacoff, H.P. and Hareven, T.K. 1979. From the empty nest to family dissolution: Life course transitions into old age. *Journal of Family History* 4:69-83.

Cicirelli, V.G. 1984. Marital disruption and adult children's perception of their siblings' help to elderly parents. *Journal of Family Relations* 33:613-621.

Clarkberg, M.E. 1999. The price of partnering: The role of economic well-being in young adults' first union experiences. *Social Forces* 77:945-968.

Clausen, J.S. 1991. Adolescent competence and the shaping of the life course. *American Journal of Sociology* 96:805-843.

Clemens, A.W. and Axelson, L.J. 1985. The not-so-empty nest: The return of the fledgling adult. *Family Relations* 34:259-264.

Cnaan, R., R.J. Gelles and Sinha, J.W. 2004. Youth and religion: The gameboy generation goes to church. *Social Indicators Research* 68:175-201.

Cohen, K.M. and Savin-Williams, R.C. 1996. Developmental perspectives on coming out to self and others. In R.C. Savin-Williams and K.M. Cohen (eds.), *The lives of lesbians, gays, and bisexuals: Children to adults* (pp. 113-151). New York: Harcourt.

Coleman, J.S. 1990. *Foundations of social theory.* Cambridge, MA: The Belknap Press of Harvard University.

Coleman, J.S. 1988. Social capital in the creation of human capital. *American Journal of Sociology* 94(Supp.):S95-S120.

Coles, B. 1995. *Youth and social policy: Youth citizenship and young careers.* London: University College London Press.

Connidis, I.A. 2001. *Family ties and aging.* Thousand Oaks, CA: Sage Publications.

Connidis, I.A. and McMullin, J. 2002. Sociological ambivalence and family ties: A critical perspective. *Journal of Marriage and the Family* 64:558-568.

Coontz, S. 1992. *The way we never were: American families and the nostalgia trap.* New York: Basic Books.

Corijn, M. 2001. Transition to adulthood in France. In M. Corijin and E. Klijzing (eds), *Transitions to adulthood in Europe* (pp. 131-151). Dordrecht: Kluwer Academic Publishers.

Corijin, M. and Klijzing, E. (eds). 2001. *Transitions to adulthood in Europe.* Dordrecht: Kluwer Academic Publishers.

Cornils, I. 1998. The struggle continues: Rudi Dutschke's long march. In G.J. Degroot (ed.), *Student protest: The sixties and after* (pp. 100-114). New York: Longman.

Côté, J. and Allahar, A. 1994. *Generation on hold: Coming of age in the late twentieth century.* Toronto: Stoddart.

Council of Europe. 1994, 1998, 1999, 2000, 2002. *Recent demographic developments in Europe.* Strasbourg: Council of Europe Press.

Council of Europe. 1991. *Seminar on present demographic trends and lifestyles in Europe.* Strasbourg: Council of Europe Press.

Crimmins, E.M., R.A. Easterlin, and Saito, Y. 1991. Preference changes among American youth: Family, work, and goods aspiration, 1976-86. *Population and Development Review* 17:115-33.

Crysdale, S. and MacKay, H. 1994. *Youth's passage through school to work: A comparative, longitudinal study.* Toronto: Thompson Educational Publishing.

Cuneo, C. 1979. State, class and reserve labour: The case of the 1941 unemployment insurance act. *Canadian Review of Sociology and Anthropology* 16:147-70.

Dalla Zuanna, G. 2001. The banquet of Aeolus: A familistic interpretation of Italy's lowest low fertility. *Demographic Research* 4:131-162.

Dempsey, J.J. 1981. *The family and public policy.* Baltimore: Paul H. Brookes.

Demos, J. 1970. *A little commonwealth: Family life in Plymouth Colony.* New York: Oxford University Press.

Dey, I. 1999. Parental support for young adults: A temporal perspective. *Time and Society* 8:231-247.

Di, Z.X., Y. Yang and Liu, X. 2002. Young American adults living in parental homes. Paper published at the Joint Centre for Housing Studies, Harvard University, W02-3, May.

Ditch, J., Barnes, H. and Bradshaw, J. 1996. *A synthesis of national family policies 1995.* Brussels: Commission of the European Communities.

Dorbritz, J. and Hohn, C. 1999. The future of the family and future fertility trends in Germany. *Population Bulletin of the United Nations* 40/41:218-234.

Dominion Bureau of Statistics. 1954, 1958, 1962, 1968. *Canada year book.* Ottawa, Ontario: Queen's Printer and Controller of Stationary.

Dranoff, L.S. 1977. *Women in Canadian life.* Toronto: Fitzhenry and Whiteside.

Duane-Richard, A.M. and Mahon, R. 2003. Sweden: models in crisis. In J. Jenson and M. Sineau (eds.), *Who cares? Women's work, childcare, and welfare state redesign* (pp. 146-176). Toronto: University of Toronto Press.

Duran-Aydintug, C. 1993. Relationships with former in-laws: Normative guidelines and actual behaviour. *Journal of Divorce and Remarriage* 19:69-81.

Duvander, A.'Z.E. 2000. *Couples in Sweden: Studies of family and work*. Edscruk: Akademitryck AB.

Eastman, M. 1996. Myths of marriage and family. In D. Popenoe, J.B. Elshtain and D. Blankenhorn (eds.) *Promises to Keep : Decline and Renewal of Marriage in America* (pp.35-68). Lanham, MD: Rowman and Littlefield.

Easterlin, R. 1980. *Birth and fortune: The impact of numbers on personal welfare*. New York: Basic Books.

Economic Commission for Europe. 1995, 1997, 1999, 2001. *Trends in Europe and North America*. New York: United Nations.

Eichler, M. 1988. *Families in Canada today: Recent changes and their policy consequences,* 2nd ed. Toronto: Gage.

Elder, G.H., Jr. 2003. The life course in time and place. In W.R. Heinz and V.W. Marshall (eds.), *Social dynamics of the life course: Transitions, institutions, and interrelations* (pp. 57-71). New York: Aldine de Gruyter.

Elder, G.H., Jr. 1998. The life course as developmental theory. *Child Development* 69:1-12.

Elder, G.H., Jr. 1995. The life course paradigm: Social change and individual development. In P. Moen, G.H. Elder, Jr. and K. Luscher (eds.), *Examining lives in context: Perspectives on the ecology of human development* (pp. 101-139). Washington, DC: American Psychological Association.

Elder, G.H., Jr. 1994. Time, human agency, and social change: Perspectives on the life course. *Social Psychology Quarterly* 57:4-15.

Elder, G.H., Jr. 1991. Lives and social change. In W.R. Heinz (ed.), *Theoretical advances in life course research* (pp. 58-86). Bremen: Deutscher Studien Verlag.

Elder, G.H., Jr. 1985. *Life course dynamics*. Ithaca, NY: Cornell University Press.

Elder, G.H., Jr. 1974. *Children of the great depression: Social change in life experience.* Chicago: University of Chicago Press.

Elder, G.H., Jr., and Caspi, A. 1990. Studying lives in a changing society: Sociological and personological explorations. In A.I. Rabin, R.A. Zucker and S. Frank (eds.), *Studying persons and lives* (pp. 201-247). New York: Springer.

Elder, G.H., Jr. and Hareven, T.K. 1992. Rising above life's disadvantages: From the Great Depression to global war. In J. Modell, G.H. Elder, Jr. and R. Parke (eds.). *Children in time and place* (pp. 47-72). New York: Cambridge University Press.

Elder, G.H., Jr. and Pellerin, L.A. 1998. Linking history and human lives. In J.Z.Giele and G.H. Elder, Jr. (eds.), *Methods of life course research: Qualitative and quantitative approaches* (pp. 264-294). Thousand Oaks, CA: Sage Publications.

Ellis, S. 1998. A demonstration of British good sense? British student protest during the Vietnam war. In G.J. Degroot (ed.), *Student protest: The sixties and after* (pp.54-69). New York: Longman.

Erikson, E. 1963. *Childhood and society*. Norton: New York.

Ermisch, J. 1997. The economic determinants of young people's household formation. *Economica* 64:627-644.

Esping-Andersen, G. 1990. *The three worlds of welfare capitalism*. Princeton, NJ: Princeton University Press.

Esping-Andersen, G. 1998. The three political economies of the welfare state. In J.S. O'Connor and G.M. Olsen (eds.), *Power, resources theory and the welfare state: A critical approach* (pp. 123-153). Toronto: University of Toronto Press.

Erikson, E.H. 1963. *Childhood and society*, 2nd ed. New York: Norton.

Ermisch, J. 1997. The economic determinants of young people's household formation. *Economica* 64: 627-644.

Eshleman, J.R. 1994. *The family*, 7th ed. Boston: Allyn and Bacon.

European Commission. 2002. *The social situation in the European union 2002*. Luxemborg: Office for Official Publications of the European Communities.

European Commission. 1993. *Age and attitudes: Main results from a Europbarometer Survey*. Brussels.

Eurostat. 2004. *Eurostat yearbook 2004: The statistical guide to Europe*. Luxembourg: Office for Official Publications of the European Communities.

Eurostat. 2003. First results of the demographic data collection for 2002 in Europe. *Statistics in focus, theme 3: population and social conditions*. Luxembourg: Office for Official Publications of the European Communities.

Eurostat. 2002. European union labour force survey. Luxembourg: Office for Official Publications of the European Communities.

Eurostat. 2001. First results of the demographic data collection for 2000 in Europe. *Statistics in focus, theme 3: population and social conditions*. Luxembourg: Office for Official Publications of the European Communities.

Faludi, S. 1991. *Backlash: The undeclared war against American women*. New York: Crown.

Ferrarotti, F. 1981. On the autonomy of the biographical method. In D. Bertaux (ed.), *Biography and society: The life history approach in the social sciences* (pp. 19-27). Beverly Hills, CA: Sage.

Fitch, C.A. and Ruggles, S. 2000. Historical trends in marriage formation: The United States 1850-1990. In L.J. Waite et al. (eds.), *The ties that bind: Perspectives on marriage and cohabitation* (pp. 59-88). New York: Aldine de Gruyter.

Field, A.M. 1999. The college student market segment: A comparative study of travel behaviours of international and domestic students at a Southeastern University. *Journal of Travel Research* 37:375-381.

Fields, J. and Casper, L.M.. 2001. America's families and living arrangements: Population characteristics. U.S. Census Bureau 2000, *Current Population Reports*, P20-537.

Fischer, L.R. 1986. *Linked lives: Adult daughters and their mothers*. New York: Harper.

Flandrin, J. 1979. *Families in former times: Kinship, household and sexuality in early modern France*. Cambridge: Cambridge University Press.

Florey, F.A. and Guest, A.M. 1988. Coming of age among U.S. farm boys in the late 1880s: Occupational and residential choices. *Journal of Family History* 13:233-249.

Folbre, N. 2002. Disincentives to care: A critique of U.S. Family Policy. Paper presented at the Public Policy and the Future of the Family conference, Syracuse University, New York, Oct. 25.

Foot, D., with Stoffman, D. 1996. *Boom, bust and echo: Profiting from the demographic shift in the 21st century*. Toronto: Stoddart.

Francese, P. 2003. Ahead of the next wave. *American Demographics* 25:42-44.

Franklin, M.B. 2003. Boomerang kids. *Kiplinger's Personal Finance* 56:114-115.

Friedan, B. 1963. The *feminine mystique*. New York: Norton.

Furedi, F. 2003. The children won't grow up. Spiked Online, July 29, 2003, retrieved July 31, 2003 at www.spiked-online.com/articles/00000006DE8D.htm.

Furstenberg, F.F. 2003. Growing up in American society: Income, opportunities, and outcomes. In W. R. Heinz and Marshall, V.W. (eds.), *Social dynamics of the life course: Transitions, institutions and interrelations* (pp. 211-233). New York: Aldine de Gruyter.

Fussell, E. 2002. Youth in aging societies. In J.T. Mortimer and R.W. Larson (eds.), *The changing adolescent experience: Societal trends and the transition to adulthood* (pp. 18-51). New York: Cambridge University Press.

Galaway, B. and Hudson, J. (eds.) 1996. *Youth in transition: Perspectives on research and policy*. Toronto: Thompson Educational Publishing.

Galland, O. 1997. Leaving home and family relations in France. *Journal of Family Issues* 18:645-670.

Galston, W. 1996. The reinstitutionalization of marriage. Political theory and public policy, In D. Popenoe, J. Elshtain and D. Blankenhorn (eds.), *Promises to keep: Decline and renewal of marriage in America* (pp. 271-290). Lanhan, MD: Rowman and Littlefield.

Garasky, S. 2002. Where are they going? A comparison of urban and rural youths' locational choices after leaving the parental home. *Social Science Research* 31:409-431.

Gardyn, R. 2001. The new family vacation. *American Demographics* 23:42-48.

Gee, E.M. 2000. Contemporary diversities. In N. Mandell and A. Duffy (eds), *Canadian families: Diversity, conflict and change*, 2nd ed. (pp. 78-111). Toronto: Harcourt Canada.

Gee, E.M. 1995. Contemporary diversities. In N. Mandell and A. Duffy (eds.), *Canadian Families: Diversity, Conflict and Change* (pp. 79-110). Toronto: Harcourt Brace.

Gee, E.M. 1990. Preferred timing of women's life events: A Canadian Study. *International Journal of Aging and Human Development* 34:281-296.

Gee, E.M. 1982. Marriage in nineteenth century Canada. *Canadian Review of Sociology and Anthropology* 19:311-325.

Gee, E.M. and McDaniel, S.A. 1994. Social policy for an aging society. In V. Marshall and B. McPherson (eds.), *Aging: Canadian perspectives* (pp. 219-231). Peterborough, Ont.: Broadview Press Ltd.

Gee, E.M. and Mitchell, B.A. 2003. One roof: exploring multi-generational households in Canada. In M. Lynn (ed.), *Voices: Essays on Canadian families*, 2nd ed. (pp. 293-313). Toronto: Thomson Nelson.

Gee, E.M., Mitchell, B.A. and Wister, A.V. 2003. Homeleaving trajectories in Canada: Exploring cultural and gendered dimensions. *Canadian Studies in Population* 30:245-270.

Gee, E.M., Mitchell, B.A. and Wister, A.V. 1995. Returning to the parental 'nest': Exploring a changing Canadian life course. *Canadian Studies in Population* 22:121-144.

Gerson, K. 2000. Resolving family dilemmas and conflicts: beyond utopia. *Contemporary Society* 29: 180-187.

Giannelli, G.C. and Monfardini, C. 2000. A nest or golden cage? Family co-residence and human capital investment decisions of young adults. *International Journal of Manpower* 21:227-245.

Giddens, A. 2000. *Runaway world: How globalization is reshaping our lives*. New York: Routledge.

Giddens, A. 1992. *The transformation of intimacy: Sexuality, love and eroticism in modern societies*. Stanford, CA: Stanford University Press.

Giddens, A. 1991a. *Modernity and self-identity: Self and society in the late modern age*. Stanford: Stanford University Press.

Giddens, A. 1991b. Structuration theory: Past, present and future. In C.G.A. Bryant and D. Jary (eds.), *Giddens' theory of structuration: A critical appreciation* (pp. 201-221). London: Routledge.

Giddens, A. 1979. *Central problems in social theory*. Basingstoke: Macmillan.

Giele, J.Z. 2004. Women and men as agents of change in their own lives. In J.Z. Giele and E. Holst (eds.), *Changing life patterns in Western industrial societies* (pp. 299-316). New York: Elsevier Jai.

Giele, J.Z. 1998. Innovation in the typical life course. In J.Z. Giele and J. H. Elder, Jr. (eds.), *Methods of life course research: Qualitative and quantitative approaches* (pp. 231-263). Thousand Oaks, CA: Sage Publications

Giele, J.Z. and Elder, G.H., Jr. 1998. *Methods of life course research: Qualitative and quantitative approaches*. Thousand Oaks, CA Sage Publications.

Giele, J.Z. and Holst, E. 2004. New life patterns and changing gender roles. In J.Z. Giele and E. Holst (eds.), *Changing life patterns in Western industrial societies* (pp. 3-21). New York: Elsevier Jai.

Gitlin, T. 1989. *The sixties: Years of hope, days of rage*. Toronto: Bantam Books.

Glenn, N.D. 1996. Values, attitudes and the state of American marriage. In D. Popenoe, J. B. Elshtain and D. Blankenhorn (eds.), *Promises to keep: Decline and renewal of marriage in America* (pp. 15-33). Lanhan, MD: Rowman and Littlefield.

Glenn, N.D. 1987. Social trends in the U.S. *Public Opinion Quarterly* 51:S109-S126.

Glick, P.C. 1992. American families: As they are and were. In A. S. Skolnick and J.H. Skolnick (eds.), *Family in transition*, 7th ed. (pp. 93-105). New York: Harper Collins Publishers.

Glick, J.E. and Van Hook, J. 2002. Parents' coresidence with adult children: Can immigration explain racial and ethnic variation? *Journal of Marriage and the Family* 64: 240-253.

Goggins, B.K. 1997. Shared responsibility for managing work and family relationships: A community perspective. In S.J. Pareasuraman and J.H. Greenhaus (eds.), *Integrating work and family: Challenges and choices for a changing world* (pp. 220-231). Westport, CT: Quorum Books.

Goldscheider, F. 1997. Recent changes in U.S. young adult living arrangements in comparative perspective. *Journal of Family Issues* 18:708-724.

Goldscheider, F. and DaVanzo, J. 1985. Semiautonomy and leaving home in early adulthood. *Social Forces* 65:187-201.

Goldscheider, F. and Goldscheider, C. 1997. The historical trajectory of the Black family: Ethnic differences in leaving home over the twentieth century. *The History of the Family: An International Quarterly* 2:295-307.

Goldscheider, F. and Goldscheider, C. 1999a. *The changing transition to adulthood: leaving and returning home*. Thousand Oaks: Sage Publications.

Goldscheider, F. and Goldscheider, C. 1999b. Changes in returning home in the U.S., 1925-1985. *Social Forces* 78:695-720.

Goldscheider, G. and Goldscheider, C. 1993. *Leaving home before marriage: Ethnicity, Familism and Generational Relationships.*. Madison: University of Wisconsin Press.

Goldscheider, G. and Waite, L.J. 1991. *New families, no families: The transformation of the American home*. Berkeley: University of California Press.

Goode, W.J. 1963. World revolution and family patterns. Glencoe, IL: The Free Press.

Goossens, L. 2001. Transition to adulthood: Developmental factors. In M. Corijin and E. Klijzing (eds), *Transitions to adulthood in Europe* (pp. 27-42). Dordrecht: Kluwer Academic Publishers.

Gordon, S. 2004. California court invalidates months of same-sex marriages. *Vancouver Sun* A10, August 13.

Gross, J. 1991. More young men hang onto apron strings. *New York Times* 1,18, 16 June.

Groves, E.R. 1928. *The marriage crisis*. New York: Longmans, Green.

Guldner, G.T. 2003. *The complete guide to long-distance relationships*. Corona, CA: JF Milne Publications.

Gutmann, M.P., S.M. Pullum-Pinon and Pullum, T.W. 2002. Three eras of young adult homeleaving in twentieth century America. *Journal of Social History* 35:533-577.

Hagestad, G.O. 1988. Demographic change and the life course: Some emerging trends in the family realm. *Family Relations* 37:405-410.

Hagestad, G.O. 1991. Dilemmas in life course research: An international perspective. In W.R. Heinz (ed.), *Theoretical advances in life course research* (pp. 23-57). Bremen: Deutscher Studien Verlag.

Hagestad, G.O. and Burton, L. 1986. Grandparenthood, life context, and family development. *American Behavioral Scientist* 29:471-484.

Hagestad, G.O. and Neugarten, B.L. 1985. Age and the life course. In R.H. Binstock and E. Shanas (eds.), *Handbook of aging and the social sciences* (pp. 35-61). New York: Van Nostrand Reinhold.

Haines, M.R. 1996. Long-term marriage patterns in the United States from Colonial times to the present. *History of the Family* 1:15-39.

Hajnal, J. 1965. European marriage patterns in perspective. In D.V. Glass and D.E.C. Eversley (eds.), *Population in history* (pp. 101-138). Chicago: Aldine.

Hall, D. 1996. Marriage as a pure relationship: Exploring the link between premarital cohabitation and divorce in Canada. *Journal of Comparative Family Studies* XXVII:1-12.

Hamon, R.R. 1995. Parents as resources when adult children divorce. *Journal of Divorce and Remarriage* 23:1/2:171-183.

Hamon, R.R. and Cobb, L.L. 1993. Parents' experience of and adjustment to their adult children's divorce: Applying family stress theory. *Journal of Divorce and Remarriage* 21:1/2:73-94.

Haskey, J. 1987. Trends in marriage and divorce in England and Wales: 1837-1987. *Population Trends* 48: 11-19.

Hareven, T.K. (ed.) 1996. *Aging and generational relations: Life-course and cross-cultural perspectives.* New York: Aldine de Gruyter.

Hareven, T.K. 1992. American families in transition: Historical perspectives on change. In A. S. Skolnick and J.H. Skolnick (eds.), *Family in transition,* 7th ed. (pp. 40-57). New York: Harper Collins Publishers.

Hareven, T.K. and Adams, K.J. 1996. The generation in the middle: Cohort comparisons in assistance to aging parents in an American community. In T.K. Hareven (ed.), *Aging and generational relations: Life-course and cross-cultural perspectives* (pp. 3-29). New York: Aldine de Gruyter.

Harkins, E. 1978. Effects of empty nest transition on self-report of psychological and physical well-being. *Journal of Marriage and the Family* 40:549-556.

Hartung, B. and Sweeney, K. 1991. Why adult children return home. *Social Science Journal* 28:467-480.

Hawkins, A.J., Nock, S.L., Wilson, J.C., Sanchez, L. and Wright, J.D. 2002. Attitudes about covenant marriage and divorce: Policy implications from a three-state comparison. *Family Relations* 51:166-175.

Heinz, W.R. 1996. Status passages as micro-macro-linkages in life-course research, In A. Weymann and W.R. Heinz (eds.), Society and biography: *Interrelationships between social structure, institutions and the life course, Vol. IX of Status passages and the life course* (pp. 51-66). Weinheim: Deutscher Studien Verlag.

Heinz, W.R. (ed.). 1991. *Theoretical advances in life course research.* Bremen: Deutscher Studien Verlag.

Hellenga, K. 2002. Social space, the final frontiers: Adolescents on the internet. . In J.T. Mortimer and R.W. Larson (eds.), *The changing adolescent experience: Societal trends and the transition to adulthood* (pp. 208-249). New York: Cambridge University Press.

Herman, E.S. and Chomsky, N. 1988. *Manufacturing consent: The political economy of the media.* New York: Pantheon.

Hermans, H.J.M. and Kempen, H.J.G. 1998. Moving cultures: The perilous problems of cultural dichotomies in a globalizing society. *American Psychologist* 53:1111-1120.

Heuveline, P. and Timberlake, J.M. The role of cohabitation in family formation: The United States in Comparative Perspective. *Journal of Marriage and the Family* 66:12-14-1230.

Hill, M.S. and Yeung, W. 1999. How has the changing structure of opportunities affected transitions to adulthood. In A. Booth, A.C. Crouter and M.J. Shanahan (eds.), *Transitions to adulthood in a changing economy: No work, no family, no future? (pp. 3-39). Westport, CT: Praeger.

Hodgson, L.G. 1995. Adult grandchildren and their grandparents: The enduring bond. Pp. 155-170 in J. Hendricks (eds.), *The ties of later life*. Amityville, NY: Baywood.

Hoem, B. 1995. Sweden. In H.-P. Blossfeld (ed), *The new role of women, family formation in modern societies* (pp. 35-55). Boulder, CO: Westview.

Hogan, D.P. 1981. *Transitions and social change: The early lives of American men*. New York: Academic Press.

Hogan, D.P. 1986. Maternal influences on adolescent family formation. In D.I. Kertzer (ed.), *Current perspectives on aging and the life cycle,* Vol. 2 (pp. 147-165). Greenwich, CT: JAI Press.

Hogan, D.P. and Astone, N.M. 1986. The transition to adulthood. *Annual Review of Sociology* 12:109-130.

Hogan, D.P., D.J. Eggebeen, and Clogg, C. 1993. The structure of intergenerational exchanges in American families. *American Journal of Sociology* 98:1428-1458.

Hooimeijer, P. and Mulder, C.H. 1998. Changing ways of leaving the parental home: With a partner or alone. In A. Kuijsten, H. De Gans and H. De Feijter (eds.), *The joy of demography... and other disciplines* (pp. 137-151). Amsterdam: Thela Thesis.

Hufton, O. 1981. Women, work and marriage in eighteenth century France. In R.B. Outhwaite (ed.), *Marriage and society: Studies in the social history of marriage*. London: Europa Publications Ltd.

Hullen, G. 2001. Transition to adulthood in Germany. In M. Corijin and E. Klijzing (eds), *Transitions to adulthood in Europe* (pp. 153-172). Dordrecht: Kluwer Academic Publishers.

Iedema, J., Becker, H.A. and Sanders, K. 1997. Transitions into independence: A comparison of cohorts born since 1930 in the Netherlands. *European Sociological Review* 13:117-137.

Institut national d'etudes deomgraphiques. 2002. *Mean age at first marriage*. Retrieved on March 18, 2003 at http://www.ined.fr/englishversion/figures/france/marriage/1ermariageA.html.

Irvine, M. 2004. We're not married – We're partners. *Vancouver Sun*, A11, April 27.

Irwin, S. 1995. *Rights of passage: Social change and the transition from youth to adulthood*. London: University College London Press.

Ishii-Kuntz, M. 1997. Intergenerational relationships among Chinese-Canadian, Japanese, and Korean Americans. *Family Relations* 46: 23-32.

Jackson, A.P., R.P. Brown, and Patterson-Stewart, K.E.. 2000. African Americans in dual-career commuter marriage: An investigation of their experiences. *The Family Journal: Counselling and Therapy for Couples and Families* 8:22-36.

Jansen, M. and Liefbroer, A. 2001. Transition to adulthood in the Netherlands. In M. Corijin and E. Klijzing (eds), *Transitions to adulthood in Europe* (pp. 209-232). Dordrecht: Kluwer Academic Publishers.

Jendrek, M.P. 1994. Grandparents who parent their grandchildren: Circumstances and decisions. *Gerontologist* 34:206-216.

Jensen, A.M. 1998. Partnership and parenthood in contemporary Europe: A review of recent findings. *European Journal of Population* 14:89-99.

Jenson, J. 2004. Changing the paradigm: Family responsibility or investing in children. *Canadian Journal of Sociology* 29:169-192.

Jenson, J. and Sineau, M. 2003. New contexts, new policies. In J. Jenson and M. Sineau (eds.), *Who cares? Women's work, childcare, and welfare state redesign* (pp. 19-55). Toronto: University of Toronto Press.

Johansson, T. and Miegel, F. 1992. *Do the right thing: lifestyle and identity in contemporary youth culture*. Malmo: Graphic Systems.

Johnson, C.L. 1998. *Ex familia: Grandparents, parents, and children adjust to divorce.* New Brunswick, NJ: Rutgers University Press.

Johnston, J.A. 1998. Student activism in the United States before the 1960s: An overview. In G.J. Degroot (ed.), *Student protest: The sixties and after* (pp. 12-26). New York: Longman.

Jones, G. 1995. *Leaving home.* Buckingham: Open University Press.

Kahn, S., Zimmerman, G., Csikszentmihalyi, M. and Getzels, J. 1985. Relations between identity in young adulthood and intimacy at midlife. *Journal of Personality and Social Psychology* 49:1316-1322.

Kain, E.L, 1990. *The myth of family decline: Understanding families in a world of rapid social changes.* Lexington, MA: Lexington Books.

Kalb, C. 1997. How old is too old? *Newsweek*, May 5.

Katz, M.B. 1974. *The people of Hamilton West.* Cambridge, MA: Harvard University Press.

Katz, M.B. and Davey, I.E. 1978. Youth and early industrialization in a Canadian city. In J. Demos and S.S. Boocock (eds.), *Turning Points: Historical and sociological essays on the family*, Supplement to *American Journal of Sociology* 84:S81-S119.

Kamerman, S.B. and Kahn, A.J. (eds.) 1997. *Family change and family policies in Great Britain, Canada, New Zealand, and the United States.* London: Clarendon Press/ Oxford.

Kamerman, S.B. and Kahn, A.J. 1978. Families and the idea of family policy. In S.B. Kamerman and A.J. Kahn (eds.), *Family policy: Government and families in fourteen countries* (pp. 1-16). New York: Columbia University Press.

Kaufman, F. and Uhlenberg, P. 1998. Effects of life course transitions on the quality of relationships between adult children and their parents. *Journal of Marriage and the Family* 60:924-938.

Kemp, C. 2003. The social and demographic contours of contemporary grandparenthood: Mapping patterns in Canada and the United States. *Journal of Comparative Family Studies* 34:187-212.

Kenney, C. 2004. Cohabiting couple, filing jointly? Resource pooling and U.S. poverty policies. *Family Relations* 53:237-247.

Kerckhoff, A.C. 2002. The transition from school to work. In J.T. Mortimer and R.W. Larson (eds.), *The changing adolescent experience: Societal trends and the transition to adulthood* (pp. 52-87). New York: Cambridge University Press.

Kerckhoff, A.C. 1990. Becoming independent: Leaving home, cohabitation, marriage, and parenthood. In *Getting started: Transitions to adulthood in Great Britain* (pp. 105-135). Boulder, CO: Westview Press.

Kerckhoff, A.C. and Macrae, J. 1992. Leaving the parental home in Great Britain: A comparative perspective. *Sociological Quarterly* 33:281-301.

Kertzer, D.I. 1983. Generation as a sociological problem. *Annual Review of Sociology*, 9, 125-149.

Kiernan, K. 2002. Cohabitation in Western Europe: Trends, issues, and implications. In A. Booth and A.C. Crouter (eds.), *Living together: Implications of cohabitation on families, children, and social policy* (pp. 53-84). Mahwah, NJ: Lawrence Erlbaum Associates.

Kiernan, K. 2000. Unmarried cohabitation and parenthood: Here to stay? Paper presented at the Conference on Public Policy and the Future of the Family, October 25, 2000, Washington, DC.

Kiernan, K. 1999a. Cohabitation in Western Europe. *Population Trends* 96:25-32.

Kiernan, K. 1999b. European perspectives on non-marital childbearing. Paper presented at the European Population Conference, The Hague, Netherlands.

Kilborn, P.T. New jobs lack the old security in time of 'disposable workers. *New York Times*, March 15.

Kines, L. 1993. Plight of street kids: No safety net to save them. *Vancouver Sun*, 29 January.

Kingsmill, S. and Schlesinger, B. 1998. *The family squeeze: Surviving the sandwich generation*. Toronto: University of Toronto Press.

Kitson, G.C. 2004 (June). The "family wars" and same sex marriage. President's Report, *National Council on Family Relations* 49:2-3.

Klang, J. 2003. Permanent mission of Sweden to the United Nations – 7 October. Retrieved July 7, 2004 at http://www.swedenabroad.com/pages/general_3040.asp.

Kobrin, F.E. 1976. The primary individual and the family: Changes in living arrangements in the United States since 1940. *Journal of Marriage and the Family* May: 233-239.

Kohli, M. 1986. The world we forgot: A historical review of the life course. In V.W. Marshall (ed.), *Later life: The social psychology of aging* (pp. 271-303). Beverly Hills, CA: Sage.

Kposowa, A. 1995. *Risk factors for divorce in the United States*. American Sociological Association.

Kreider, R.M. and Fields, J.M. 2001. Number, timing and duration of marriages and divorces: Fall 1996. *Current Population Reports* P70-80. Washington, DC: U.S. Census Bureau.

Kreider, R.M. and Simmons, T. 2003. *Marital status: 2000, Census 2000 brief*. U.S. Census Bureau, U.S. Department of Commerce.

Kurdeck, L.A. 1998. Relationship outcomes and their predictors: Longitudinal evidence from heterosexual married, gay cohabiting, and lesbian cohabiting couples. *Journal of Marriage and the Family* 60:553-568.

Kurdeck, L.A. 1988. Perceived social support in gays and lesbians in cohabiting relationships. *Journal of Personality and Social Psychology* 54:504-509.

Lamanna, M.A. and Riedmann, A. 1999. *Marriages and families: Making choices in a diverse society*, 7th ed. Belmont, CA: Wadsworth Thomson Learning.

Lapierre-Adamcyk, É. and Charvet, C. 2000. Cohabitation and marriage: An assessment of research in demography. *Canadian Studies in Population* 27:239-254.

Larson, R. 2002. Globalization, societal change, and new technologies: What they mean for the future of adolescence. *Journal of Research on Adolescence* 12:1-30.

Lasch, C. 1979. The culture of narcissism : American life in an age of diminishing expectations. New York: Norton.

Laslett, P. 1969. Size and structure of the household in England over three centuries. *Population Studies* 23:199-224.

Laslett, P. 1979. *The world we have lost*. London: Methuen.

Laslett, P. and Wall, R. (eds.). 1972. *Household and family in past time*. Cambridge: Cambridge University Press.

Lauterbach, W. and Klein, T. 2004. The change of generational relations based on demographic development: The case of Germany. *Journal of Comparative Family Studies* 35:651-64.

Lawton, L., Silverstein, M., and Bengtson, V. 1994. Affection, social contact, and geographical distance between adult children and their parents. *Journal of Marriage and the Family* 56:57-68.

Le Bourdais and Juby, H. 2002. The impact of cohabitation on the family life course in contemporary North America: Insights from across the border. In A. Booth and A.C. Crouter (eds.), *Living together: Implications of cohabitation on families, children, and social policy* (pp. 107-118). Mahwah, NJ: Lawrence Erlbaum Associates.

Lee, A.B. and Levy, S.D. 1997. Parent adult-child coresidence: Consequences of grown children in parental households for mid and later life parenthood for mid and later life parenthood and family socialization. Introductory remarks at symposium at the 59th Annual National Council on Family Relations, Arlington, Virginia, November.

Lehrer, E.L. 2000. Religion as a determinant of entry into cohabitation and marriage. In L.J. Waite, C.A. Bachrach, M. Hinden, E. Thomson, and A.T. Thornton (eds.), *The ties that bind: Perspectives on marriage and cohabitation* (pp.227-252). New York: Aldine de Gruyter.

Lesthaeghe, R. 1983. A century of demographic and cultural change in Western Europe: An explanation of underlying dimensions. *Population and Development Review* 9:411-435.

Lesthaeghe, R. and Surkyn, J. 1988. Cultural dynamics and economic theories of fertility change. *Population and Development Review* 14:1-14.

Lesthaeghe, R. and van de Kaa, D.J. 1986. Twee deomgrafische transities? In D.J. van de Kaa and R. Lesthaeghe (eds.), *Bevolking: groei en krimp*. Mens en Maatschappij: 9-42.

Letablier, M.T. 2004. Work and family balance: A new challenge for policies in France. . In J.Z. Giele and E. Holst (eds.), *Changing life patterns in Western industrial societies* (pp. 189-209). New York: Elsevier Jai.

Levin, I. 2004. Living apart together: A new family form. *Current Sociology* 52:223-241.

Levy, F. 1998. *The new dollars and dreams: American incomes and economic change.* New York: Russell Sage.

Lewis, J. 2003. *Should we worry about family change?* Toronto: University of Toronto Press.

Li, J.H. and Wojtkiewicz, R.A. 1994. Childhood family structure and entry into first marriage. *The Sociological Quarterly* 35:247-268.

Liefbroer, A. 2003. Transitions to adulthood in Europe: Empirical results and theoretical considerations. Paper presented at workshop on "Immigration, family, and the transition to adulthood: Sweden in the European Context." Bergendal, Sweden, May 23-25.

Liefbroer, A. 1999. From youth to adulthood: Understanding changing patterns of family formation from a life-course perspective. In L. van Wissen and P.A. Dykstra (eds.), *Population issues: An interdisciplinary focus* (pp. 53-85). New York: Plenum Press.

Liefbroer, A. and de Jong Gierveld, J. 1995. Standardization and individualization: The transition from youth to adulthood among cohorts between 1903 and 1965. In J. C. Van Den Brekel and F. Deven (eds.), *Population and family in the low countries* (pp.57-80). Dordrecht: Kluwer Academic Publishers.

Lin, C. and Liu, W.T. 1999. Intergenerational relationships among Chinese immigrants from Tawian. In H.P. McDoo (ed.), *Family ethnicity: Strength in diversity*, 2nd ed. (pp. 235-251). Thousand Oaks, CA: Sage Publications.

Liv-Bacci, M. 1997. *A history of Italian fertility during the last two centuries*. Princeton, NJ: Princeton University Press.

Logan, J.R and Spitze, G.D. 1996. *Family ties: Enduring relations between parents and their grown children.* Philadelphia: Temple University Press.

Looker, E.D. 1993. Interconnected transitions and their costs: Gender and urban/rural differences in the transitions to work. In P. Anisef and P. Axelrod (eds.), *Transitions: Schooling and employment in Canada* (pp. 43-64). Toronto: Thompson Educational Publishing, Inc.

Loram, D. 1996. *Born at the right time: A history of the baby boom generation.* Toronto: University of Toronto Press.

Lowenstein, A., R. Katz, D. Prilutzky, D. and Melhousen-Hassoen, D. 2003. A comparative cross-national perspective on intergenerational solidarity. *Retraite et Societe* 38:52-80.

Luescher, K. 2000. A heuristic model for the study of intergenerational ambivalence. University of Konstanz, Arbeitspapier No. 29.

Luescher, K., and Pillemer, K. 1998. Intergenerational ambivalence: A new approach to the study of parent-child relations in later life. *Journal of Marriage and the Family* 60: 413-25.

Luxton, M. 1987. Thinking about the future. In Anderson et al. (eds.), *Family matters: Sociology and contemporary Canadian families* (pp. 237-260). Toronto: Methuen.

MacDonald, G. 2001. Love goes global. *The Globe and Mail*, F1, May 26.

Mackey, R.A., B.A. O'Brien and Mackey, E.F. 1997. *Gay and lesbian couples: Voices from lasting relationships*. Westport, CT: Praeger.

MacRae, D. 1985. *Policy indicators: Links between social science and public debate*. Chapel Hill: University of North Carolina Press.

Mandel, W. 1987. Back to the future: how we thought we'd live in 1987. *San Francisco Examiner*, August 9.

Majete, C.A. 1999. Family relationships and the interracial marriage. Paper presented at the annual American Sociological Association Meeting

Mannheim, K. 1952. The problem of generations. In P. Kecskemeti (ed. and trans.), *Essays on the sociology of knowledge* (pp. 276-322). New York: Oxford University Press.

Manning, W.D. 2002. The implications of cohabitation for children's well-being. In A. Booth and A.C. Crouter (eds.), *Living together: Implications of cohabitation on families, children, and social policy* (pp. 121-152). Mahwah, NJ: Lawrence Erlbaum Associates.

Manning, W.D. 2001. Childbearing in cohabiting unions: Racial and ethnic differences. *Family Planning Perspectives* 33: 217-223.

Margolis, M. 1984. *Mothers and such*. Berkeley: University of California Press.

Marshall, V.W., F.L. Cook, and Marshall, J.G. 1993. Conflict over generational equity: Rhetoric and reality in a comparative context. In V.L. Bengtson and W. A. Achenbaum (eds.), *The changing contract across the generations* (pp. 119-40). New York: Aldine de Gruyter.

Marshall, V.W., W.R. Heinz, H. Krüger and Verma, A. 2001. *Restructuring work and the life course*. Toronto: University of Toronto Press.

Marshall, V.W. and Mueller, M.M. 2003. Theoretical roots of the life-course perspective. In W. R. Heinz and V.W. Marshall (eds.), *Social dynamics of the life course: Transitions, institutions and interrelations* (pp. 3-32). New York: Aldine de Gruyter.

Martin, J.A., Hamilton, B.E., Sutton, P.D., Ventura, S.J., Menacker, F., Munson, M.L. 2003. Births: Final data for 2002. *National Vital Statistics Reports*, Vol. 52, No. 10. Hyattsville, MD: National Center for Health Statistics.

Martin, S.P. 2002. *Delayed marriage and childbearing: Implications for measurement of diverging trends in family timing*. Retrieved January 31, 2002 at www.http://www.ressell-sage.org/special_interest/socialinequality/revmartin01.pdf.

Matthews, S.H. and Sprey, J. 1984. The impact of divorce on grandparenthood: An exploratory study. *The Gerontologist* 24:41-47.

Matthews, T.J.and Hamilton, B.E. 2002. Mean age of mother, 1970-2000. *National Vital Statistics Reports*, Vol. 51, No. 1. Hyattsville, MD: National Centre for Health Statistics.

Mayer, K.U. 1991. Life courses in the welfare state. In W.R. Heinz (eds.), *Theoretical advances in life course research,* Vol. 1 (pp. 146-158). Weinheim: Deutscher Studien Verlag.

Mayer, K.U. and Tuma, N.B. 1990. *Event history analysis in life course research*. Madison: University of Wisconsin Press.

Mazzuco, S. 2003. The impact of children leaving home on the parents' wellbeing: A comparative analysis of France and Italy." Paper presented at the NIDI Euresco Conference 2003-174: The Second Demographic Transition in Europe, Spa, Belgium, June.

McDaniel, S. 1996. The family lives of the middle-aged and elderly in Canada. In M. Baker (ed.), *Families: Changing Trends in Canada, 3rd ed.* (pp. 195-211). Toronto: McGraw-Hill Ryerson.

McDaniel, S. and Tepperman, L. 2004. *Close relations: An Introduction to the sociology of families,* 2nd ed. Scarborough, Ont.: Prentice-Hall.

McDaniel, S. and Tepperman, L. 2000. *Close relations: An Introduction to the sociology of families.* Scarborough, Ont.: Prentice-Hall.

McKenzie, R.H. 1991. Consensual public policy in an adversarial culture. *National Forum* (The Phi Kappa Phi Journal): 20-21.

McLanahan, S. and Casper, L. 1995. Growing diversity and inequality in the American family. In R. Farley (ed.), *State of the union: America in the 1990s* Vol. 2 (pp. 1-45). New York: Russell Sage Foundation.

McLanahan, S. and Sandefur, G. 1994. *Growing up with a single parent: What hurts, what helps.* Cambridge, MA: Harvard University Press.

McPherson, B. D. 1983. *Aging as a social process: An introduction to individual and population aging.* Toronto: Butterworths.

Meyer, S. and Schulze, E. 1988. Unmarried cohabitation: An opportunity to change gender relationships? *Kölner Zeitschrift für Soziologie and Sozialpsychologie* 40:337-356.

Miall, C. 1989. The stigma of involuntary childlessness. In A.S. Skolnick and Skolnick (eds.), *Family in transition,* 6th ed. (pp. 387-405). Boston: Little, Brown.

Miles, S. 2000. *Youth lifestyles in a changing world.* Philadelphia: Open University Press.

Mills, C.W. 1959. *The sociological imagination.* New York: Oxford University Press.

Mills, M. 2000. *The transformation of partnerships: Canada, the Netherlands, and the Russian Federation.* Amsterdam: Thela Thesis.

Minkler, M. and Roe, K.M. 1996 Spring. Grandparents as surrogate parents. *Generations* 20:30-38.

Minkler, M. and Robinson-Beckley Jr., R. 1994. Raising grandchildren from crack-cocaine households: Effects on family and friendship ties of African-American women. *American Journal of Orthopsychiatry* 64:20-29.

Minnerup, G. 1998. Germany 1968 and 1989: The marginalized intelligentsia against the cold war. In G.J. Degroot (ed.), *Student protest: The sixties and after* (pp. 201-215). New York: Longman.

Mitchell, B.A. in press. Social capital and intergenerational coresidence: How families and ethnic communities shape transitions to adulthood. In R. Johnston and F. Kay (eds.), *Diversity, Social Capital and the Welfare State.* Vancouver, B.C.: University of British Columbia Press.

Mitchell, B.A. 2004. Home, but not alone: Social and economic aspects of young adults living at home. *Atlantis: A Journal of Women's Studies* 35:423-443.

Mitchell, B.A. 2002. Life course theory. In J.J. Ponzetti (ed.), *The international encyclopedia of marriage and family relationships,* 2nd ed. (pp. 1051-1055). New York: Macmillan Reference, USA.

Mitchell, B.A. 2001. Ethnocultural reproduction and attitudes towards cohabiting relationships. *Canadian Review of Sociology and Anthropology* 38:391-413.

Mitchell, B.A. 2000. The refilled nest: Debunking the myth of families-in-crisis. In E.M. Gee and G. Gutman (eds.), *The overselling of population aging: Apocalyptic demography, intergenerational challenges, and social policy* (pp. 80-99). Toronto:Oxford University Press.

Mitchell, B.A. 1998. Too close for comfort? Parental assessments of boomerang kid living arrangements. *Canadian Journal of Sociology* 23:21-46.

Mitchell, B.A. 1994. Family structure and leaving home: A social resource perspective. *Sociological Perspectives* 37:651-671.

Mitchell, B.A. and Gee, E.M. 1996a. Boomerang kids and midlife parental marital satisfaction. *Family Relations* 45:442-448.

Mitchell, B.A. and Gee, E.M. 1996b. Young adults returning home: Implications for social policy. In B. Galaway and J. Hudson (eds.), *Youth in transition: Perspectives on research and policy* (pp. 61-71). Toronto: Thompson Educational Publishing.

Mitchell, B.A., Wister, A.V. and Gee, E.M. 2004. The family and ethnic nexus of home leaving and returning among Canadian young adults. *Canadian Journal of Sociology* 29:543-575.

Mitchell, B.A., A.V. Wister and Gee, E.M. 2002. There's no place like home: An analysis of young adults' mature coresidency in Canada. *International Journal of Aging and Human Development* 54:1-28.

Mitchell, B.A., Wister, A.V. and Gee, E.M. 2000. Culture and coresidence: An exploration of variation in home-returning among Canadian young adults. *Canadian Review of Sociology and Anthropology* 37:197-222.

Modell, J. 1989. *Into one's own: From youth to adulthood in the United States, 1920-1975*. Berkeley: University of California Press.

Modell, J., Furstenberg, F., and Hershberg, T. 1976. Social change and transitions to adulthood in historical perspective. *Journal of Family History* 1:7-32.

Moen, P. and Jull, P.M. 1995. Informing family policies: The use of social research. *Journal of Family and Economic Issues* 16:79-107.

Moore, O. 2003. Bush wants to 'codify' heterosexual unions," *Globe and Mail*, retrieved July 31, 2003 at www.http./theglobeandmail.com.

Morales, E.S. 1990. Ethnic minority families and minority gays and lesbians. In F. W. Bozett and M.B. Sussman (eds.), *Homosexuality and family relations* (pp. 217-239). New York: Harrington Park.

Mortimer, J.T. and Larson, R.W. 2002. Macrostructural trends and the reshaping of adolescence. In J.T. Mortimer and R.W. Larson (eds.), *The changing adolescent experience: Societal trends and the transition to adulthood* (pp. 1-17). New York: Cambridge University Press.

Moynihan, D.P. 1965. A family policy for the nation. *America*, 280-283. [Cited in Family and nation, The Godkin Lectures, Harvard University, April 8-9, 1985].

Murdock, G.P. 1949. *Social structure*. New York: The Free Press.

Myles, J. 1995. Pensions and the elderly. *Review of Income and Wealth* 41:101-106.

Myrdal, A. 1968. *Nation and family*. Cambridge, MA: MIT Press.

Myrdal, A. 1941. *Nation and family: The Swedish experiment in democratic family and population policy*. New York: Harper.

National Centre for Health Statistics. 1996. *Vital statistics of the United States, 1988: Volume III Marriage and Divorce*. Hyattsville, MD: National Center for Health Statistics.

National Marriage Project. 2000. *The state of our unions: The social health of marriage in America, 2000*. New Brunswick, NJ: Author.

Nault, F. and Belanger, A. 1996. The Decline of Marriage in Canada, 1981-1991. Ottawa: Statistics Canada. Catalogue no. 84-536-XPB.

Nave-Herz, R. 1997. Still in the nest: The family and young adults in Germany. *Journal of Family Issues* 18:671-689.

Nazio, T. and Blossfeld, H.P. 2003. The diffusion of cohabitation among young women in West Germany, East Germany and Italy. *European Journal of Population* 19:47-82.

Nett, E. 1981. Canadian families in social-historical perspective. *Canadian Journal of Sociology* 6:239-59.

Newman, D.M. and Grauerholz, L. 2002. *Sociology of families*, 2nd ed. Thousand Oaks, CA: Pine Forge Press.

Nilsson, K. and Strandh, M. 1999. Nest leaving in Sweden: The importance of early educational and labour market careers. *Journal of Marriage and the Family* 61:1068-1079.

Nock, S.L. 1998. *Marriage in men's lives*. New York: Oxford University Press.

Nock, S.L. 1995. A comparison of marriages and cohabiting relationships. *Journal of Family Issues* 16:53-76.

Norris, J.E. and Tindale, J.A.. 1994. *Among generations: The cycle of adult relationships*. Toronto: W.H. Freeman and Company.

Nye, F.I. and McDonald, G.W. 1982. Family policy research: Emergent models and some theoretical issues." In F.I. Nye (ed.), *Family relationships: Rewards and costs* (pp. 185-204). Beverly Hills, CA: Sage.

OECD (Organization for Economic Co-operation and Development). 2002. *Society at a glance*. Paris: OECD.

Office of Population Censuses and Surveys. 1982 and 1992. *Marriage and divorce statistics*. Series FM2. London: Her Majesty's Stationary Office.

Office of Population Censuses and Surveys. 1982. *Birth statistics*. Series FM1 no. 7. London: Her Majesty's Stationary Office.

Official Statistics of Sweden. 1992. *Statistical yearbook of Sweden 1993*. Stockholm, Statistics Sweden.

Okimoto, J.D. and Stegall, P.J. 1987. *Boomerang kids: How to live with adult children who return home*. Boston: Little, Brown and Co.

Olds, D.L., R. Tatelbaum, C.R. Henderson, Jr., J. Robinson, H. Kitzman, L.M. Pettitt, J. Eckenrode, R. O'Brien, R. Cole and Hill, P. 1998. Prenatal and infancy home visitation by nurses: A program of research. In C. Rovee-Collier, L.P. Lipsitt and H. Hayne (eds.), *Advances in Infancy Research, Vol. 12*. Stanford, CT: Ablex Publishing Corporation.

Oliver, M.L. and Shapiro, T.M. 1995. *Black wealth/white wealth: A new perspective on racial inequality*. New York: Routledge.

Olsen, G.M. 2002. *The politics of the welfare state: Canada, Sweden and the United States*. Toronto: Oxford University Press.

Ongaro, F. 2001. Transition to adulthood in Italy. In M. Corijin and E. Klijzing (eds), *Transitions to adulthood in Europe* (pp. 173-208). Dordrecht: Kluwer Academic Publishers

Ooms, T. 1998. Towards more perfect unions: Putting marriage on the public agenda. Washington, DC: Family Impact Seminar.

O'Rand, A.M. 1996. Precious and the precocious: understanding cumulative disadvantage and cumulative advantage over the life course. *The Gerontologist* 36:230-238.

O'Rand, A.M. and Henretta, J.C. 1999. *Age and inequality: Diverse pathways through later life*. Boulder, CO: Westview.

Owram, D. 1996. *Born at the right time: A history of the baby boom generation*. Toronto: University of Toronto Press.

Pampel, F.C. 1998. *Aging, social inequality and public policy*. Thousand Oaks, CA: Pine Forge Press.

Paul, P. 2003. The permaparent trap. *Psychology Today*. Retrieved October 11, 2003 at http://www.psychologytoday.com/thdoscs/prod/PTOArticle/Pto-2003.

Paul, P. 2001. Echo boomerang. *American Demographics* 23:44-50.

Pearson, J.L. 1993. Parents' reactions to their children's separation and divorce at two and four years: Parent gender and grandparent status. *Journal of Divorce and Remarriage* 20:3/4:25-43.

Peck, R.C. 1968. Psychological development in the second half of life. In B.L. Neugarten (ed.), *Middle age and aging* (pp. 88-92). Chicago: Chicago Press.

Peplau, L.A., R.C. Veneigas Campbell, S.M. 1996. Gay and lesbian relationships. In R.C. Savin-Williams and K.M. Cohen (eds.), *The lives of lesbians, gays, and bisexuals* (pp. 250-269). Fort Worth, TX: Harcourt Brace.

Pike, R. and Allen, C. 2002. Mamma mia, *Guardian*, May 14.

Plantenga, J. 2004. Changing work and life patterns: Examples of new working-time arrangements in the European member states. In J.Z. Giele and E. Holst (eds.), *Changing life patterns in Western industrial societies* (pp. 119-135). New York: Elsevier Jai.

Portes, A. 1998. Social capital: Its origins and applications in modern sociology. *Annual Review of Sociology*, 24:1-24.

Preston, S.H., Heuveline, P., and Guillot, M. 2001. *Demography: Measuring and modeling population processes*. Oxford, England: Blackwell.

Price, S.J., McKenry, P.C. and Murphy, M. 2000. *Families across time: A life course perspective*. Los Angeles, CA: Roxbury Publishing Co.

Prinz, C. 1995. *Cohabiting, married, or single*. Aldershot et al.: Avebury.

Putnam, R.D. 2000. *Bowling alone: The collapse and revival of American community*. New York: Simon and Schuster.

Raabe, P.H. 2003. Policy inequalities: Inequalities in work-family and other social policy coverage in the United States. Paper presented at the annual Southern Sociological Society meetings.

Raley, R.K. 2000. Recent trends and differentials in marriage and cohabitation: The United States. In L.J. Waite, C.A. Bachrach, M. Hinden, E. Thomson, and A.T. Thornton (eds.), *The ties that bind: Perspectives on marriage and cohabitation* (19-39). New York: Aldine de Gruyter.

Ravernera, Z.R., F. Rajulton and Burch, T.K. 1992. A cohort analysis of homeleaving in Canada, 1910-1975. Paper presented at the annual meeting of the Canadian Population Society, Charlottetown, PEI, June 2-4.

Rhodes, A.R. 2002. Long-distance relationships in dual-career commuter couples: A review of counselling issues. *The family journal: Counselling and therapy for couples and families* 10:398-404.

Riedmann, A., M. Lamanna and Nelson, A. 2003. *Marriages and families*. Scarborough, Ont.: Thomson Nelson.

Ries, P. and Stone, A.J. (eds.) 1992. *The American woman 1992-93: A status report*. New York: Norton.

Rigaux, F. 2003. Same-gender marriage: A European view. *Journal of Family History* 28:199-207.

Riley, M.W. 1996. Discussion: What does it all mean? *The Gerontologist* 36:256-258.

Riley, M.W. 1987. On the significance of age in sociology. *American Sociological Review* 52:1-14.

Riley, M.W. and Riley, J.W. 1996. Generational relations: A future perspective. In T.K. Hareven (ed.), *Aging and generational relations: Life course and cross-cultural perspectives* (pp. 283-291). New York: Aldine de Gruyter.

Riley, M.W. and Riley, J.W. 1994. Structural lag: Past and future. In M.W. Riley, R.L. Kahn, R. Louis; A. Foner, and Mack, K.A.. (eds.). *Age and structural lag: Society's failure to provide meaningful opportunities in work, family, and leisure* (pp.15-36). Oxford, England: John Wiley and Sons.

Riley, M.W. and Riley, J.W. 1993. Connections: Kin and cohort. In V.L. Bengtson and W. A. Achenbaum (eds.), *The changing contract across generations* (pp.169-189). New York: Aldine de Gruyter.

Rindfuss, R.R. 1991. The young adult years: Diversity, structural change, and fertility. *Demography* 28: 493-512.

Roan, C.L. and Raley, R.K. 1995. Changes in intergenerational relationships across the life course. Research report No. 95-329, Population Studies Center, University of Michigan.

Rodgers, R.H. and White, J.M. 1993. Family development theory. In P.G. Boss, W.J. Doherty, R. LaRossa, W.R. Schumm and S.K. Steinmetz (eds.), *Sourcebook of family theories and methods: A contextual approach* (pp. 225-54). New York: Plenum.

Roe, J. 1998. *Governing America: Our choices, our challenges.* Dayton, OH: National Issues Forums Research.

Rosenmayr, L. and Kockeis, E. 1963. Propositions for a sociological theory of aging and the family. *International Social Science Journal* 15:410-426.

Rosenzweig, M.R., and Wolpin, K.I. 1993. Intergenerational support and the life-cycle incomes of young men and their parents: Human capital investments, coresidence, and intergenerational financial transfers. *Journal of Labor Economics* 11:84-112.

Rossi, A.S. and Rossi, P.H. 1990. *Of human bonding: Parent-child relations across the life course.* New York: Aldine de Gruyter.

Rossi, G. 1997. The nestlings: Why young adults stay at home longer: The Italian case. *Journal of Family Issues* 18:627-644.

Rothman, S.M. 1978. *Women's proper place: A history of changing ideals and practices, 1870 to the present.* New York: Basic Books.

Rubin, L. 1992. The empty nest. In J.M. Heaslin (ed.), *Marriage and Family in a Changing Society.* New York: Free Press.

Ryff, C.D. and Seltzer, M.M. 1996. The parental experience in midlife: Past, present and future. In C.D. Ryff and M.M. Seltzer (eds.), *The parental experience in midlife* (pp.641-661). Chicago: University of Chicago Press.

Sardon, J.P. 1990. Cohort fertility in member states of the Council of Europe. *Population studies series*, no. 21. Strasbourgh, Ont.: Council of Europe.

Savin-Williams, R.C. 2001. *Mom, dad, I'm gay. How families negotiate coming out.* Washington, DC: American Psychological Association.

Schnaiberg, A. and Goldenberg, S. 1989. From empty nest to crowded nest: The dynamics of incompletely-launched young adults. *Social Problems* 36:251-269.

Schor, J.B. 1991. *The overworked American: The unexpected decline of leisure.* New York: Basic Books.

Seccombe, K. and Warner, R.L. 2004. *Marriages and families: Relationships in social context.* Belmont, CA: Wadsworth/Thomson Learning.

Seltzer, M.M. 1976. Suggestions for the examination of time-disordered relationships. In F.J. Gubrium (ed.), *Time, roles and self in old age* (pp. 111-125). New York: Human Sciences Press.

Serovich, J. and Price, S.J. 1994. In-law relationships: A role theory perspective. *International Journal of Sociology of the Family* 24:127-146.

Settersten, R.A., Jr. and Hagestad, G.O. 1996. What's the latest? Cultural age deadlines for family transitions. *Gerontologist* 36:178-188.

Seward, R., D. Yeatts, and Zottarelli, L.K. 2002. Parental leave and father involvement in child care: Sweden and the United States. *Journal of Comparative Family Studies* 33: 387-399.

Shanahan, M.J. 2000. Pathways to adulthood in changing societies: Variability and mechanisms in life course perspective. *Annual Review of Sociology* 26:667-692.

Shanas, E. 1979. Social myth as hypothesis: The case of the family relations of old people. *The Gerontologist* 19:3-9.

Shaw, Crouse, J. (ed.) 1999. The state of marriage in 20th century America: Implications for the next millennium. Retrieved August 16, 2002 at www.http/beverlayhayeinstitute.org.

Sherrod, L.S. 1996. Leaving home: The role of individual and familial factors. In *Leaving home: Understanding the transition to adulthood.* New Directions for Child Development (pp. 111-119). San Francisco: Jossey-Bass Publishers.

Shorter, E. 1975. *The making of the modern family.* New York: Basic Books.

Shragge, E. 2003. *Activism and social change: Lessons for community and local organiz-ing*. Peterborough, Ont.: Broadview Press.

Simmons, T. and O'Connell, M. 2003. Married-couple and unmarried partner households: 2000. *Census 2000 special reports*. U.S. Census Bureau, CENSR.5.

Silverstein, M., Giarrusso, R., and Bengtson, V.L. 1998. Intergenerational solidarity and the grandparent role. In M. Szinovacz (ed.), *Handbook on grandparenthood* (pp. 144-58). Westport, CT: Greenwood.

Siurala, L. 2002. *Can youth make a difference? Youth policy facing diversity and change*. Strasbourg, France: Council of Europe Publishing.

Skoepol, T. 1997. A partnership with American families. In S.B. Greenberg and T. Skocpol (eds.), *The new majority: Toward a popular progressive politics* (pp. 104-129). New Haven, CT: Yale University Press.

Skolnick, A.S. 1996. *The intimate environment: Exploring marriage and the family*, 6th ed. New York: HarperCollins College Publishers.

Slater, S. 1995. *The lesbian family life cycle*. New York: Free press.

Smith, P.K. (ed.). 1991. *Psychology of grandparenthood: an international perspective*. New York: Routledge.

Smock, P.J. 2000. Cohabitation in the United States: An appraisal of research themes, findings, and implications. *Annual Review of Sociology* 26:1-12.

Smock, P.J. and Gupta, S. 2002. Cohabitation in contemporary North America. In A. Booth and A.C. Crouter (eds.), *Living together: Implications of cohabitation on fami-lies, children, and social policy* (pp. 53-84). Mahwah, NJ: Lawrence Erlbaum Associ-ates.

Spanier, G.B. 1983

Social Policy Action Network. 2001. *Second chances homes national directory*. Washing-ton, DC: SPAN Publications.

Soares, C. 2000. Aspects of youth, transitions, and the end of certainties. *International Social Science Journal* 52:209-218.

South, S.J. 1995. Do you need to shop around? Age at marriage, spousal alternatives, and marital dissolution. *Journal of Family Issues* 16:432-449.

South, S.J. Trent, K.and Shen, Y. 2001. Changing partners: Toward a macrostructural opportunity theory of marital dissolution. *Journal of Marriage and the Family* 63:743-754.

Spanier, G.B. 1983. Married and unmarried cohabitation in the United States: 1980. *Jour-nal of Marriage and the Family* 83:277-289.

Stack, S. and Eshleman, J.R. 1998. Marital status and happiness: A 17-nation study. *Journal of Marriage and the Family* 60:527-537.

Statistics Canada. 2004a. Births, 2002. *The Daily*, Monday, April 19.

Statistics Canada. 2004b. Divorces, 2001 and 2002. *The Daily*, Tuesday May 4.

Statistics Canada. 2003a. Marriages, *The Daily*, Thursday, February 6.

Statistics Canada. 2003b. Couples living apart. *The Daily*, Tuesday, June 10.

Statistics Canada. 2002a. 2001 Census: Profile of Canadian families and households: Diversification continues. Census release 22 October, 2002, www.statcan.ca.

Statistics Canada. 2002b. 2001 census: Marital status, common-law status, families, dwell-ings and households. *The Daily*, Tuesday, October 22.

Statistics Canada. 2002c. *Changing conjugal life in Canada. The Daily*, 11 July.

Statistics Canada. 2002d. *General social survey—Cycle 15: Family History*. Ottawa: Sta-tistics Canada.

Statistics Canada. 1999. *Vital statistics compendium, 1996*. Catalogue no. 84-214-XPE. Ottawa: Statistics Canada.

Statistics Canada. 1993. *Selected birth and fertility statistics, Canada 1921-1990*. Cata-logue no. 82-553. Ottawa: Statistics Canada.

Statistics Canada. 1973, 1978, 1985, 1990. *Canada year book*. Ottawa, Ontario: Statistics Canada.

Statistics Netherlands. 2003. *Key figures marriages and partnership registrations*. Retrieved on March 18, 2003 at http://statline.cbs.nl/StatWeb.

Strong, B. and DeVault, C.1992. *The marriage and family experience*, 5th ed. New York: West Publishing Co.

Szinovacz, M.E. 1998. Grandparents today: A demographic profile. *The Gerontologist* 38:37-52.

Takahashi, H. and Voss, J. 2000. 'Parasite Singles' – A uniquely Japanese phenomenon? *Japan Economic Institute* report, No. 31A, Washington, DC

Tang, S. 1997. Repeated home leaving behavior of American youth. *Journal of Comparative Family Studies* 28:147-159.

Teachman, J.D. 2002. Childhood living arrangements and the intergenerational transmission of divorce. *Journal of Marriage and the Family* 64:717-729.

Teeple, G. 2000. *Globalization and the end of social reform: Into the twenty-first century*. Aurora, Ont.: Garamond Press.

Tennant, P. 1992. Cut the cord before sharing the house. *Kitchener-Waterloo Record*, F1, 6 March.

Therborn, G. 2004. *Between sex and power: Family in the world, 1900-2000*. London: Routledge.

Thomas, M. and Venne, R. 2002. Work and leisure: A question of balance. In D. Cheal (ed.), *Aging and demographic change in Canadian context* (pp. 190-223). Toronto: University of Toronto Press.

Thomas, W.I. and Zhaniecki, F. 1927. *The polish peasant in Europe and America*. New York: Alfred A. Knopf (originally published 1918-1920).

Thornton, A.T., Axinn, W.G. and Hill, D. 1992. Reciprocal effects of religiosity, cohabitation and marriage. *American Journal of Sociology* 96:868-894.

Tischler, B.L. 1998. The refiner's fire: Anti-war activism and emerging feminism in the late 1960s. In G.J. Degroot (ed.), *Student protest: The sixties and after* (pp. 186-215). New York: Longman.

Tomaini, C., Wolf, D.A. and Rosina, A. 2003. Parental housing assistance and parent-child proximity in Italy. *Journal of Marriage and the Family* 65:700-715.

Torjman, S. and Battle, K. 1999. *Good work. Getting it and keeping it*. Ottawa: Caledon Institute of Social Policy.

Travel Industry Association of America. 2005. U.S. travel expenditures hit $600 billion for the first time. Retrieved July 30, 2005 from http://www.hospitalitynet.org/news/4023247.search

Troll, L.E. 1985. The contingencies of grandparenting. In V.L. Bengtson and J.F. Robertson (eds.), *The ties of later life* (pp. 63-74). Amityville, NY: Baywood.

Turcotte, P. and Bélanger, A. 1997. *The dynamics of formation and dissolution of first common-law unions in Canada*. Ottawa: Statistics Canada.

Uhlenberg, P. and Hammill, B.G. 1998. Frequency of grandparent contact with grandchild sets: Six factors that make a difference. *The Gerontologist* 38:276-285.

Uhlenberg, P. and Miner, S. 1996. Life course and aging: A cohort perspective. In R.H. Binstock and L.K. George (eds.), *Handbook of aging and the social sciences,* 4th ed. (pp. 208-228). San Diego, CA: Academic Press.

Umberson, D. 1992. Relationships between adult children and their parents: Psychological consequences for both generations. *Journal of Marriage and the Family* 50:1037-1047.

UN (United Nations). 1969, 1975, 1984, 1992, 1995, 1999, 2002. *Demographic yearbook*. New York: United Nations.

UNECE (United Nations Economic Commission for Europe). 2003. *Table 2: Selected demographic indicators.* Retrieved on March 18, 2003 at http://www.unece.org/ead/pau/ffs/f_home1.htm.

U.S. Bureau of the Census. 2002. International data base. Retrieved July 30, 2005, from http://blue.census.gov/cgi-bin/ipc/idbagg.

U.S. Bureau of the Census. 2001a. Table MS-2: Estimated median age at first marriage, by sex: 1890 to the present. Retrieved May 8, 2003 at http://www.census.gov/population/socdemo/hh-fam/tabMS-2.txt.

U.S. Bureau of the Census. 2001b. *Profile of general demographic characteristics for the United States: 2000.* Quick Table-02. Retrieved August 6, 2001 at http://factfinder.census/Gov/home/en/C2ss.html.

U.S. Bureau of the Census. 2000. *Statistical abstract of the United States.* Washington, DC: U.S. Government Printing Office.

U.S. Bureau of the Census. 2000. *Living together, living alone: families and living arrangements, Population profile of the United States 2000.* Retrieved Oct. 5, 2004 at http://www.census.gov/population/pop-profile/2000/Chap5.pdf.

U.S. Bureau of the Census. 1998.*Current Population Survey* (March). Washington, DC: U.S. Government Printing Office.

U.S. Bureau of the Census. 1993. *Current Population Reports*, Table 608 and Table 744, Poverty in the United States. Washington, DC: U.S. Government Printing Office.

U.S. Bureau of the Census. 1992. *Current Population Reports,* Table 219, Poverty in the United States. Washington, DC: U.S. Government Printing Office.

U.S. National Center for Health Statistics. 2000. Births: Final data for 1998. *National Vital Statistics Reports*, Vol. 48.

Van Hekken, S., L de May and Schulze, H. 1997. Youth inside or outside the parental home: The case of the Netherlands. *Journal of Family Issues* 18:690-707.

Veevers, J.E., E.M. Gee and Wister, A.V. 1996. Homeleaving age norms: Conflict or consensus? *The International Journal of Aging and Human Development* 43: 277-295.

Veevers, J. and Mitchell, B.A. 1998. Intergenerational exchanges and perceptions of support within 'boomerang kid' family environments. *International Journal of Aging and Human Development* 46:91-108

Ventura, S.J., Mathews, M.S. and Hamilton, B.E. 2002. *Teenage births in the United States: State trends, 1991-2000, an update.* National vital statistics reports, vol. 50, no. 9. Hyattsville, MD: National Center for Health Statistics.

Villeneuve-Gokalp, C. 2002. Les jeunes partent toujours au même âge de chez leurs parents. *Économie et statistique* 337-338, 61-80.

Vobejda, B. 1991. Declaration of independence: It's taking longer to become an adult. *Washington Post Weekly Edition* pp. 23-9, Sept. 9-10.

Ward, R., J. Logan and Spitze, G. 1992. The influence of parent and child needs on coresidence in middle and later life. *Journal of Marriage and the Family* 54:209-221.

Wall, R. 1978. The age at leaving home. *Journal of Family History* 3:181-201.

Wall, R. 1983. Introduction. In R. Wall and Laslett (eds). *Family forms in historic Europe* (pp. 1-63). Cambridge: Cambridge University Press.

Ward, M. 2002. *The family dynamic: A Canadian perspective.* 3rd ed. Scarborough, Ont.: Nelson Thomas Learning.

Waters, J.L. 2002. Flexible families? 'Astronaut' households and the experiences of lone mothers. *Social and Cultural Geography* 3:117-134.

Webster, S.W., Benson, D.E. and Spray, S.L. 1994. Gender, marital status and social support. *Sociological Focus* 27:131-146.

Weigert, J. 1991. *Mixed emotions: Certain steps toward understanding ambivalence.* Albany, NY: State University of New York Press.

Weitzman, L.J. and Dixon, R.B. 1992. Divorce and remarriage: The transformation of legal marriage through no-fault divorce. In A.S. Skolnick and J.H. Skolnick (eds.), *Family in transition,* 7th ed. (pp. 217-230). New York: Harper Collins Publishers.

White, L. 1994. Coresidence and leaving home: Young adults and their parents. *Annual Review of Sociology* 20:81-102.

Whittington, L.A. and Peters, H.E. 1996. Economic incentives and financial and residential independence. *Demography* 33:82-97.

Willetts, M.C. 2003. An exploratory investigation of heterosexual licensed domestic partners. *Journal of Marriage and the Family* 65:939-952.

Wilson, A.E., Shuey, K.M. and Elder, G.H., Jr. 2003. Ambivalence in the relationship of adult children to aging parents and in-laws. *Journal of Marriage and the Family* 65:1055-1072.

Wilson, S.J. 1991. *Women, families and work,* 3rd ed. Toronto: McGraw-Hill Ryerson Ltd.

Wolf, R. 1996. *Marriages and families in a diverse society.* New York: Harper Collins College Publishers.

Wolfinger, N. 2000. Beyond the intergenerational transmission of divorce: Do people replicate the pattern of marital instability they grew up with? *Journal of Family Issues* 21:1061-1086.

Wolfinger, N. 1999. Trends in the intergenerational transmission of divorce. *Demography* 36:415-420.

Wu, Z. 2000. *Cohabitation: An alternative form of family living.* Toronto: Oxford University Press.

Wu, Z. and Balakrishan, T.R. 1995. Dissolution of premarital cohabitation in Canada. *Demography* 32:521-532.

Wu, Z. and Schimmele, C.M. 2003. Cohabitation. In J.J. Ponzetti (ed.), *The International encyclopaedia of marriage and family relationships,* 2nd ed. (pp. 315-323). New York: Macmillan Reference, USA.

Yi, Z., A. Coale, M. Choe, L. Zhiwu and Li, L. 1994. Leaving the parental home: Census-based estimates for China, Japan, South Korea, United States, France, and Sweden. *Population Studies* 48: 65-80.

Young, C.M. 1987. Young people leaving home in Australia: The trend toward independence. Australian Family Formation Project, Monograph No. 9, Canberra.

Youniss, J. and Ruth, A.J. 2002. Approaching policy for adolescent development in the 21st century. In J.T. Mortimer and R.W. Larson (eds.), *The changing adolescent experience: Societal trends and the transition to adulthood* (pp. 250-271). New York: Cambridge University Press.

Zhao, J.Z., R. Fernando and Ravanera, Z.R. 1995. Leaving parental homes in Canada: Effects of family structure, gender, and culture. *Canadian Journal of Sociology* 20:31-50.

Zimmerman, S.L. 2001. *Family policies: Constructed solutions to family problems.* Thousand Oaks, CA: Sage Publications.

Zimmerman, S.L. 1999. Family policy research: A system's view. *Family Science Review* 12:113-130.

Zimmerman, S.L. 1992. *Family policies and family well-being: The role of political culture.* Newbury Park, CA: Sage.

# Index